Brexit – The Road to Freedom
by
Will Podmore
ISBN: 978-1-9164271-7-4

Published by

i2i

PUBLISHING

i2i Publishing.
Manchester M25 0NL UK
www.i2ipublishing.co.uk

Acknowledgements

To our local Leave team in Redbridge and Epping, so ably led by Lucy Bostick, with huge contributions from Dave Dorrell and Pete and Gill Wrobel. Also to Nick and Val Bateson, Anna McKeown, Keith Turner, Rolfe Birch, Eddie McGuire and Kate Brown.

To Phil Thompson for writing the foreword.

To all my wonderful colleagues at the UCO, especially Husaina Waliji, James Barclay, Claire O'Donovan, Adele Sharp, Cormac O'Dalaigh, Karl Holder, Michael Murphy, Chris Lambert, Ugo Ejionye, Richard Pierce, Humaira Khan, Henal Ganatra, Myles King, Martin Webb, Rob McCoy, Chris Thomas, Hilary Abbey, Stephen Tyreman and Charles Hunt.

Also to the late Dorothy Birch, Phil Lenton and Eric Roberts – gone but not forgotten.

To Lucy Harris and the Leavers of London, David Axe and Invoke Democracy Now and to the team at Brexit Central.

To all my lovely family.

Contents:

Foreword

There's a case for saying that Will Podmore's important book doesn't quite reach far enough back into our history. True, it begins in 1215 with Magna Carta Libertatum, but evidence does exist of the roots of Britain's creation of a form of democracy stretching back before then. Before the Conquest some parts of the country, Nottinghamshire for one, had evolved a system of ploughing land that covered very long single strips. This led to ploughmen ploughing next to one another, and this in turn led to them being able to talk while they worked. To such a seemingly obscure fact could well be attributed the birth of our democracy, for without the ability and opportunity to converse there is little hope of political progress.

And talking together marked out the months before June 2016, when all manner of views were expressed about how Britain should live, how it should be governed, and from where it should be governed. The view was touted that a vote to leave would bring calamity. Another bruited that independence allowed the people a degree of control not known in most of our lifetimes. The former view was espoused, without any exceptions, by those institutions which hold and exercise power in Britain (except the monarchy, perhaps showing how little power it really has). The latter was cleaved to by most working people who expressed a view (although by almost none of their Trade Unions), as well as by a brave and independent assortment of others not prepared to be intimidated by 'Project Fear'.

Many Trade Unions, including my own, accepted money from the EU to support a remain vote, having what was described as 'only a paper-thin mandate' to do so. The President-elect of UNISON at the time, now sadly deceased, ambulance worker Eric Roberts, argued forcefully but unsuccessfully in UNISON's National Executive Council that UNISON should not make a recommendation to its members, arguing that the response to an internal consultation exercise was so sparse that it did not provide a mandate. Some Unions didn't consult members at all, just told them which way they thought they should vote. There were exceptions to a pro-remain view being espoused among Unions, principally the RMT, and among non-governmental organisations, War on Want being the best example. Those who think that Brexit is a 'right wing' project gratuitously insult such organisations.

The outcome of the Referendum we know. The historic outcome though, we don't.

It should have come as no surprise that a vote to leave, opposed by what can appropriately be called 'The Establishment', would not of itself lead to 'Brexit'. Yes, it was the most significant vote in the biggest turnout ever recorded. Yes, all sides of the debate insisted that the outcome would be respected, acted upon even. But there are many who now argue that a struggle for independence from the EU will be (at least) a two-stage process. First is the declaration, which was made in June '16. Second is the actual enactment of that decision; that's the phase we're in, two years later. Many think that those who voted for independence must come to see that independence will not be delivered by the very establishment which seeks to prevent it. Together with increasing numbers of those who voted to remain, but who genuinely *do* respect the wishes of the British people, those who voted to leave will have to grapple with that deficiency. Increasing weight is being given to the view that if the organs of power in Britain: Government, Parliament, the Courts, will not carry out the freely-expressed choice of the sovereign people, then the people sovereign will have to find ways & means of asserting their view democratically expressed. In this inheres the real deep-down significance of 23 June 2016; business most certainly cannot be carried on in the old way.

The years since the referendum have shown in the evolving view of many, that Britain's independence, and parliamentary democracy, are incompatible. Either we have the former, or we have the latter, it is increasingly believed. Such a realisation may be a long time coming, but we've taken a long time to reach where we are and come it probably will. We lean on history, but we live in times when we might make it.

Phil Thompson, member of UNISON

Chapter 1 Democracy and sovereignty

Our long tradition of democracy since 1215

The roots of our commitment to sovereignty and national independence go very far back into our history. Magna Carta Libertatum, the great charter of liberties, was agreed in 1215. It established the principle that the king, like his people, was subject to the law. The Pope condemned it within days of its being signed.

In 1353, 1365 and 1393 the three Acts of Praemunire were passed, which made it a criminal offence to appeal to or obey a foreign court. In the second half of the 14th century English began to displace French and Latin. The 1362 Pleading in English Act first permitted courtroom business to be done in English. The English language has always been an instrument of democracy, both in Britain and in the USA.

"The King's Majesty hath the chief power in this Realm of England ... and is not, nor ought to be, subject to any foreign Jurisdiction. ...The bishop of Rome hath no jurisdiction in this realm of England." This is part of the 37th of the 39 articles of religion, which still govern the Church of England. The articles were agreed in 1562 and are printed at the back of the Book of Common Prayer.

The Reformation, like the Renaissance, the enlightenment, abolitionism, the industrial revolution, the struggle for the vote, anti-colonialism and the anti-war movement, were all great popular movements, in which huge numbers of people acted to make progress. When Britain broke away from the universal Church of Rome in the Reformation, the Pope at once denounced the British as insular and xenophobic. The Pope tried to focus on Henry VIII's flaws as the key issue of the Reformation, deliberately missing the point that it was about national independence. Henry was a king who was also a revolutionary.

The Petition of Right of 1628 affirmed the rights of all not to be taxed or confined without 'common consent by act of parliament' and 'due process of law'. In 1641 the English state stopped torturing political suspects to get information.

Some made the case for government by popular consent. In 1646 the Levellers William Walwyn, Henry Marten and Richard Overton wrote of "the choice of the People, from whom the power that is just must be derived." The Leveller John Lilburne wrote, "The only and sole legislative and law-making power is originally inherent in the people and derivatively in their commissions chosen by themselves by common consent and no other. In which the poorest that lives has as true a right to give a vote, as well as the richest and greatest."

Colonel Thomas Rainsborough said in 1647 in the course of the New Model Army's Putney debates with Oliver Cromwell, "For really I think that the poorest he that is in England hath a life to live, as the greatest he; and therefore, truly, Sir, I think it's clear that every man that is to live under a government ought first by his own consent to put himself under that government; and I do think that the poorest man in England is not at all bound in a strict sense to that government that he hath not had a voice to put himself under ..."

Some denounced the colonial war against Ireland. For example, in 1649 William Walwyn said, "it is an unlawful war, a cruel and bloody work to go to destroy the Irish natives for their consciences ... and to drive them from their proper natural and native rights." The Levellers asked, "whether it be not the character of a true patriot to endeavour the just freedom of all as well as his own?"

The Digger Gerard Winstanley wrote in 1652, "No man can be rich, but he must be rich either by his own labours, or by the labours of other men helping him. If a man have no help from his neighbour, he shall never gather an estate of hundreds and thousands a year. If other men help him to work, then are those riches his neighbours' as well as his; for they be the fruits of other men's labours as well as his own."

Many defended the people's right to revolution. In 1653 Peter English wrote, "it is undoubtedly lawful for the people, or their Representative, to resist the King ... The people's power is the higher, yea the supream power." William Prynne wrote in defence of Parliament's revolutionary acts against King Charles I, "if the Parliaments War be necessary, and a necessary War is just, certainly a just War, cannot justly be called a Rebellion." Many quoted the *Magnificat*: "He hath put down the mighty from their seats and hath exalted them of low degree." And many quoted the prophet Ezekiel, "Thus saith the Lord God: remove the diadem and take off the crown. ... Exalt him that is low and abase him that is high. I will overturn, overturn, overturn ..." Later, John Locke agreed: "the Legislative being only a Fiduciary Power to act for certain ends, there remains still *in the People a Supream Power* to remove or *alter the Legislative*, when they find the *Legislative* act contrary to the trust reposed in them ..." The idea that sovereignty lay in the people was revolutionary.

In 1685 Richard Rumbold's last words on the scaffold were, "I am sure there was no man born marked of God above another; for none comes into the world with a saddle on his back, neither any booted and spurred to ride him."

Many also backed the practice of deciding by majority voting. The Dutch jurist Hugo Grotius wrote, "it is altogether unreasonable, that a greater Number should be governed by a less ... the Majority would naturally have the Right and Authority of the Whole." Thomas Hobbes agreed: "the wish of the majority shall be taken as the will of all ... they are bound by the decisions made by agreement of the majority. And that is a *Democracy* ..." And, "every one, as well as he that *Voted for it*, as he that *Voted against it*, shall *Authorise* all the Actions and Judgements, of that Man, or Assembly of men, in the same manner, as if they were his own."

After the deposition of James II in 1688, parliament became supreme over the monarchy. Parliament could make laws concerning anything; no parliament could bind a future parliament (that is, it could not pass a law that could not be changed or reversed by a future parliament); and a valid Act of Parliament could not be questioned by even the highest court. This refusal to bind itself to its previous decisions is a revolutionary doctrine, very different from the EU's adherence to all its treaties, the 120,000 pages of its irreversible acquis, and very different from the US Constitution. It was more democratic to have an unwritten constitution than a written one for the same reason that in a conflict between two legislative acts of equal status, the more recent one took precedence – the familiar legal maxim. Similarly, in a wise democracy, the more recent decision took precedence over the earlier one, because we have learnt from our experience and were now proposing a better way.

The Electors Right Asserted with the Advices and Charges of Several Counties, Cities and Burroughs in England to their Respective Members of Parliament of 1701 reminded Members of Parliament that "the power with which he is intrusted, must be larger and fuller in the People who chuse and give him that Trust, than it can be in Him, their Delegate and Substitute." In any conflict between Parliament and people, the people are supreme.

The British ruling class opposed the American revolutionary struggle for independence (1776-83). Should we have never let America go, because independence would be so bad for it? After America won its independence, some said that it would weary of its independence, it would want to come back, all was in confusion, the economy was in distress, the government was falling apart.

The American revolutionary John Adams objected to the 'sneers and snubs' of those who, presuming 'Airs of Wisdom and Superiority', had only contempt for 'the multitude, the million, the populace, the vulgar, the mob, the herd and the rabble, as the great always delight to call them'.[1] Edmund Burke wrote of 'the swinish multitude'.

The American struggle for national liberation gave the world lessons in democracy.[2] A decade before the American revolution, the patriot James Otis defined democracy in its purest and simplest form as 'a government of all over all', in which 'the votes of the majority shall be taken as the will of the whole', and where the rulers were the ruled.[3]

The USA's Declaration of Independence, of 4 July 1776, stated, "We hold these truths to be self-evident, that all men are created equal, that they are endowed by their Creator with certain unalienable Rights, that among these are Life, Liberty and the pursuit of Happiness. — That to secure these rights, Governments are instituted among Men, deriving their just powers from the consent of the governed, — That whenever any Form of Government becomes destructive of these ends, it is the Right of the People to alter or to abolish it, and to institute new Government, laying its foundation on such principles and organizing its powers in such form, as to them shall seem most likely to effect their Safety and Happiness. Prudence, indeed, will dictate that Governments long established should not be changed for light and transient causes; and accordingly all experience hath shewn, that mankind are more disposed to suffer, while evils are sufferable, than to right themselves by abolishing the forms to which they are accustomed. But when a long train of abuses and usurpations, pursuing invariably the same Object evinces a design to reduce them under absolute Despotism, it is their right, it is their duty, to throw off such Government, and to provide new Guards for their future security."

The Pennsylvania Constitution of September 1776 was a landmark in the history of democracy. It ended all property and wealth qualifications for voting and holding office and said that "every freeman of the full age of twenty-one years, having resided in this state for the space of one whole year next before the day of election for representatives, and paid public taxes during that time, shall enjoy the right of an elector." This included those free black people who paid taxes.

In May 1778 the state of Massachusetts submitted its constitution to the people in the first general referendum ever held anywhere. Its constitution of 1780 stated, "All power residing originally in the people, and being derived from them, the several magistrates and officers of government, vested with authority, whether legislative, executive, or judicial, are their substitutes and agents and are at all times accountable to them."

James Wilson, one of the founders of the USA, said in 1787, "The majority of people wherever found ought in all questions to govern the minority." James Madison, another founder, said, "the censorial power is in the people over the Government, and not in the Government over the people."[4]

President Thomas Jefferson acknowledged the rancor of the 1801 election but suggested that it was no more than the normal to-and-fro of a people able 'to think freely and to speak and to write what they think'. Now that the people had voted they would all 'of course, arrange themselves under the will of the law, and unite in common efforts for the common good'.[5] Jefferson said in his first inaugural address, of 4 March 1801, "All … will bear in mind this sacred principle, that though the will of the majority is in all cases to prevail, that will to be rightful must be reasonable; that the minority possess their equal rights, which equal law must protect, and to violate would be oppression. Let us then, fellow citizens, unite with one heart and one mind."

This raised the question of whether the slave minority possessed equal rights, which equal law must protect, which to violate would be oppression.

If one man could rightfully own another, he could rightfully own the product of that other's labour. But he could not rightfully do so. Jefferson said that government should 'not take from the mouth of labor the bread it has earned'. (Nor should capital.)

President Abraham Lincoln opposed slavery. He wrote, "If A. can prove, however conclusively, that he may, of right, enslave B. – why may not B. snatch the same argument, and prove equally, that he may enslave A? – You say A. is white, and B. is black. It is *color*, then; the lighter having the right to enslave the darker? Take care. By this rule, you are to be slave to the first man you meet, with a fairer skin than your own. You do not mean *color* exactly? – You mean the whites are intellectually the superiors of the blacks, and, therefore, have the right to enslave them? Take care again. By this rule, you are to be slave to the first man you meet, with an intellect superior to your own."[6]

Historian Harry Jaffa commented, "Every attempt to deny the Negro equality of right, as distinct from equality of reward, Lincoln called that 'old serpent', the root of all despotism, 'You work; I'll eat.'"[7] But capitalism exploited the same 'old serpent'.

Abolitionist Owen Lovejoy said that Lincoln was riding in a carriage being pulled by 'the Radical steed … If he does not drive as fast as I would, he is on the same road'.[8] The mass movement for abolition drove Lincoln, and made the leaders do the right thing.

Britain initiated many acts of progress. In 1689 the Bill of Rights criminalised 'cruel and unusual punishments'. In 1783 public hangings were ended. In 1834 the display of corpses on gibbets was ended. Until 1838, children, like adults, could be sentenced to death for a very large number of felonies. British law allowed the death penalty for 'strong evidence of malice in a child 7-14 years of age'. Only in the 1908 Children's Act was the minimum age for execution raised to 16.

Acts promoting the welfare of animals were passed. In 1822 Parliament passed the Ill-Treatment of Cattle Act and in 1835 extended its protections to bulls, bears, dogs and cats.

There was progress in international affairs too. Britain abolished the slave-trade in 1807. In the 1820s the Spanish Empire in the Americas was reaching the end of a long process of dissolution and the new republics of Latin America were gaining independence. George Canning (Foreign Secretary

1822-27) recognised these new republics, normalised relations with them, and worked to prevent the European colonial powers from seizing them.

In the late eighteenth and early nineteenth century the country moved to abolish property in office as part of a sustained attack on 'Old Corruption'. Parliament, court circles and the embryonic civil service had used public office to gain private wealth. The executive had used the politics of patronage to give its favourites unmerited pensions, lucrative sinecures and gratuitous emoluments. This system of patronage was enriched by bribery. Elections usually floated on tides of alcohol. For example, in 1784 the Grosvenor family paid for 1,187 barrels of ale, 3,756 gallons of rum and brandy and more than 27,000 bottles of wine, all to sway the votes of the 1,500 voters in the seat of Chester.[9]

An Act of 1828 removed the most important legal barriers against dissenters. The Catholic Emancipation Act of 1829 did the same for Catholics. In 1846 Parliament passed the Religious Disabilities Act which removed the last restrictions against dissenters and Catholics. It also extended to Jews the same rights and freedoms on education, property and the administration of charities. In 1858, after a ten-year campaign led by David Salomons, the first Jewish lord mayor of London, the Jewish Relief Act was passed granting full civil and political rights to Jews. The first Jewish MP, Baron Lionel de Rothschild, took his seat the same year. Benjamin Disraeli, who was from a Jewish family, became Prime Minister in 1868. In 1872 the secret ballot was introduced.

In Britain in the early nineteenth century, the working class could influence public policy, despite not having parliamentary representation. The people, not parliament or the courts, were the agents of progress. Public sentiment was the key battleground where issues were decided, not parliament or the courts. For example, the working class held mass demonstrations that helped to achieve trade union rights to organise, the voting reforms of 1832, and the ten-hour working day.

Each time, the people rejected the old vision and approved the new, either directly or by supporting those politicians who supported the new principles. In 1830 alone, the public sent 645 petitions for reform to Parliament. The Tory leader in the Commons Sir Robert Peel opposed the Reform Act of 1832, but then accepted the outcome. The Duke of Wellington opposed the Act, writing in June to a fellow Tory peer, the Duke of Buckingham, "The Government of England is destroyed. A Parliament will be returned, by means of which no set of men will be able to conduct the administration of affairs, and to protect the lives and property of the King's subjects."[10] Horace Twiss, a junior minister in Wellington's government, said in 1831 that the great Reform Act would call in "shopkeepers and attorneys, persons of narrow minds and bigoted views ... to counsel the nation."[11] The Whig MP and historian Thomas Babington Macaulay said, "We say, and we say justly, that it is not by mere numbers but by property and intelligence that the nation ought to be governed."[12] He wrote that universal suffrage was 'incompatible with the very existence of civilization'. But the anti-democrats lost the vote on the vote.

The 1832 reform led at once to the abolition of slavery throughout the Empire in 1833. Peel also passed the Factory Act of 1844 and repealed the Corn Laws in 1848, infuriating employers and large landowners.

In 1845 Parliament passed the Museums Act, in 1847 Joseph Paxton designed Birkenhead Park, the first public park in the world. Also in 1847 Scottish obstetrician James Young Simpson of Edinburgh was the first to use chloroform as a general anesthetic on a human. In 1848 Parliament passed the Public Health Act and in 1850 the Public Libraries Act. In 1851 the Great Exhibition was held. In 1854 the Birmingham Parks Act was passed. In 1854 John Snow identified a water pump in Soho as the source of the cholera outbreak in London. In 1870 the Education Act was passed.

As Macaulay wrote, our history has been one of governments "sometimes peaceably, sometimes after a violent struggle, but constantly giving way before a nation that has been constantly advancing." Even then, some protested that the press was responsible for the countrywide calls for reform, which was to mistake effect for cause. Wellington complained that "we are governed by the mob and its organ – a licentious Press."

During the American civil war (1861-65), despite the dire consequences of the Union blockade on employment, and despite the unremitting pro-South propaganda of the British press, British workers backed the Union against the secessionist slaveholding South. In the first three months of 1863, the class held at least 56 rallies calling for the abolition of slavery.

The class opposed the government schemes to intervene on the slaveowners' side. Karl Marx wrote, "It was not the wisdom of the ruling classes, but the heroic resistance to their criminal folly by the working classes of England, that saved the west of Europe from plunging headlong into an infamous crusade for the perpetuation and propagation of slavery on the other side of the Atlantic ... The fight for such a foreign policy forms part of the general struggle for the emancipation of the working classes."

Democracy was the continuous extension of the democratic rights of the people, achieved through revolutionary acts like 1534, 1641, 1689, 1832, 1945 and 2016. People won extensions of the right to vote in 1867, 1884, 1918, 1928 and 1948. Personal freedom, personal property, free inquiry, trial by jury, due process, habeas corpus, the rule of law, and limited, constitutional government were all great achievements and we the people upheld them all. Similarly, with the clipping of the House of Lords' veto in 1911, the recognition of the Irish Free State in 1922, and the acceptance of India's independence in 1947.

In 1948, the Labour government abolished university constituencies along with all other examples of plural voting. (University constituencies represented the members of one or more universities rather than residents of a geographical area. They involved plural voting, where some voters could vote in both a university constituency and a geographical constituency.)

Similarly, the Conservative party accepted the democratic reforms achieved after 1945 – the National Health Service, education and welfare reforms, support for the arts, the nationalisation of rail. After its Suez fiasco, the Conservative party generally accepted the independence of the colonies. And in 2016 it generally accepted the referendum result, thereby winning the support of many of those who voted to leave and winning the support of those who thought that in a democracy the majority vote should be respected, even if they themselves had not voted to leave.

Similarly, some wrote about those who voted to leave the EU in the same terms that reactionaries used to write about national liberation struggles in the colonies – ignorant natives were misled by lying demagogues. For example, American journalist James Traub in his 28 June 2016 article in *Foreign Policy*, "It's Time for the Elites to Rise Up Against the Ignorant Masses", claimed that our vote to leave the EU showed that the 'political schisms of our time' are between 'the sane vs. the mindless angry'.

Some who opposed having a referendum in the first place openly doubted whether people could decide matters of this importance. Like 19th century reactionaries, they doubted the value of universal suffrage. Some said that some voters were too uneducated to be allowed to vote. It was odd how some pro-EU progressives echoed this.

Some have explained all history as resulting from the irrationality of the masses. They saw, for example, the American civil war as a needless war, because reasonable people would have found a compromise between slavery and freedom, and the American people did not do so, therefore they must have been irrational. Similarly, some explain the world wars as caused by the masses' irrational attachment to nation. Ignorant, irrational peoples were misled by irresponsible agitators. Reactionaries applied this trope to all actions by organised workers, from trade union action to revolution.

But all progress comes from the people. When the people tell the government what to do there is progress. When the government tell the people what to do, there is no progress.

In Britain we pioneered trial by jury in the modern world, the presumption of innocence, and free speech. We ensured that no-one could be arbitrarily detained by government order. We set up the first free parliament. We forced our rulers to accept that they ruled by consent not by divine right. We tamed religious privilege and zealotry. We led the world in abolishing slavery. We established free education for all, national insurance, the National Health Service and a national broadcaster respected across the world. We pioneered industries, railways, urban sewerage systems, underground railways, and the jet engine.

These were Britain's practical achievements, the values we upheld, not the old discredited ideals of the Empire. We rejected those as far back as 1945 when the British people voted for Attlee's welfare nationalism rather than Churchill's imperial nationalism. As leave campaigner Sebastian Handley wrote, asserting Enlightenment ideals, "There is no moral relativism between British culture and the alternative models on offer in China, the Middle East, Africa or Russia. Our way *really is* better. Freedom of expression *is* better than censorship. People telling the government what to do *is* better than the government telling the people what to do. Gender equality, *is* better than patriarchy. Reason *is* better than belief. Philosophy *is* better than religion. In short, our great, sophisticated culture is imperilled by its indulgence of inferior thuggish ideologies, and if saying so risks accusations of nationalism then we will have to live with the accusation, because indulging brutal ideologies risks the rise of *real* right wing extremism."[13]

The Referendum is 'your decision'

Lawyers for Britain stated, "It is true that the Act does not contain a section at the end expressly saying that the government is under a legal duty to proceed to implement the result of the vote. But that does not mean that the referendum result is 'advisory'. The Act itself does not say that it is advisory. At no point did ministers in their public statements either to Parliament or outside say that the referendum result would only be advisory. On the contrary, they repeatedly said that the referendum would allow the British people to *decide* the question of whether we remain or leave."[14]

Lord Norton of Louth said on 7 July 2016, "We asked the electors to make a decision on whether we should remain in or leave the European Union. They made the decision - perhaps by a small majority but it was a decision. In the past two days we have heard various people arguing, 'But it was only advisory and there was a small majority. We should have had some sort of threshold or there should have been a much larger majority'."

He also pointed out, "As for whether we should have applied some rules, we did not. At Second Reading of the European Union Referendum Bill, I raised the question of a threshold but there was clearly no desire to pursue it, so we put it to the people. It was a simple choice based on a majority. We cannot rerun it; we cannot apply rules that were not in place at the time."

He continued, "To say that the referendum was advisory is misleading. We did not say to the electors, 'Please tell us what you think and then we'll decide whether to accept what you've said'. It was non-binding but that is a very different matter. There is no statutory obligation on Ministers to trigger Article 50 but there most certainly is a compelling political argument for doing so. The Government are bound by that political dimension. Yesterday I quoted Dicey, who distinguished between parliamentary and political sovereignty. The latter matters." Referendums did not have immediate, direct legal effect, but they did oblige the state to do as the people decided. Imagine if the Stay camp had won, and the government had then said that we have listened to the debates and have now decided that leaving the EU is the right thing to do, your vote was only advisory.

Both campaigns ruled out any need for a second referendum. Parliament made no provision for a second referendum, though it could have done so in the Referendum Act if it had wanted to. David Cameron repeatedly said this was 'a once in a lifetime vote'. Lord Norton said a second referendum was 'an extremely dangerous path to pursue', "It would convey [that] the political class weren't prepared to accept what the electors had decided, and I think that would undermine trust in the political process at a time when that trust is already fragile," he said. "We cannot second-guess the electors."

When parliament passed a law authorising a referendum, it accepted that the people had sovereignty. After the referendum, Parliament's job was to give effect to the will of the political sovereign, that is, the nation.[15] The people were the sovereign. Parliament had no sovereignty over the people. As Professor Vernon Bogdanor pointed out, "The sovereignty of the people trumps the sovereignty of Parliament."[16] In a democracy the people were sovereign. In the EU the state is sovereign, because the people are seen as inherently untrustworthy. R. G. Collingwood wrote that sovereignty "is merely the name for political activity, and those who would banish sovereignty as an outworn fiction are really only trying to shirk the whole problem of politics."[17]

The point of a referendum is that the whole people decide, it is sovereignty, it is democracy. It is control, it is power, it is responsibility. We the people are in charge – but only for a day. It should be for longer. After the vote, we needed to keep this control, to hold this responsibility.

Our referendums in Britain were about constitutional issues – the method of voting (2011), national unity (2004 and 2014), national independence (1975 and 2016). What could be more democratic than asking all the sovereign people to decide vital national matters? Our Supreme Court was the people. We were called upon to decide and settle constitutional questions. We did not give advice. The people were part of government, the fourth estate, the fourth power, rightly able to overrule all the others, because the people are the ultimate source of sovereignty. Parliament did not embody democracy. The people did. The whole overruled the part. In a democracy, who else should have the authority to settle constitutional questions?

Parliament should represent the expressed and collective decision of the people. It was a national vote, not one counted constituency by constituency. So, all MPs, however their constituents voted, were obliged to respect our decision, as they had voted to do. They should all uphold that decision. All MPs whose constituents voted to Remain and all MPs whose constituents voted to leave should honour our majority, democratic decision to leave the EU, just as Sir Robert Peel had opposed the Reform Act of 1832 but accepted the outcome. Every democrat was obliged to accept the result. Or should elections be decided on who conducted the nicer campaign, not on the votes cast? Democracy is a system of rule where the people's preferences govern policies, where elected representatives carried out the people's will and did not instead impose their own preferences.

Some enemies of democracy tried to use parliament to overturn the will of the people. Parliament, they said, was sovereign. It was, in the sense that no force outside Britain, no foreign country or organisation, could tell it what to do. But parliament was not sovereign over the people. Once you departed from the principle that parliament derived its authority from the people and must serve the people, you were going down a road leading to fascism. In a democracy, politicians are the servants of the people and do what we the people tell them to do. Tony Blair and some other pro-EU politicians thought that the people must do what politicians told them to do. This anti-populism has become a greater threat to democracy than populism. The greatest threat to democracy was not our majority vote to leave the EU, but the minority attempt to overthrow that decision.

Those who rejected our referendum decision would, by the same argument, reject the results of all elections. The referendum was a free, fair, universal, secret ballot, legally mandated and constitutionally legitimate. Calling a referendum did not conflict with parliamentary sovereignty because if parliament could do whatever it liked, then it could call a referendum.

Arguments against the validity of the referendum could equally be deployed against all elections, indeed against the very idea of having elections. For any government to try to reverse the referendum result would set a most dangerous precedent. Some EU-lovers wanted the PM to say, "I know you Remainers are sore because the country did not vote to agree with you. Therefore, as Prime Minister, I will overrule the majority democratic decision taken at the Referendum. With this precedent set, we can then ignore any future General Election results too if you don't like them, just let me know." Elections would become just advisory, like the elections to the EU's advisory parliament.

In his foreword to Labour's manifesto for the February 1974 general election, Harold Wilson promised, "We shall restore to the British people the right to decide the final issue of British membership of the Common Market." Labour's manifesto for the October 1974 general election pledged to make the referendum result binding not advisory. So, since the 1975 vote was binding, it was right that our 2016 decision was binding too.

In 2009 the LibDems called for a referendum on Europe, saying that "Only a real referendum on Britain's membership of the EU will let the people decide our country's future." Note, "let the people decide", not, let the people advise MPs and then MPs will decide for you.

Cameron said in January 2013, "It is time for the British people to have their say. It is time to settle this European question in British politics. I say to the British people: this will be your decision." Did that sound like promising an advisory referendum?

The 2015 Conservative election manifesto said, "We believe in letting the people decide: so we will hold an in-out referendum on our membership of the EU before the end of 2017." And, "We will hold that in-out referendum before the end of 2017 and respect the outcome." "We will honour the result of the referendum, whatever the outcome." These were pledges to let the people decide. The electorate mandated the Conservative government to hold a referendum. After the election, Parliament passed the European Union Referendum Act by 544 votes to 53. Only the Scottish National Party's MPs voted against.

The European Union Referendum Act of 2015 [An Act to make provision for the holding of a referendum in the United Kingdom and Gibraltar on whether the United Kingdom should remain a member of the European Union] said, "A referendum is to be held on whether the United Kingdom should remain a member of the European Union." The referendum question was, "Should the United Kingdom remain a member of the European Union or leave the European Union?" The question was not, "Do you think that the United Kingdom should remain a member of the European Union or leave the European Union?" Parliament delegated to the people the decision on whether Britain should stay in the EU. Parliament decided to let the people decide, it did not promise to hold an advisory poll, leaving Parliament to take the final decision.

The government leaflet of 16 April sent to all 27 million households stated on the page headed 'A once in a generation decision': "The referendum on Thursday 23rd June is your chance to decide if we should remain in or leave the European Union. ... This is your decision. The Government will implement what you decide." Note the words decision, decide, your decision, implement and decide. Not the words advice, advise, your advice, consider and advise. It did not say "it is your chance to *advise on* whether we should remain, *the actual decision being taken by Parliament.*"

The Britain Stronger in Europe leaflet said, "On 23rd June, you will get to vote in the EU referendum, and decide whether Britain remains in or leaves Europe. This vote will affect you and your family's future." Note, "you will ... decide." Both official campaigns were asked if the decision was binding, both confirmed that it was. Labour In's leaflet said, "On 23 June you face a big decision about our future."

Some claimed that the referendum was no more than a glorified opinion poll. What opinion poll ever made a Prime Minister, indeed a whole government, go? Referendums were not opinion polls. Polls were indicative, telling us what people said now they might do in an election or a referendum, they were hypothetical. Elections, referendums, were the actual decisions, they were consequential, binding, decision-making devices. They were not advice to government and parliament, but instructions. Government must act on the sovereign's instructions.

It was part of our unwritten constitution that our referendum decisions were binding. In practice, governments took them as binding. As Professor Richard Tuck wrote, "Characteristically this has happened without a formal or legal acknowledgment of their fundamental role, and technically they are merely consultative; but the idea that they could be disregarded seems to most people about as fanciful as the idea that the Queen could actually use the power, still technically in her hands, to veto a Parliamentary statute."[18] All this gave rise to the not unreasonable expectation that if we voted to stay in the EU, we would stay in, and if we voted to leave, we would leave.

In 1975 we voted to stay in the EEC, so we stayed in the EEC for 40 years. In the 2014 referendum in Scotland, if the SNP had won, Scotland would have seceded. If the pro-Alternative Vote camp had won the 2011 referendum, we would have used the Alternative Vote in general elections. So, when the British people voted to leave the EU, we left the EU. The majority decided.

If Scotland had voted 'Yes' in 2014 the government would not have been free to ignore or to seek to overturn the result. Similarly, in 2016, after the government asked the people for their decision it was duty bound to give effect to it. Britain was leaving the EU not because the Tories wanted it – May, Cameron and Major all campaigned to remain – but because parliament had decided in the European Union Referendum Act 2015 to ask the people whether we should leave or remain, and the people gave their answer.

As Philip Hammond, the Foreign Secretary at the time, said, in opening the second reading debate (Hansard) on the Referendum Bill on 9 June 2015, "This is a simple, but vital, piece of legislation. It has one clear purpose: to deliver on our promise to give the British people the final say on our EU membership in an in/out referendum by the end of 2017 … whether we favour Britain being in or out, we surely should all be able to agree on the simple principle that the decision about our membership should be taken by the British people, not by Whitehall bureaucrats, certainly not by Brussels Eurocrats; not even by Government Ministers or parliamentarians in this Chamber. The decision must be for the common sense of the British people."

Speaking for the Labour Party, Hilary Benn said that the Bill might only consist of eleven words, "but the answer will have profound consequences for the future of our country, as the people of the United Kingdom make the most important decision on our place in the world for 40 years."

In September 2016 LibDem MP Norman Lamb said, "For better or worse we all voted to hold the referendum. You can't now say we reject the result."[19] Also in September 2016 Vince Cable rejected calls for a second referendum: "The public have voted. It's seriously disrespectful and politically utterly counter-productive to say, 'sorry guys, you've got it wrong, try again.'" But by 19 September 2017 Mr Cable was calling for a second referendum. On 11 March 2018 he told the LibDem conference that "my own initial reaction to the referendum was to think maybe there was little choice but to pursue Brexit. I thought, you know, the public had voted to be poorer - well, that was their right. What changed my mind was the evidence that Brexit had overwhelmingly been the choice of the older generation." The LibDems' Constitution still says, "We believe that sovereignty rests with the people and that authority in a democracy derives from the people." Fine words butter no parsnips.

So Mr Cable at first thought the public had the right to vote as they chose, but then that we only had the right to vote the way he chose. So, he used to believe in democracy, until he didn't.

Mr Cable was saying that if older people's votes made up a large part of a majority democratic vote, then that majority democratic vote was invalid and had to be overturned. Mr Cable was calling into question the basis of democracy, of 'One Person, One Vote': the belief that the vote of the poor man is equivalent to the vote of the rich man, that the vote of a woman has the same power as the vote of a man, that the vote of a 65-year-old carries the same weight as the vote of a 21-year-old. If Mr Cable's view prevailed, it would destroy democracy. He was prepared to override our democracy to keep us in the EU.

Mike Gapes, the Labour MP for Ilford South, said on 16 June 2015, "If I lose an election or a referendum, I recognise the result. ... It is a pity that Scottish nationalists do not accept the result of the referendum they lost last year." In June 2018 he was one of the London Labour MPs who called for a second referendum.

1951 - Creating a State

The 1951 Schuman Declaration which launched the European Coal and Steel Community called it 'the first step in the federation of Europe'. A federation was of course a state. The EU still commemorates the date of this Declaration, 9 May, as 'Europe Day'. Prime Minister Winston Churchill rejected this, saying in May 1953, "We are not members of the European Defence Community, nor do we intend to be merged in a federal European System."

Clement Attlee said in 1962, "We are told that we have to accept the Treaty of Rome. I have read the Treaty of Rome pretty carefully, and it expresses an outlook entirely different from our own. It may be that I am insular, but I value our Parliamentary outlook, an outlook which has extended throughout the Commonwealth. That is not the same position that holds on the Continent of Europe. No one of these principal countries in the Common Market has been very successful in running Parliamentary institutions: Germany, hardly any experience; Italy, very little; France, a swing between a dictatorship and more or less anarchic Parliament, and not very successfully. As I read the Treaty of Rome, the whole position means that we shall enter a federation which is composed in an entirely different way. I do not say it is the wrong way. But it is not our way. In this set-up it is the official who really puts up all the proposals; the whole of the planning is done by officials. It seems to me that the Ministers come in at a later stage — and if there is anything like a Federal Parliament, at a later stage still. I do not think that that is the way this country has developed or wishes to develop. I am all for working in with our Continental friends. I was one of those who worked to build up NATO; I have worked for European integration. But that is a very different thing from bringing us into a close association which, I may say, is not one for defence, or even just for foreign policy. The fact is that if the designs behind the Common Market are carried out, we are bound to be affected in every phase of our national life. There would be no national planning, except under the guidance of Continental planning—we shall not be able to deal with our own problems; we shall not be able to build up the country in the way we want to do, so far as I can see. I think we shall be subject to overall control and planning by others. That is my objection."

In the same speech, Lord Attlee said, "But as a matter of fact the idea of an integrated Europe is historically looking backward, and not forward. The noble Viscount was looking at the Holy Roman Empire. We never belonged to the Holy Roman Empire, and we never belonged to the reactionary organisation after 1815. We have always looked outward, out to the New World; and to-day we look out to the New World, and to Asia and Africa. I think that integration with Europe is a step backward. By all means let us get the greatest possible agreement between the various continents, but I am afraid that if we join the Common Market we shall be joining not an outward-looking organisation, but an inward-looking organisation. I think that Germany, for instance, which has probably the most powerful influence in the organisation, will not escape from looking at what she thought she was going to gain, and what she has lost. I do not think we have a new look there. I think that by marrying into Europe we are marrying a whole family of ancient prejudices and ancient troubles, and I would much rather see an Atlantic organisation. I would much rather work for the world organisation."[20]

In another speech he said, "Unfortunately, in this country the propaganda for entering the Common Market has been largely based on defeatism. We are told that unless we do it we are going to have a terrible time. That is no way to go into a negotiation. You ought to go into a negotiation on the basis that they have need of you, not just you of them.

"My noble friend Lord Morrison of Lambeth rather suggested that it was a really good Socialist policy to join up with these countries. I do not think that comes into it very much. They are not Socialist countries, and the object, so far as I can see, is to set up an organisation with a tariff against the rest of the world within which there shall be the freest possible competition between capitalist interests. That might be a kind of common ideal. I daresay that is why it is supported by the Liberal Party. It is not a very good picture for the future...I believe in a planned economy. So far as I can see, we are to a large extent losing our power to plan as we want and submitting not to a Council of Ministers but a collection of international civil servants, able and honest, no doubt, but not necessarily having the best future of this country at heart...I think we are parting, to some extent at all events, with our powers to plan our own country in the way we desire. I quite agree that that plan should fit in, as far as it can, with a world plan. That is a very different thing from submitting our plans to be planned by a body of international civil servants, no doubt excellent men. I may be merely insular, but I have no prejudice in a Britain planned for the British by the British. Therefore, as at present advised, I am quite unconvinced either that it is necessary or that it is even desirable that we should go into the Common Market."[21]

Hugh Gaitskell, the leader of the Labour party, said in 1961, "The people are being told they are not capable of judging this issue. The government knows best, the top people are the only people who can really understand it. The classic argument of every tyranny in history."

Sir Edward Heath told us on 24 May 1971, "Joining the community does not entail a loss of national identity or an erosion of essential national sovereignty." Yet the Foreign

Office disagreed: "The long-term objectives of EMU ... go well beyond the full establishment of a Common Market and the formal provisions of the Treaty of Rome (which would require amendment). With exchange control, uniform rates of tax on goods and companies, a unified currency ... and strong central direction of individual budgets, the economies of the members of the EMU would be as interlocked as those of the states of the USA. Indeed, it could be argued that the independence of the members would be less than that of the States, for the latter have more autonomy over their budgets ... State taxes are not harmonised in the USA ... At the ultimate stage economic sovereignty would to all intents and purposes disappear at the national level ... The degree of freedom which would then be vested in national Government's [sic] might indeed be somewhat less than the autonomy enjoyed by the constituent States of the USA."[22] The Heath government knew quite well, as it acknowledged in its White Paper, that "the Six have firmly and repeatedly made clear that they reject the concept that European unity should be limited to the formation of a free trade area."[23]

Mr Justice Hoffmann explained in 1990 the effect of the EU's legal primacy as illustrated by the Factortame case: "The Treaty of Rome is the supreme law of this country, taking precedence over Acts of Parliament. Our entry into the Community meant that (subject to our undoubted but probably theoretical right to withdraw from the Community altogether) Parliament surrendered its sovereign right to legislate contrary to the Treaty on the matters of social and economic policy which it regulated."[24]

The ECJ spelled out its thinking in 1992 in the *European Economic Area Agreement* Case: "An international treaty is to be interpreted not only on the basis of its wording, but in the light of its objectives. ... The Rome Treaty aims to achieve economic integration leading to the establishment of an internal market and economic and monetary union. Article 1 of the Single European Act makes it clear that the objective of all the Community treaties is to contribute together to making concrete progress towards European unity. It follows from the foregoing that the provisions of the Rome Treaty on free movement and competition, far from being an end in themselves, are only means for attaining those objectives. ... As the Court of Justice has consistently held, the Community treaties established a new legal order for the benefit of which the States have limited their sovereign rights, in ever wider fields, and the subjects of which comprise not only the member-States but also their nationals."

Every EU widening led to an EU deepening. The accession of Spain and Portugal in 1986 led to the Single European Act, the accession of the Nordic countries in 1994 led to the Amsterdam Treaty, the accession of the Eastern European countries in 2004 led to the Lisbon Treaty. Now its narrowing was also leading to yet more deepening.

How much of our law came from the EU? Liberal Democrat MEP for the East Midlands Nick Clegg said on 8 December 2003, "Probably half of all new legislation now enacted in the UK begins in Brussels." Full Fact said on 19 March 2015, "Claim: The European Union makes two thirds of UK law. Conclusion: That's about right if you count EU regulations as part of 'UK law'." EU Commissioner Viviane Reding said, "70 per cent of British laws are made in the EU."

The EU not democratic

The EU was anti-democratic; therefore, we the demos could not reform it. For nearly 60 years British governments tried and failed to reform the EU. In 1961, before we even joined, Harold Macmillan said that by joining we could reform away its commitment to 'ever closer union'. In 1986 Neil Kinnock said, "We believe there should be reforms in the EEC which would benefit all the members."

Cameron thought he could reform the EU. But Chancellor Merkel said on 27 February 2014, "some expect my speech to pave the way for a fundamental reform of the European architecture which will satisfy all kinds of alleged or actual British wishes. I am afraid they are in for a disappointment."[25] In 2015 Cameron promised 'Treaty change that I'll be putting in place before the referendum'. France's President François Hollande at once replied, "No revision of the Treaties is planned." Cameron promised 'fundamental change' in the EU. The President of the European Parliament replied that it was 'not possible' to change the EU. German finance minister Wolfgang Schäuble said on 11 February 2015 at the Eurogroup (the meeting of eurozone finance ministers), "Elections cannot be allowed to change economic policy."

In early 2016 Cameron promised again to get change from the EU. But, as his friend Steve Hilton commented, his "modest demands were treated with total contempt." Just before the referendum, the pro-EU camp talked once more of changing the EU. An EU spokesperson at once replied that this is 'totally, fully and entirely ruled out'. On 21 September 2016, EU Economics Commissioner Pierre Moscovici said, "It is right to aim for a better functioning of the Stability and Growth Pact to make it more understandable and easier to apply. But we are talking about small improvements within a framework – not a change. This is out of the question."

The EU was not a democracy; by contrast in our nation-states we could oust leaders we opposed. The EU's unreformable treaties enforced bankers' rule, privatisation and mass unemployment. Inside the EU we were stuck with these policies whoever formed the government. The EU broke the links between people and government. It aimed, in short, to save capitalism from democracy. By leaving the EU we escaped these EU policies.

Since we joined in 1973, we have opposed 55 regulations and have had to accept every one. We have been outvoted all the 72 times we have voted against an EU measure. In the European Parliament, 9.7 per cent of MEPs were from Britain: even if they had voted as a bloc, they would always be outvoted. For example, MEPs voted to overturn Britain's requirement that Internet companies provided filters so that parents of young children could screen out obscene sites. In the Council of Ministers, the British government had one vote out of 28.

Giles Merritt, who founded the pro-EU think-tank 'Friends of Europe', admitted, "The EU's institutions are dysfunctional and poorly organized. ... Distant, remote, inscrutable, politically unanswerable, untouched by the new austerity, and seemingly indifferent to criticism, the EU's institutions have increasingly fewer friends for even sympathetic ears."[26] He rightly called the 2014 Euro-election with its record low 42 per cent turnout 'a massive rejection of the EU'.[27]

He noted that the European parliament "isn't a real parliament; it can't raise taxes, it can't declare war, and it doesn't provide the EU executive with any sort of democratic legitimacy. That's the nub of the EU's problem: when things go wrong, there's no mechanism for ousting those who have been responsible for taking far-reaching political decisions on behalf of the peoples of Europe."[28] Elections should be about the public being able to choose who made the laws. Instead, all our politicians had to do what the EU said - not what we said.

In the European Parliament the three party groupings voted in common far more often than the parties in national parliaments ever did. Analyst Roland Vaubel concluded that they were one large party, 'the party of EU centralisation. The European parliament represents itself.'[29]

The Council of Ministers was the real legislature, but it operated in secret, with no public record of its speeches or votes. Merritt summed up, "the EU and its mid-twentieth-century ramshackle institutional compromises are no longer fit for purpose in the twenty-first-century."[30] The European Court of Auditors refused to give the annual €133.6 billion EU budget a clean bill of health for 21 years in a row.

Some claimed that the EU was democratic, largely because we elected the MEPs. But this parliament was not even allowed to propose any laws. The unelected and supra-national European Commission was the only EU body that could initiate legislation. It was both executive and legislative. The EU's elected bodies were not allowed to initiate legislation. The European parliament was just advisory, like Britain's monarchy. Parliamentary committees formulated legislative proposals and took these into 'trilogue' negotiations between representatives of the Commission, the Council and the Parliament. The resulting legislation was then taken to Parliament, where 81 per cent of proposals were passed at first reading. It voted them in or not, dozens of votes every hour. Only 3 per cent ever reached third reading, where texts were debated. This was not democratic control.

As Chris Bickerton pointed out, "The trilogues of the Council, and the Parliament, the consultations of the European Commission, the intensive deliberations of the European Council in moments of tension and crisis – are all bound by the common thread of secrecy. Decision-making in Europe is done overwhelmingly behind closed doors. ... We are accustomed to diplomatic negotiations being conducted in secret, but not common legislative business. ... The virtue of the EU for national politicians and officials is the freedom it gives to them to discuss with one another, unencumbered by their domestic publics." [31] He summed up: "We saw that Europe's peoples do not rule through the Parliament as this institution has sacrificed its representative role in favour of being an influential insider in the EU's legislative machine."[32] Where the peoples did not rule, there was dictatorship.

The EU's democratic deficit was perhaps best shown in the much-vaunted Citizens' Initiative. This set a high threshold to trigger; a million signatures, with a set number from at least seven member states. This was supposed to result in a legislative proposal from the Commission. In the first three years after it came into force, 51 petitions got more than a million signatures. How many generated any legislative proposals from the Commission? Not one.

The EU gave £52 million of taxpayers' money to European political parties to fight the 2014 election. It also gave money to the IMF, the CBI, the National Farmers Union, the OECD, the Institute for Fiscal Studies, the Rand Corporation, the Centre for Economic Performance, Oxford Economics, Universities UK, the London School of Economics, the Royal United Services Institute, PricewaterhouseCooper, Standard & Poor's, the TUC, the GMB, Unison, the National Union of Students, and the European Trades Union Congress.

In 2006 alone, the EU gave 43 million euros in total to the National Society for the Prevention of Cruelty to Children, Oxfam, ActionAid and One World Action. The EU also gave money to Friends of the Earth, the Royal Society for the Protection of Birds, and the World Wildlife Fund. In 2007-14 it gave the RSPB £15 million. Over the period 2007-2012, the EU paid the World Wildlife Fund €53,813,343. Friends of the Earth was lead recipient for grants worth €13,674,033. Over this period, nine environmental Non-Governmental Organisations were primary or lead recipients of €126,610,677 disbursed by the European Commission.

The EU had only a voluntary register of the 10-15,000 lobbyists talking to Commissioners, MEPs and EU civil servants, pushing for junk food, tobacco, dangerous chemicals, dodgy drugs, the giant banks, etc. Finance spent 120 million euros a year on lobbying the EU, hiring 1700 lobbyists via 700 organisations. Deutsche Bank spent 3,962,000 euros lobbying in the first six months of 2015 alone. The CEOs of the 36 FTSE-100 firms who signed a pro-EU letter to the *Financial Times* had spent 21.3 million euros lobbying the EU and got back 120.9 million euros in EU grants, a 600 per cent return on their investment.

There were two key questions. One, can we trade with the EU without being in it? If the answer is yes, Leave wins the argument on the economy. We can trade with the EU without being in it. 160 other countries, none of which are in the EU, happily trade with the EU.

Two, could we make our own decisions when we were in the EU? If the answer was no, Leave wins the argument on the politics. Inside the EU we were part of a larger whole which took the decisions. So, we could not make our own decisions when we were in the EU. Outside it, we can make our own decisions. Outside the EU we could oust leaders whose policies we opposed. Outside the EU we could reject those responsible for taking decisions on our behalf. Outside the EU we could choose who made our laws. Outside the EU we could change policies when we disagreed with them. Outside the EU we could ensure that governments carried out policies which we supported. Outside the EU we could reform our institutions as we wished.

Chapter 2 The economy

EU austerity

Before we joined the EEC, its members were in catch-up growth after World War Two. Almost as soon as we joined, it started to stagnate. The more integrated we were into the EEC, the worse our exports and balance of payments became. Britain had relatively balanced trade (equal imports and exports) until Margaret Thatcher signed the 1986 Single European Act, at which point our exports started to fall. To get this Act, Thatcher gave away our national veto. She downplayed the Act's commitment to closer political union even though this was integral to the single market she wanted.[33]

Adair Turner, former director-general of the CBI, explained why Thatcher wanted Economic and Monetary Union [EMU]: "EMU ... seemed justified as an impeccably free-market project, driving forward completion of the single market and supporting in particular the free flow of capital." [34] The European employers' organisation, the Union of Industrial and Employers' Confederations of Europe, wanted EMU because it would put downward pressure on wages and on the social wage.

Blair then embraced Thatcher's single market and its freedom of movement of labour. Then Jeremy Corbyn with his 'no borders' policy continued the Labour party's embrace of free market liberalism.

In 1988 Thatcher told the House of Commons that "Monetary union would be the first step, but progress towards it would not necessarily involve a single currency or a European central bank."[35] But it did involve a single currency and a European central bank.

The EU wanted its members to remove all national controls over their economies. Especially, it wanted countries no longer to run their own central banks. Article 109e (5) of the 1992

Maastricht Treaty stated, "Each Member State shall, as appropriate, start the process leading to the independence of its central bank." The 1997 Labour government's first act (never mentioned in its manifesto) was to make the Bank of England independent.

The experiences of Venezuela and Greece showed what happened when countries had no control over banking. Without control of the central bank, there was no control of finances. Without control of the finances, there was no control of investment. Without control of investment, there was no control of productivity. Without control of productivity, there was no control of growth. Without control of growth, there was no control of tax revenue. Without control of tax revenue, there were inadequate funds for services.

The single currency has done what its backers designed it to do. It removed governments' control over their currency, preventing them from using monetary and fiscal policy to pull countries out of recession. The euro's founder Robert Mundell explained, "the euro is the way in which congresses and parliaments can be stripped of all power over monetary and fiscal policy. Bothersome democracy is removed from the economic system."[36]

In the 1993 debate about the Maastricht Treaty Jeremy Corbyn said that the Treaty "takes away from national parliaments the power to set economic policy and hands it over to an unelected set of bankers who will impose the economic policies of price stability, deflation and high unemployment." Deflation – austerity - pushed down investment, productivity, growth and living standards and forced up unemployment, debt levels and inequality. The Institute for Fiscal Studies estimated that austerity had cost each household in Britain £1,127 a year, with low-income families with children bearing the brunt.

The single market did not increase trade within the EU and it did not improve productivity in its members. The 2007 European Commission report *Steps towards a deeper economic integration: the Internal Market in the 21st century* acknowledged the single market's failure. It referred to the 'slowdown of trade growth within the EU15 and euro-zone relative to trade growth with third partners ...' It stated that "... since 2000 the trade effect of the enlargement process and particularly intra-EU15 trade integration, seem to have stalled." And, "... the share of extra EU suppliers in apparent consumption (AC) has gradually increased at the expense of domestic production."[37] It observed, "Not only are EU firms less active in fast growing markets but also they have not managed to improve their performance in fast growing sectors at world level although this was one of the main goals of the 1992 Single Market programme. ... the Internal Market ... has not led to a sufficient shift of the specialisation of the production sector towards the more technology intensive sectors where EU competitiveness can be more sustainable in the long-run."[38]

From 1999 to 2014 the overall growth of the EU founders was 87 per cent. The growth of EU members that were not in the euro was 116 per cent, of non-EU European countries 163 per cent. The more integrated into the EU a country was, the less its GDP grew.

The eurozone's growth rate for 2008-2017 was only 0.6 per cent. Its nominal GDP fell from 14.1 trillion euros in 2008 to 11.9 trillion in 2016. In 2018 its GDP per head was still less than it was in 2003. This was even after the EU issued a regulation in 2014 adding revenues from illegal drug sales, smuggling and prostitution to its measure of GDP.

So in Italy, for example, this added 1.3 per cent to its 2014 GDP. Jobs, living standards and public welfare were all better protected in the 1950s and 1960s than they have been in the EU's single market. Two-thirds of households in the relatively advanced economies, including the EU member states – up to 580 million people – saw their incomes (before benefits and other forms of state top-up) fall or stagnate between 2005 and 2014.[39] As the former European Commissioner Frits Bolkestein said, "The party is over ... we shall all have to work longer and harder, more hours in the week, more weeks in the year, and no state pension before the age of sixty-seven."[40] As the TUC acknowledged in 2017, "The EU's promotion of liberalisation has done huge damage to the services working people rely on, widened inequality by enriching private corporations, and brought greater insecurity and lower pay to working people."[41]

Even before the crash of 2008, the EU was failing its people, particularly its young people. In the years 1993 to 2003 more than a third of young people in Italy, Ireland, Belgium, the Netherlands, Portugal, Spain and Greece were unemployed for more than a year. The EU's youth unemployment rate averaged 19.3 per cent from 2000 to 2018. In February 2018 it was 15.9 per cent. It was 45 per cent in Greece (December 2017 figure), 35.5 per cent in Spain, 32.8 per cent in Italy, and 21.6 per cent in France.

Over the first 23 years of the single market (1990-2013), its 12 founding members had 9.4 per cent unemployment, while in the other OECD member countries it was 5.4 per cent. Among 15 to 24-year-olds the EU average was 31.8 per cent, more than three times the 8.7 per cent average of the other OECD countries. In February 2018, 17.6 million people in the EU were unemployed, a rate of 8.5 per cent. In Greece in December 2017, 20.8 per cent were unemployed.

The EU, locked into the euro, dragged us down with it. Lord King, ex-governor of the Bank of England, concluded that 'The tragedy of monetary union in Europe is not that it might collapse but that, given the degree of political commitment among the leaders of Europe, it might continue, bringing economic stagnation to the largest currency bloc in the world and holding back recovery of the wider world economy. It is at the heart of the disequilibrium in the world today."[42]

After the euro's crisis, Britain and other relatively wealthy EU members (even those outside the eurozone) had to pay to fix it. Under 'Target2', the European Central Bank's secret intra-eurozone payments system, creditor members made huge covert payments to weaker states, notably Italy, to keep the euro afloat. By May 2018 Germany was owed 871 billion euros. So, the ECB must print ever-increasing amounts of money (quantitative easing) to prop up its failing currency. It was no surprise that the EU wanted to keep us in and keep our payments coming in.

The European Commission and the European Council used the debt crisis to impose the Europe 2020 programme, the Barroso-van Rompuy economic plan, the Euro Plus Pact and the Single Market Act. All increased the power of capital over labour and all increased the EU's powers over member states.[43] The 2009 Lisbon Treaty took away workers' rights to job contracts and collective agreements, ending 'social Europe'.

The Euro Plus Pact, pushed through by Chancellor Merkel and France's President Nicholas Sarkozy in 2011, imposed pay cuts and freezes in the public sector. National collective bargaining systems were 'reformed' to allow companies to reduce 'downward wage rigidity'. A 2012 report by the European Commission's Directorate General for Economic and Financial Affairs called for 'employment-friendly reforms'. The EU 2020 programme spelt these out: each member state must reform its pensions, benefits and labour market rules to maximise labour flexibility, minimise 'disincentives to work' (that is, cut benefits) and prevent 'early exit from the labour market', that is, postpone retirement and state pension age. These were not employment-friendly, they were employer-friendly. The 2000 Lisbon Programme's 'flexicurity' was all flexibility, no security.

EU Treaties and Pacts relentlessly enforced austerity.[44] The EU Council Recommendation 2015/1029 of 19 June 2015 was: "(1) The United Kingdom should put an end to the present excessive deficit situation by 2016-2017 at the latest. (2) The United Kingdom should reach a headline deficit of 4.1 per cent of GDP in 2015-2016 and 2.7 per cent of GDP in 2016-2017 … (5) The Council sets the deadline of 15 October 2015 for the

United Kingdom to (i) take effective action; and (ii) to report in detail the consolidation strategy that is envisaged to achieve the targets." This was not so much a recommendation as an order. Orders had deadlines, recommendations did not.

But in President Barack Obama's brilliant analogy, "Cutting the deficit by gutting our investments in innovation and education is like lightening an overloaded aeroplane by removing its engine. It may feel like you're flying high at first, but it won't take long before you'll feel the impact."[45]

The EU's debt-to-GDP ratio rose from 68.6 per cent in 2008 to 89.2 per cent in 2016. This, after the decade of austerity that we were told was necessary to prioritise getting this ratio down. The EU's austerity policy failed to stop debts growing across the EU, unlike in Argentina, which cut its debt by doing the opposite of the austerity that the IMF had told it to impose. As Keynes asserted decades ago, "It is a complete mistake to believe that there is a dilemma between schemes for increasing employment and schemes for balancing the Budget – that we must go slowly and cautiously with the former for fear of injuring the latter. Quite the contrary. There is no possibility of balancing the Budget except by increasing the national income, which is much the same thing as increasing employment."[46]

Joseph Stiglitz showed that the EU's austerity policy 'would *inevitably* lead to deep recessions and depressions'. As he wrote, "austerity has *never* worked." He pointed out that there was a "fundamental difference between the Swabian housewife, which Germany's chancellor Angela Merkel so famously talks about, and a country: the Swabian housewife has to live within her budget, yes, but when she cuts back on her spending, her husband doesn't lose his job. If he did, the family would obviously be in much worse shape. Yet that's exactly what happens when austerity is imposed on a country: the government cuts spending, and people lose their jobs."[47]

Stiglitz commented, "The worst myths are that austerity will bring recovery and that more government spending will not. ... Recessions are caused by *lack of demand* – total demand is less than what the economy is capable of producing. When the government cuts back on spending, demand is lowered even more, and unemployment increases. ... Underlying the myth that austerity will bring confidence is often another myth – the myth that the national government's budget is like a household's budget. Every household, sooner or later, has to live within its means. When an economy has high unemployment, the simple rule does not apply to the national budget. This is because an expansion of spending can actually expand production by creating jobs that will be filled by people who would otherwise be unemployed. A single household, by spending more than its revenues, cannot change the macro-economy. A national government can. And the increase in GDP can be a multiple of the amount spent by the government."[48]

Inside the EU we could not adopt any economic policy other than this EU-driven 'austerity' (poverty) policy because we had no sovereignty. Of special importance, EU membership prevented us from having an effective policy for industry. The Cameron government allocated only around £4 billion a year to its industrial strategy. It had no industrial equivalent of its commitment to spend 0.7 per cent of gross national income on international development aid, a commitment of £11 billion a year that was met.

In 2016, total investment as a proportion of GDP, including intellectual property, was 15.6 per cent, physical investment was 12.6 per cent, and the critical investment able to produce the most increase in GDP – mechanisation, technology and power – was only 2.7 per cent. Even as recently as 2008 it was one third higher at 3.6 per cent.

'£350 million a week'

The Treasury figures for our gross payments to the EU were: 2009 £14.129 billion, 2010 £15.197 billion, 2011 £15.357 billion, 2012 £15.746 billion, 2013 £18.135 billion and 2014 £18.777

billion. According to the Institute of Fiscal Studies (based on official figures), in 2015 our gross (pre-rebate) payment to the EU was £17.8 billion.[49] In 2016 our gross payment was £20.5 billion, which was £394 million a week.[50] The Office for National Statistics' Pink Book listed our annual payment to EU institutions as £20 billion, which was £384.6 million a week. This figure included payments to EU institutions by UK households.[51]

We usually used gross figures in discussing money matters. For example, if you tell me your salary, you tell me the gross figure, not the amount after tax. The basic rate of income tax is 20 per cent: we do not count it as zero because we get it back in the form of schools, hospitals etc.

The slogan on the red bus was "We send the EU £350 million a week." It then said, "Let's fund our NHS instead." Inside the EU we had to give the EU this £350 million a week, which we could not spend as we wished. Outside the EU, we will not be giving the EU that £350 million a week; we could spend it as we wished. So, outside the EU we had the power to spend £350 million more on our NHS; inside the EU we did not have that power. This was not a promise, more a statement of fact. If we wanted the money to be spent on the NHS, we would have to make that happen. Only the government was able to deliver on any promises made in the campaign but instead it only made threats about what it would do if it lost, rather than promises about what it would do if it won. "Let's fund our NHS instead" was an aspiration that indeed could not be realized inside the EU.

In addition, some European Court rulings have exposed the taxpayer to massive liabilities for tax refunds to big businesses. The Office of Budget Responsibility forecast that HM Revenue & Customs would pay out £7.3 billion from 2016-2017 to 2020-2021, an average of £270.43 per household.[52] If HMRC also lost every case currently pending (a further £35.6 billion), we would be forced to pay out £42.9 billion, the equivalent of £1,589 per household.[53] The UK has tried to block these payouts but the

Court has overruled our tax legislation.[54] Leaving means we can end these vast tax payments, protecting our public services by saving between £7.3 billion and £42.9 billion by 2020-21.

Crystal balls

Before the crash of 2008, Alan Greenspan, chairman of the US Federal Reserve, saw nothing wrong. He said in 2005, "These increasingly complex financial instruments have contributed to the development of a far more flexible, efficient, and hence resilient financial system than the one that existed just a quarter-century ago."[55] Chancellor Gordon Brown told us on 20 June 2007 that growth was "expected to be stronger this year than last and stronger next year than this. We will succeed if like London we think globally ... advance with light-touch regulation, a competitive tax environment and flexibility."

Simon Lee commented, "Brown became a convert to the neo-liberal approach to globalisation, the political economy of Alan Greenspan, and a risk-based approach to financial regulation. It was this framework, which was fundamentally flawed, as Greenspan has admitted, which ultimately gave the freedom to bankers and markets to originate and distribute risk irresponsibly, in pursuit of short-term profit but without regard to the longer-term health of either their own institution or the wider economy. To this extent, Gordon Brown must be held responsible for the transition from boom to bust."[56] As Stiglitz noted, "it was the so-called experts in the financial sector who developed regulatory and macro-management models that led to the crisis of 2008. It was the experts who believed that the euro would lead to stronger economic performance."[57]

On 6 June 2016 Michael Gove said on Sky News that "the people of this country have had enough of experts ...." The pro-EU camp leapt on the remark, claiming that Gove was denigrating all experts. As Robert Peston commented, "the truth ... was that he was traduced, because a few vital words in what he said were ignored."[58] The full quote was, "the people of this country have had enough of experts from organisations with acronyms, saying that they know what is best, and getting it consistently wrong."

President Obama made a similar comment to the UN on 20 September 2016: "In Europe, a well-intentioned Brussels often became too isolated from the normal push and pull of national politics. Too often, in capitals, decision-makers have forgotten that democracy needs to be driven by civic engagement from the bottom up, not governance by experts from the top down." Nobody howled him down.

We should be sceptical of all claims, even those made by people who claimed expertise. Government and official institutions, like the OECD, the IMF, the Bank of England and the Treasury, all failed to warn of the crash of 2008, and they all warned of a great crash in late June 2016 if we voted to leave the EU – a crash which did not happen.

In 2010 the IMF projected that Italy's income per head would be 3 per cent higher by 2015 than it was in 2010. Instead, it was more than 4 per cent lower. IMF economists forced austerity on poor countries, making them even poorer. All too many foreign policy experts backed disasters like the attack on Suez, the Bay of Pigs fiasco, the Vietnam War, the war against Iraq, etc.

The experts in the Treasury have been wrong about every major economic issue since the Great Depression. The Treasury told us that joining the EU's disastrous exchange rate mechanism would be good for us: it led to mass unemployment and 'Black Wednesday'. The Treasury told us it would be a disaster if we left the ERM. But after we left the ERM on 16 September 1992, inflation fell, interest rates were cut, and the economy recovered. The Treasury urged us to sell half our gold reserves for less than $300 an ounce; gold then rose more than six-fold. The Treasury told us that we were doomed if we failed to join the euro. We kept the pound and survived. Before the 2008 crash, the Treasury told us that the big banks were safe. No comment. The Treasury said in the March 2016 Budget documents, "Voting to leave the EU would create a profound economic shock and years of uncertainty." The Treasury warned of a 'downside scenario … a much more profound shock … credible risk this more acute scenario could materialise'.

Before the referendum, the Bank of England warned that a vote to leave the EU would increase unemployment, hit economic growth and cause a recession. Its Governor, Mark Carney, said in March 2016 that a vote to leave 'would be likely to have a negative impact in the short term. I certainly think that would increase the risk of recession."

Leaving the EU would be bad for us, said the OECD that received €30,000,000 from the EU between 2007 and 2014, the OECD that said that we would get 'great benefits' from joining the ERM, the OECD that recommended that we join the euro. The OECD said that if we left the EU our GDP would fall by 1.25 per cent in the short term. Its secretary-general Angel Gurria said in April 2016 that "Brexit would be a major negative shock to the UK economy."

The OECD warned us in May 2016 that leaving the EU would impose 'a persistent and rising cost on the economy' amounting to the equivalent of £2,200 per household by 2020. Mr Gurria said the OECD had tried to persuade voters of the danger of a 'Brexit tax' on their living standards if they voted to leave the EU. After the referendum, Gurria said, "The quality of life (in Britain after leaving the EU), you know, will probably remain to a very great extent as it is today, because the values will remain the same. There may be some things that change. We do not know to what extent – it's very early." He changed his mind after looking at the evidence.

The IMF said that in the third quarter of 2016 GDP would fall by 0.3 per cent. Christine Lagarde, the IMF's managing director, said of the consequences of a Leave vote, "It's going to be pretty bad to very, very bad." The IMF later accepted that its forecast of a crash after a vote to leave was wrong. Pierre Moscovici, European Commissioner for Economic and Financial Affairs, said that the EU must acknowledge that our growth has been 'more resilient than was anticipated' after our decision to leave.

Robert Azevedo, the World Trade Organisation's director general, warned before the referendum that voting to leave would spark 'tortuous' negotiations to re-enter the WTO and would face 'billions in annual costs'.[59] But after the vote he said that leaving would be 'relatively straightforward' and 'smooth': "The UK is a member of the WTO today, it will continue to be a member tomorrow. There will be no discontinuity in membership. ... Trade will not stop, it will continue and members negotiate the legal basis under which that trade is going to happen. But it doesn't mean that we'll have a vacuum or a 'disruption' in terms of trade flows or anything of the kind ..."[60] He too changed his mind after looking at the evidence.

The CBI told us we should stay in the EU. Previously, it had told us that we should join and stay in the European Exchange Rate Mechanism (which cost us a million jobs in 1990-92) and that we should join the euro. Richard Fletcher, *The Times'* Business Editor, reported, "The independence of the CBI has been undermined because it received more than £800,000 in funding from the European Commission over the past five years."[61]

Reports by the Bank of England, the Treasury, the London School of Economics, the Organisation for Economic Cooperation and Development, the International Monetary Fund and the National Institute of Economic and Social Research did indeed get their forecasts consistently and systematically wrong. Yet Cameron and Chancellor of the Exchequer George Osborne (should that be spelt Ausborne?) "cited the results of this handful of economic studies as though they were objective 'facts' rather than economic simulations based upon a range of often questionable assumptions."[62]

After the referendum, the OECD, the IMF, the Bank of England and the European Commission all admitted that they had been wrong about the short-term impact of the vote to leave. The Bank of England's chief economist publicly admitted that his profession had failed to foresee the 2008 financial crisis and had also misjudged the impact of the vote to leave.

Experts in the private sector did no better. Goldman Sachs said on 26 June 2016, "We now expect the economy to enter a mild recession by early 2017." On 5 September Goldman Sachs said, "We now expect the UK economy to avoid even the technical recession that we had foreseen immediately after the Referendum." Morgan Stanley admitted that it was 'eating humble pie' over its forecast that Britain would suffer an immediate recession if it voted to leave. Credit Suisse said in January, "If the UK votes to leave the EU, it is likely to entail an immediate and simultaneous economic and financial shock for the UK." On 6 September Credit Suisse said, "The impact of the vote to leave the EU on the UK economy seems to be materially less negative than we expected." HSBC forecast that a vote to leave would push inflation up by five points, would force interest rates up and cut nearly two points off economic growth in 2017. All wrong.

Three days before the vote, speculator George Soros warned us not to vote to leave, threatening a 'Brexit crash'. A week after the referendum, 71 per cent of City economists surveyed by Bloomberg expected a recession in 2016. Yet Britain grew faster in the six months after the vote than in the six months before it. A survey by Reuters found a consensus among economists that unemployment would rise by 9,000 a month in the second half of 2016; in fact, it fell by almost exactly that amount.

Politicians made their forecasts too. Nick Clegg said that 3 million jobs depended on our being in the EU. By this logic, millions of American jobs depended on the USA being in the EU. The Executive Director of the In Campaign, Will Straw, told the Treasury Select Committee on 2 March 2016, "We have not and have never claimed that 3 million jobs would be lost if we left the EU." But ex-TUC leader Brendan Barber said in the In campaign's 8 June broadcast, "The wages, the jobs, the living standards of millions of British workers, directly depend upon our trading relationship with the rest of Europe." Labour In's leaflet claimed in its very first sentence, "Millions of jobs depend on our EU membership ..."

Alan Johnson of Labour In said on 23 February 2016, "That's two thirds of our manufacturing base reliant on that single market access and Britain's membership of the EU." Full Fact, on 9 March, responded, "These claims are wrong. ... Newer figures suggest roughly 15 per cent of manufacturing jobs were directly associated with demand from other EU countries in 2014. ... The report that the original figures were based on spells out that this doesn't mean this many jobs would be lost if the UK left the EU."

This report, by the National Institute of Economic and Social Research, had claimed that "up to 3.2 million jobs are now associated directly with exports of goods and services to other EU countries." Associated with, not dependent on. Professor Ian Begg, one of the report's authors, pointed out that "there is no a priori reason to suppose that many of these, *if any*, would be lost permanently if Britain were to leave the EU." (My emphasis)

Anna Soubry, Cameron's small business minister, claimed that outside the EU, our exports to the EU would 'fall to almost absolutely zero'. Cameron said that leaving the EU would put a 'bomb under the economy'. But some disagreed: one Conservative MP said, "If we were outside the EU altogether, we'd still be trading with all these European countries. Of course we would. ... There's a lot of scaremongering on all sides of this debate. Of course the trading would go on."[63] The same person said in November 2015, "Some people seem to say that really

Britain couldn't survive, couldn't do okay outside the European Union. I don't think that is true." Who was this MP? David Cameron.

Cameron and Osborne wrote in the *Daily Telegraph* of 22 May 2016, "Mortgages would be harder to get and more expensive." Mortgage rates have fallen since the referendum. Cameron wrote in the *Daily Telegraph* of 11 June, "if we leave, pensioner benefits would be under threat, and the triple lock could no longer be guaranteed in the long term." The Prime Minister's office stated in August, "The manifesto contains a commitment to protect the triple lock. That commitment still stands."

Cameron said that if we voted to leave the EU, "the shock to the economy ... would tip the country into recession." Osborne said it was a 'fact' that "a vote to leave would represent an immediate and profound shock to our economy. That shock would push our economy into a recession and lead to an increase in unemployment of around 500,000, GDP would be 3.6 per cent smaller, average real wages would be lower, inflation higher, sterling weaker, house prices would be hit and public borrowing would rise compared with a vote to remain.... the shock could be much more profound, meaning the effect on the economy would be worse still. The rise in uncertainty could be amplified ... We already know the long-term effects of a vote to leave: Britain would be permanently poorer. Now we know the short-term shock too: an economy in recession, major job losses and a self-inflicted blow to living standards and aspirations of the British people."[64]

A letter by Cameron and Osborne said: "A few weeks ago, the Treasury published analysis which shows Britain would be worse off to the tune of £4,300 for every household every year by 2030. ... The analysis produced by the Treasury today shows that a vote to leave will push our economy into a recession that would knock 3.6 per cent off GDP and, over two years, put hundreds of thousands of people out of work right across the country, compared to the forecast for continued growth if we vote to remain in the EU. ... This would be, for the first time in our history, a recession brought on ourselves: a DIY recession."[65] They forgot that the recession of the early 1990s was a DIY recession: the Major government put the economy into recession to keep the pound in the EU's Exchange Rate Mechanism in the interests of closer integration with the EU.

On the 8 June 2016 Andrew Neil Show on BBC1, Neil asked Osborne, "The Treasury report doesn't show that we would be £4,300 worse off, does it? On either scenario, in or out, the Treasury report shows substantial growth in the economy through 2030." Neil then cited the House of Commons Treasury Select Committee: "Neither government departments nor other spokespeople for the remain side should repeat [this] mistaken assertion ... to persist with this claim would be to misrepresent the Treasury's own work." Osborne could only respond weakly that this was a selective quote. On 11 June, Cameron repeated this 'mistaken assertion'. Even Will Straw called the £4,300 claim 'a spurious specificity'.

The warning that leaving the EU would make every household £4,300 worse off was not believed. The Conservative-supporting *Spectator* described it as 'breathtaking dishonesty'. Its editor Fraser Nelson wrote: "I'm a Europhile, but these are the kinds of tactics that make me want to vote 'out' – the appalling level of dishonesty with which the government is making the case."[66]

The Treasury warned that if voters backed Brexit, the economy would contract by 1 per cent between July and September, compared to the same quarter in 2015, before shrinking another 0.4 per cent from October to December. So just the decision to leave, as opposed to leaving, would push us into recession. The pro-EU camp repeatedly described this forecast as 'fact'.[67] This did not happen. The economy did not decline after the referendum. It grew in every quarter by an average of 0.4 per cent. By November 2017 GDP was 2.5 per cent higher in real terms than on the day before the referendum. That was 6.1 per cent better than the Treasury forecast, equivalent to £135 billion of extra annual production over their estimate, or just over £2000 for every man, woman and child.

In May 2016 Osborne forecast 500,000 job losses in the year after any Leave vote. In fact, by August 2017 there were 137,000 more people in work than a year earlier. By April 2018 unemployment was at its lowest in more than four decades, at 1.42 million, and a record 32.2 million people were in work. Osborne and the Treasury could not even forecast accurately events just a few months ahead, yet some believed their forecasts of events 30 years ahead!

Cameron was caught on camera at Davos in January 2018 admitting that Brexit was 'not a disaster' and was turning out 'less badly than we first thought'. Gisela Stuart, who had chaired the Vote Leave campaign, welcomed the former Prime Minister's realisation that "his claims of doom and gloom were baseless scaremongering."

The EU's customs union

Trade did not require a customs union, and more than half our trade happened without it. We already sold 56 per cent of our exports outside the EU, most sold to countries where the EU had no free trade agreement or customs union. The customs union put a tariff wall around the EU, imposing charges on all the goods that we imported from the rest of the world. Inside the EU customs union we could not set our own tariffs at levels which suited our economy but had to implement across the board a tariff schedule set for the benefit of EU producers. So, we had to pay more to buy goods like food, clothing and footwear.

The EU imposed tariffs on imports from the 93 per cent of the world that is not a member of the bloc. The EU kept prices high by imposing tariffs on more than 12,000 imported products, including rice, coffee, oranges, new world wine, and children's shoes and clothes.The House of Commons Library said that "consumer prices across a range of other goods imported from outside the EU are raised as a result of the common external tariff and non-tariff barriers to trade imposed by the EU. These include footwear (a 17 per cent tariff), bicycles (15 per cent tariff) and a range of clothing (12 per cent tariff)."[68] It also included an average of 23 per cent on food. For example, we would be required to impose a 16 per cent tariff on oranges to protect the interests of Spanish orange growers. 80 per cent of these tariff revenues went straight to the EU. Since 2011 we have sent the EU £15.7 billion in customs union tariffs.

The EU-funded CBI told us that we could stay in the EU's customs union while 'respecting the vote to leave the EU'. Not so – the customs union is enshrined in the 1957 Treaty of Rome, the EU's legal essence. Staying in the EU's customs union would prevent us from negotiating trade deals on our own behalf and we would be rule takers not rule makers, leaving us with no say over how third countries could access our market. Customs union membership would mean even less control over trade than we had now. It would mean that we would have no power to stop the EU granting US companies access to all our public services, including the NHS. We would be obliged to open ourselves up to goods from nations the EU cut deals with, but with no reciprocity. It would be the Transatlantic Trade and Investment Partnership (TTIP) reborn. Many people opposed the Transatlantic Trade and Investment Partnership but did not see that the first and greatest of these 'Partnerships' was in fact the European Union. The EU was Britain's TTIP.

The only country in the world to have a customs union with the EU was Turkey, which had a deal under which the EU signed away access for third countries to Turkish markets, with Turkey often getting no reciprocal access itself. So, for example, it must import Mexican cars tariff-free, while Mexico slaps 20 per cent on its clothing. A European Parliament report on EU-Turkey relations concluded, "In sum, the existing legal and institutional framework of the CU translates into an overall relationship of general dependency both economically and politically of Turkey upon the EU. Turkey is obliged to adopt a considerable part of the acquis in several fields and to align its custom and commercial legislation with the EU legislation, without involvement in the EU's external trade decision-making processes with regard to negotiating FTAs with third parties. Without setting out a binding roadmap to membership these systemic weaknesses undermine the legitimacy of the relationship and creates for Turkey a sovereignty shortfall."

The Turkish diplomat Mehmet Ogutcu, who helped to negotiate his country's customs deal with the EU, said, "Being part of the Customs Union but not being able to make favourable trade deals with the rest of the world, and being subjected to unilateral EU rules and decisions in which you are not allowed to participate, do not look the most intelligent and win-win way of integration in terms of protecting your national interests. ... With no influence in decisions on free trade agreements with the rest of the world and no membership prospects, the Customs Union has effectively reduced Turkey to a semi-colonial status, as some politicians argue."[69]

EU negotiator Michel Barnier rejected the idea of a special customs union for the UK, saying, "We can't change our rules, our rules will remain the same. When you're in a customs union for goods, like Turkey for example, you become part of a common trade policy. You don't have autonomy anymore."

As the International Trade Secretary Liam Fox said at Bloomberg on 27 February 2018, "There has been much debate in recent days about the EU's customs union. As we are leaving the European Union, necessarily, we cannot remain in the Customs Union which is open only to EU Member States. The alternative has been proposed that we enter a new customs union with the European Union. But what would this mean?

"First of all, for goods, we would have to accept EU trade rules without any say in how they were made, handing Brussels considerable control of the UK's external trade policy. Secondly, it would limit our ability to reach new trade agreements with the world's fastest-growing economies. And thirdly, it would limit our ability to develop our trade and development policies that would offer new ways for the world's poorest nations to trade their way out of poverty.

"And what would a customs union actually consist of? Which sectors would be covered? Would it be like Turkey which has a customs union but only for industrial goods and some agricultural products? Whatever it covered, should such a customs union be negotiated, we would be forced to allow goods from other countries into our market tariff-free, on terms set by Brussels, without any tariff-free access to the markets of other countries in return. And, if we were to disagree, Brussels could simply overrule us.

"Those on the political left who opposed TTIP, the agreement between the European Union and the United States, might want to consider that in a customs union, they would have to implement any elements of TTIP, whether they like them or not, in any sectors covered by a customs union. As rule takers, without any say in how the rules were made, we would be in a worse position than we are today. Not only does the EU have a high average external tariff – 5.1% compared to the US 3.5% – but it continues to operate tariffs in a way that particularly disadvantages countries who want to add value to their primary commodities and move up value chains.

"As we leave the EU we are committed to maintaining preferential access for developing countries. Outside the Customs Union, we would have the freedom to expand access and tackle barriers to trade to enable poorer countries genuinely to trade their way out of poverty and become less dependent on our aid budgets."

In February 2018, senior officials in the Treasury, with the assistance of officials from the Department for Exiting the European Union and the Cabinet Office's Europe Unit, all acting under their own initiative without permission from ministers or Downing Street, produced a report that said that the only thing to do was stay in the customs union. This ran directly against government policy. These senior officials then leaked the report to the press at a critical moment in the political debate, before ministers from the Department for Exiting the European Union had even seen it.

Retired top civil servants Lord O'Donnell, Lord Turnbull and Lord Butler then criticised those who criticised these senior Treasury officials. Lord Turnbull likened criticism of top civil servants to Nazi lies. All was fair in debate, but it should be remembered that, as *The Economist* remarked in 2007, "a good rule in most discussions is that the first person to call the other a Nazi automatically loses the argument."

The EU's single market

Neither the British state nor the EU had ever published an assessment of the single market's effects. No trade association or business had ever presented evidence that EU membership had enabled member companies to outperform their non-member competitors in trading with the single market. Nick Clegg wrote of the single market's 'untold benefits', which he declined to tell us about, and of its 'immeasurable benefits', which he declined to measure.

By comparison with the Common Market years from 1973 to 1992, the single market years from 1993 to 2015 were an era of falling UK export growth to the EU. We were 36th out of the 40 fastest-growing exporters to the other founder members of the single market. We had been overtaken by many of the countries that traded with the EU under WTO rules. In general, countries that exported to the EU under WTO rules were the fastest growing exporters to it, faster than countries which traded with the EU as fellow EU members, or under bilateral treaties, or as European Economic Area (EEA) members. China, the USA, Japan, Australia and many other countries had increased their exports to customers in countries in the single market faster from outside than we did from inside.

Most of our trade was conducted under WTO rules. Our biggest single-country trading partner and biggest export destination was the USA, where we sold around 17 per cent of our exports, under WTO rules. We did not have to be part of the USA to trade with it. Our trade under WTO rules was growing and was in surplus. Our EU trade was shrinking and in deficit. £111 billion of the total £115 billion foreign payments deficit we had in 2016 was with the EU27 and only £4 billion with the rest of the world. If membership of the single market and customs union worked for us, this would be the other way around.

Moreover, our exports to the 111 countries with which we had traded under WTO rules since 1993 grew four times more than our exports to the EU.[70] Our exports to the EU grew by only 10 per cent between 2010 and 2017, while our sales to the USA were up 41 per cent, to China 60 per cent, New Zealand 40 per cent, Japan 60 per cent and South Korea 100 per cent.

The Cameron government's pro-EU leaflet said, "No other country has managed to secure significant access to the Single Market, without having to ... pay into the EU; accept EU citizens living and working in their country." But the EU was not a hermit kingdom, where you had to beg its permission before you could trade with it. Access to the single market meant being able to trade with businesses in single market countries. Membership of the single market meant being bound by single market rules. Access was consistent with the vote to leave the EU. Membership was not. Access did not require membership. Michael Wohlgemuth, Founding Director of the pro-EU body Open Europe Berlin, acknowledged that "one does not have to be a *member* of the single market in order to have *access* to it."[71] By being a member of the EU, we were paying for access to a market that other countries got for free.

Access to the single market was not granted or withheld by the EU but was available to all nations. Businesses traded across borders not because politicians signed trade deals but because it made good business sense. We did not need trade agreements to trade. As Lord Bamford of JCB often said, to trade, you just trade.

The USA and China both sold more goods to the EU's single market than we did. Imports and exports worth $686 billion flowed between the USA and the EU in 2016, under WTO rules. The USA and China had $649 billion of trade, the EU and China $613 billion – all under WTO rules.

Some 160 or more countries all not in the EU still somehow sold to EU members - so we could too. We did not have to be a member to sell goods and services to customers in EU member countries. China was not in the single market yet exported 374 billion euros' worth of goods to the EU in 2017. The USA was not in the single market yet exported 256 billion euros' worth of goods to the EU in 2017. Russia was not in the single market yet exported 145 billion euros' worth of goods to the EU in 2017. Japan was not in the single market yet exported 68.8 billion euros' worth of goods to the EU in 2017. They all accessed the single market without being in the single market. None had a trade deal with the EU. All traded quite happily with the EU, under WTO rules.

Trade in services also flourished between EU members and non-EU members. EU financial regulations allowed non-members to access EU financial markets, as companies from the USA, Singapore, Hong Kong and others all did. Countries outside the EU sold service-sector exports into the EU worth more than 600 billion euros in 2015. From 2004 to 2012 the services exports of 27 non-members to the EU grew faster under WTO rules than the intra-EU services exports of EU members. Since a single market in services barely existed, there was little to be lost by leaving it.[72]

The OECD said that EU nations had 'ample room' to keep trading in financial services after we left. It pointed out that "Erecting new barriers to financial services in the post-Brexit environment will not be in the collective interest of the global economy, where London plays such a key role in international banking, bonds and foreign exchange."[73]

On 30 October 2017, the Bank of England claimed that up to 75,000 jobs could be lost in financial services after we left the EU. But the Bank was contradicting what businesses were saying. A Reuters poll of more than 100 finance firms suggested that the number of job losses would be just below 10,000 in the 'few years' after we leave. London was still the world's leading financial centre and after the referendum it even extended its lead.[74]

Trading with the EU under WTO rules was 'perfectly manageable', said Roberto Azevedo, the WTO's director general. 98 per cent of world trade was conducted under WTO rules, including trade in services and intellectual property through the WTO's roughly 30 constituent agreements. Tariffs under WTO rules were relatively low and falling. If talks broke down and the UK had to rely on WTO rules (average tariffs 1.5 per cent), the impact would be small. Worldwide the average tariff had declined from about 40 per cent in the early 1940s to 13 per cent in 1947, when the General Agreement on Tariffs and Trade was signed, to 6 per cent in 1994 when the WTO was signed, to its current record low. So, we were better off paying tariffs that were getting smaller all the time, rather than an EU membership fee that was getting bigger all the time.

Rules set by global bodies like the WTO increasingly governed world and EU trade. After leaving the EU, we will have our own seat at the WTO, instead of being represented (or misrepresented) there by the EU. Even if we were challenged in the WTO, our trade would continue. The WTO only accepted the EU's 2004 schedules in late 2016. Trade continued during that twelve-year gap.

EU members wanted to trade with Britain. We bought far more from them than we sold to them. The EU's GDP growth has lagged every other region for a generation. The eurozone economy was stagnant, hardly bigger than in 2003. The 85 per cent of the world economy outside the EU was growing far faster, offering us all kinds of trading opportunities. In 1999, 61 per cent of our trade was with the EU; by 2015 it was 43 per cent.

The rest of the EU sold us around £291 billion in goods and services a year but bought only £223 billion in goods and services a year in return. It had a trade surplus with us of £68 billion. They did not want to harm trade with us. We should be able to use our position as the EU's major buyer of export goods to negotiate trade in goods and access to financial services. Any attempt to make access to the EU market dependent upon mirroring EU regulatory regimes should be firmly rejected. The rest of the EU had a simple choice. Did they want to retain tariff-free access to our market or not? If not, then their access and our access would be under Most Favoured Nation WTO rules.

The WTO has Agreements whereby countries recognise each other's product standards - Technical Barriers to Trade (TBTs) and Sanitary and Phytosanitary (SPS) measures in the case of foods. Since the UK already had regulatory convergence with the EU, the EU would not be allowed to discriminate against UK goods entering the EU on grounds such as health and safety, because any discrimination would violate the Agreements. Under the TBT, product safety testing procedures were not allowed to be more onerous or be applied more strictly than necessary to give importers confidence that products conformed to the relevant technical standards. So, the EU was not allowed to impose regulatory barriers on UK goods without justification, if product and safety standards remained aligned. New EU barriers would be illegal under WTO rules, even with no deal.

Companies in EU member countries would want to stay tariff-free. If the EU imposed a vindictive policy (against the interests of member states and of business), then we would enjoy tariff-free trade on what we were good at like aerospace and services, whilst French agriculture would face quite high tariffs and German cars would face a 10 per cent tariff.

Obviously, every exporter must comply with the standards of the country to which it was exporting. For example, Jaguar Land Rover's auto exports to the USA differed from those to the EU regarding emission standards; in fact, even their exports to California must meet emission standards that differ from those in other US states. Companies sold to customers in the EU by meeting EU regulatory standards on specific goods and, where necessary, paying the low tariffs. These companies' home countries did not have to accept EU rules and laws, pay annual fees and embrace the EU's four freedoms of capital, labour, goods and services. The EU uncompromisingly always treated these four freedoms as indivisible.

Leaving the EU meant leaving the European Economic Area (EEA). Being in the EEA meant being subject to the single market. The EU briefing on its Agreement with the EEA and the European Free Trade Association (EFTA) said, "The Agreement guarantees equal rights and obligations within the Internal Market for citizens and economic operators in the EEA. ... Whenever an EEA-relevant legal act is amended or a new one adopted by the EU, a corresponding amendment should be made to the relevant Annex of the EEA Agreement." It acknowledged that the EEA and EFTA had 'little influence on the final decision on the legislation on the EU side', while 'all the EEA countries are subject to the Internal Market legal framework.' Additionally, "Efta countries are part of the Schengen area." One of the components of the EEA Agreement is the EFTA Court, which resolves disputes. The Agreement requires this Court to follow the rulings of the ECJ.

Switzerland has single market access through a series of agreements where they agree to adopt elements of the EU rulebook. They have also committed to the four freedoms and Schengen membership. This also means that Switzerland pays to support 'economic and social cohesion' in the new EU member states. The model does not grant Swiss companies unrestricted access to the single market for services. Any agreement that we made with the EU must mean no membership of a customs union, the EEA or EFTA, and freedom to make our own deals with third countries.

The EU was all about free trade. Free trade was aggressive economic competition. The German employing class waged trade war in and through the EU, against its fellow EU members and against other countries too. Capital was accumulated through free trade. Some wanted worldwide free trade. When the EU said free trade, it meant treaties against national sovereignty like the North American Free Trade Agreement, the Trans-Pacific Partnership and TTIP. These were not free trade agreements, not even trade agreements, but investor-protection agreements. We needed to escape TTIP, the Trade in Services Agreement and the EU-Canada Comprehensive Economic and Trade Agreement, which all privileged foreign investors and multinational companies. They were forms of economic aggression and political interference which the EU tried to impose on us. But with the EU there was no such thing as free trade. EU members either paid a membership fee and no tariffs or paid tariffs and no membership fee.

Economist Michael Burrage summed up, "Overall, the evidence shows that the disadvantages of non-membership of the EU and Single Market have been vastly exaggerated and that the supposed benefits of membership, whether for exports of goods and services, for productivity, for world-wide trade, or for employment, are largely imaginary. ... The benefits of

EU and Single Market membership have been illusory, while its costs are real, onerous, and unacceptable to a majority of the British people."[75]

Ameet Gill, Cameron's former director of strategy, said, "I remember in the campaign, the most significant moment of the campaign that we saw on the Remain side was in mid-April when Michael [Gove] made that speech saying we're going to leave the single market. Now, we spent the next three months trying to hang that round Leave's neck. We went round saying, 'Look, a vote to leave is a vote to leave the single market.' So I do find it a bit weird with some politicians coming now saying that was never on the ballot paper." Cameron said on 13 June 2016, "What the British public will be voting for is to leave the EU and leave the single market." Nick Clegg acknowledged during the referendum campaign that a vote for Brexit meant leaving the single market. On the *Daily Politics* show, presenter Andrew Neil showed Clegg the video of this, yet Clegg stuck to his claim that there was no mandate for leaving the single market.

On 8 January 2017, on BBC1, Andrew Marr said to Nicola Sturgeon, "you have made it very clear that what you mean by a 'soft' Brexit or an 'acceptable' Brexit involves staying inside the single market and the customs union. The problem is that people were told all the way through the referendum that leaving the EU meant leaving those things." Sturgeon said, "I'm not sure … I don't think that's the case." Marr replied, "It is the case, if I may say so. I interviewed David Cameron, George Osborne, Michael Gove, Boris Johnson and I asked all of them, and they all said yes, it means leaving the single market."

After the referendum, the RMT's Mick Cash pointed out that membership of the single market meant de facto membership of the EU. He said, "The trade union movement needs to be extremely careful if it is not to be accused of seeking to undermine the democratic decision of the British people on leaving the EU. It was the millions of votes of working people across the country that swung the vote to leave and that must not be ignored. The constant flagging up of continued membership of the Single Market sends out all the wrong signals and is a diversion from the opportunities that leaving the EU presents for a strong and ambitious trade union movement in the fields of jobs, workers' rights and public services. As a movement we need to make it clear that there is no back door open to continued EU membership and we need to be promoting a strong, alternative vision for the future that unites our communities."

Being outside the single market gave us control over our laws and borders and freed us from EU regulations and from its external tariff. Leaving the single market was the only way to take back control of our borders and of our laws. We would get the same free access to the same market without having to pay the £350,000,000 weekly membership fee.

Greece, the canary in the mine.

In 2001 Greece's Pasok government paid Goldman Sachs hundreds of millions of dollars in fees for fixing deals that hid the government's real level of borrowing. This enabled Greece to meet the Maastricht Treaty guideline of debt of no more than 60 per cent of GDP and so to join the euro. Goldman Sachs hedged its exposure to Greece by buying a credit default swap on the deal from Deutsche Pfandbriefbank. The European Central Bank refused to disclose any documents related to the case.

But when Greece joined the euro, the currency's over-valuation harmed Greece's manufacturing and shipping industries. Cheap imports displaced Greek-made goods. Then came the EU bailouts, which saved the banks, not the Greeks. The EU told the Greeks in 2010 that under its bailout measures Greece's economy would grow by 1.1 per cent in 2011 and by 2.1 per cent in 2012. Not so – it contracted by 7.1 per cent in 2011 and by 6.4 per cent in 2012.

The Left Syriza government's fantasy of a 'good EU' led Greece to disaster. In June 2015 the Syriza government called a national referendum on the next proposed bailout. But when on 5 July 61.5 per cent voted against the EU's 'austerity' package, Syriza then imposed it anyway. Syriza had said Greece had to stay in the EU so that Syriza could help to reform the EU away from austerity. Instead the EU reformed Syriza and turned it into the enforcer of even harsher austerity. A single claw ensnared, and the bird was caught.

Lord King commented, "Since the agreement implied an increase in Greece's already unsustainable debt burden and no measures to boost overall demand, it was unclear why either side saw any benefit to it other than preserving the shackles of euro membership. The Greek Prime Minister, Mr Tsipras, called the proposals 'irrational' but said he was willing to implement them to 'avoid disaster for the country'."[76] It was irrational to accept these proposals because they did indeed bring disaster to the country. As Stiglitz pointed out, "Greece's depression wasn't because Greece didn't do what it was supposed to; it was because it did."[77]

The EU had agreed that we would not have to contribute towards Eurozone bailouts, but Osborne later had to admit that the EU had torn up that agreement: "out of the blue, in flagrant breach of the agreement we'd all signed up to, and without even the courtesy of a telephone call, we were informed we would have to pay to bail out Greece." On SkyNews on 2 June 2016 Cameron had said, "we can never be asked to bail out eurozone countries." Yet in September 2015 the European Court had confirmed that article 122(2) 'enables the Union to grant ad hoc financial assistance to a Member State'.[78]

Only €15 billion of the €410 billion total aid to Greece went into Greece's economy. The greatest part went to its main creditors – German and French banks. Economist Paul Krugman observed, "You get a picture of a European policy elite always ready to spring into action to defend the banks, but otherwise completely unwilling to admit that its policies are failing the people which the economy is supposed to serve."[79]

According to the OECD the 2016 annual average wage in Greece was lower than in 2000. The wage share of GDP fell from 61.1 per cent in 2010 to 56.7 per cent in 2015. But this enforced austerity did not even cut the debt: Greek sovereign debt rose from 115 per cent of GDP in 2010 to 181 per cent in 2018. From January 2018 the Greek government stopped publishing the usual monthly statistics of births and deaths. In 2017 the annual total of deaths was 123,700, up from 118,623 in 2016. In 2013 the total had been 70,830. Before the financial crisis the total averaged 60,000. The austerity imposed by the EU and the IMF caused this huge increase in mortality by imposing poverty and unemployment and by destroying Greece's national health service, which in turn caused hunger, despair and an increase in suicides.

Lord King wrote, "It is evident, as it has been for a very long while, that the only way forward for Greece is to default on (or be forgiven) a substantial proportion of its debt burden and to devalue its currency so that exports and the substitution of domestic products for imports can compensate for the depressing effects of the fiscal contraction imposed to date. ... if the alternative is crushing austerity, continuing mass unemployment, and no end in sight to the burden of debt, then leaving the euro area may be the only way to plot a route back to economic growth and full employment. The long-term benefits outweigh the short-term costs."[80]

Stiglitz agreed that Greece would gain from leaving the euro: "Indeed, freed from the conditions imposed as part of the 'assistance', freed from austerity and counterproductive structural reforms, the country would actually be in better shape."[81]

Tax haven man

In 2012 Cameron criticised the comedian Jimmy Carr, describing him as 'morally wrong' for seeking to avoid taxes. But the *Financial Times* reported that Cameron personally intervened in 2013 to weaken an EU proposal that would have forced member states to create public registers disclosing the true owners of shell companies and trusts. Cameron wrote to then President of the European Council Herman van Rompuy, "It is clearly important we recognise the important differences between companies and trusts. This means that the solution for addressing the potential misuse of companies, such as central public registries, may well not be appropriate generally." The *Financial Times* noted that this resulted in the EU placing less scrutiny on trusts than originally intended. The ECJ's case law in this area made it hard for countries to tax the activities of multi-national companies who used the tax avoidance structures set up under laws like Luxembourg's, for example.

One reason that tax havens were not illegal in Britain was that City of London corporate lawyers - who profited from tax havens - wrote the laws with island-sized loopholes to help the very rich to dodge tax. The City was the world's money launderer, the tax haven of all tax havens, the receiver of the world's stolen capital. Barclays Bank for example had set up an entire unit for tax dodging, the structured capital markets division, which made £1 billion profit a year. It marketed a product called Structured Trust Advantaged Repackaged Securities, which a US court found to be 'an abusive tax avoidance scheme'. Barclays itself paid only £82 million tax in 2012, on £7 billion profits, an effective tax rate of just one per cent.

Being in the EU's single market helped many multinational companies to dodge tax. They used the EU's freedom of establishment to trade within the single market out of companies incorporated in the EU states with favourable tax regimes, like Luxembourg, Ireland, and the Netherlands. So, these firms could then steer their Britain-derived income away from Britain, as tax-deductible costs of a separate company, and paid minimal tax.[82] In this way, large corporations have been the main beneficiaries of the EU's single market.[83]

The EU had its own in-house tax haven Luxembourg, whose Prime Minister used to be European Commission President Jean-Claude Juncker. When Juncker was Prime Minister, he gave sweetheart tax deals to more than 340 giant corporations, including many of the leading US tech giants, enabling them to evade most of their taxes. The public record proved that, as he boasted at the time, he was instrumental in many of these deals. Later, he said he knew nothing about them.

Stiglitz commented, "While the Troika has criticized tax avoidance in Greece, dominant countries in the eurozone have been among those most adamant *against* changing the international framework for taxation in ways that would reduce tax avoidance, and the head of the European Commission, Jean-Claude Juncker, in his role as premier of Luxembourg, perfected that country's role as a center for tax avoidance."[84]

At a 2015 UN conference on Finance for Development, the developing countries, led by India, nearly unanimously backed changing the international framework for taxation in ways that would reduce tax avoidance. But, as Stiglitz commented, "Unfortunately, none of the eurozone countries supported the initiative, and with the strong opposition of the United States, it died."[85]

Luxembourg was also quite good at avoiding other payments. It is the EU member country with the highest GDP per head, yet it had not contributed a single euro to it over the past fifteen years, while it received the highest proportion of the funds given out by the Commission. The Commission had not redistributed income from the wealthier to the poorer but had taken from all but the wealthiest to give to the wealthiest.

'market economics apparently incapable'

The 20 per cent devaluation of the pound was the equivalent to putting a 20 per cent tariff on all imported goods and offering a 20 per cent subsidy to all our exports. The weaker pound pushed up demand for British-made goods. A 2017 CBI survey showed manufacturing output growing at its fastest rate since 1995. UK manufacturing order books swelled in June 2017 as the highest level since August 1988. Export orders also rose, to a two-decade high. Factories raised their output at the fastest pace since the mid-1990s. Optimism among exporting manufacturers was at a 40-year high. Construction activity grew to its highest level ever. Those who thought that our economy would collapse after the referendum were very wrong.

2017 saw the strongest two quarters of productivity growth since 2008. Output per hour rose 0.8 per cent in the three months to December 2017, following growth of 0.9 per cent in the previous quarter. There was also a better than expected rise in wages. Excluding bonuses, earnings rose by 2.5 per cent year-on-year.

Before the referendum Osborne told us that inflation would rise by 4.7 per cent, unemployment would rise by 820,000 (a jobless rate of 7.6 per cent), borrowing would rise to £77.8 billion and the economy would shrink by 2.1 per cent.

The April 2018 figures were: inflation at 2.4 per cent, unemployment down by 215,000 to a 43-year low, employment at a record high, up by 609,000 since the referendum, a jobless rate of 4.2 per cent, borrowing at £40.5 billion, the lowest level for 16 years, and the economy had grown by 2.9 per cent.

HM Revenue & Customs reported on 7 December 2017 that, in the year to September, England exported 14 per cent more goods than a year earlier, reaching £241.1 billion, while Scotland's goods exports rose by 19.9 per cent to £28 billion. Wales' exports of goods rose by 18.9 per cent to £16.4 billion and Northern Ireland's by 13.3 per cent to £8.5 billion. The UK goods trade deficit fell by £12.8 billion to £28.8 billion.

The ONS figures released on 9 March 2018 showed that overall UK exports had risen by 11.5 per cent to £625.9 billion in the past year, with service exports up 10.1 per cent and goods exports up 12.6 per cent. The ONS described 'strong manufacturing figures' as 'leading the way in making the biggest contribution to growth', as the UK manufacturing sector recorded its ninth consecutive month of growth - the longest stint of uninterrupted expansion since records began in 1968.

On 2 April 2018, the ONS released the latest figures for Gross Fixed Capital Formation (GFCF) which covered investment across the whole economy, public and private sectors, manufacturing, construction, services and extractive industries. Investment had grown by 1.1 per cent in the fourth quarter of 2017, to a total of £84.1 billion. Over 2017 it had grown by 4 per cent compared with 2016. This was higher than for any other G7 country – with Italy following on 3.7 per cent, France on 3.5 per cent, and the USA on 3.1 per cent. This important news did not make the business news on the BBC's *Today* programme, nor did the story appear on the business section of the BBC website. The *Guardian* did not mention it, nor did the *Times*.

After the 2008 crash, the government threw billions of our money into restoring banks' balance sheets, but never asked for a guarantee that any of this money would go into productive industry. The quest for nationally-based development was jettisoned in favour of 'globalisation': the transnationalisation of investment, production and consumption. The money that we raise must be invested in the real economy, into industry and services. We needed to increase domestic demand and we needed to control the banks and to create special purpose banks, like housing banks and development banks.

A balanced economy needed all regions to be developed, which meant planned. Only through planning could a country achieve balanced, equitable development. Without independence there could be no planning. We needed new infrastructure, to connect our regions better than ever before. We needed to put Britain, and Britain's industry, first, and employ our people in making what we needed. A planned economy needed both output targets and efficiency targets to maximise the ratio of output to input. During World War Two, the US government used input/output tables to help it to direct material inputs to strategically vital lines of production. We needed to do likewise.

Jeremy Warner wrote in the *Daily Telegraph* of 3 August 2011, "If the Government is serious about rebalancing, it must be bolder in its measures to boost investment. Tax incentives can be helpful, but they are not enough. With normal market economics apparently incapable of providing answers, it may be necessary to move quickly towards applying some of the policy tools used in command economies such as China – cheap loans, land and energy for publicly determined business and infrastructure investment. Namby pambying around with market incentives simply isn't working. If there is to be another bout of quantitative easing, as now seems likely, some way of ensuring that it is applied to cheap business lending rather than disappearing into the pockets of bankers must be found. Extreme circumstances call for extreme solutions."

Chapter 3 Scotland

"Secession is the essence of anarchy" - Abraham Lincoln

The 1707 Act of Union was not an agreement between states in which both states retained their paramountcy. It was not a treaty. Its Clause 1 said "That the two Kingdoms of Scotland and England shall ... be united in one Kingdom." As John Locke wrote, "When any number of men have so consented to make one community or government, they are thereby presently incorporated, and make one body politic, wherein the majority have a right to act and conclude for the rest."[86]

Similarly, Presidents James Madison and Thomas Jefferson argued in 1798 that the US Constitution was not a 'compact' between 'sovereign states'. As US Chief Justice John Marshall later wrote, "The government of the Union ... is emphatically, and truly, a government of the people."

This meant rejecting the doctrine of nullification, the notion that the individual states of the USA had the right to void any law created by the federal government that they judged unconstitutional. Senator Daniel Webster stated: "those who espouse the doctrines of nullification reject ... the first great principle of all republican liberty: that is, that the majority must govern."[87] President Andrew Jackson said in 1832 when he faced the threat of separatism by the leaders of South Carolina, "the crisis must be now met with firmness, our citizens protected, and the modern doctrine of nullification and secession put down forever."[88]

President Abraham Lincoln always opposed secession. In his first inaugural address, of 4 March 1861, he said, "Plainly, the central idea of secession, is the essence of anarchy. A majority, held in restraint by constitutional checks, and limitations, and always changing easily, with deliberate changes of popular opinion and sentiments, is the only true sovereign of a free people. Whoever rejects it, does, of necessity, fly to anarchy or to despotism. Unanimity is impossible; the rule of a minority, as a permanent arrangement, is wholly inadmissible; so that, rejecting the majority principle, anarchy or despotism in some form, is all that is left ..."

Eric Foner pointed out that "Lincoln couched his argument as a defence of a basic principle of democracy – that the minority must acquiesce in the rule of the majority, so long as that rule accords with constitutional principles. ... Secession, by contrast, not only was illegal but would lead to an endless splintering of authority as disgruntled minorities seceded from polities they deemed oppressive. ...."[89] Historian Henry Jaffa observed, "Lincoln held that the alleged constitutional right of secession, as distinct from the natural right of revolution, was a prescription for anarchy."[90]

The Scottish National Party and the 2014 referendum

Devolution did not create independent governments, despite the SNP's pretensions. As Fishing for Leave commented, "In effect, Devolved Assemblies are branch offices for Brussels with limited autonomy."[91]

The Scottish National Party was built on the demand for secession. Yet the SNP appeared to value EU membership above the wishes of the people of Scotland: in 1995 Nicola Sturgeon said, "Europe is our flagship policy." (Odd, some might have thought that Scottish independence was its key policy.)

Even so, the SNP has twisted and turned over the EEC/EU. It was for European integration in the 1950s but against the EEC in the 1960s and 1970s, urging a vote to leave in the 1975 referendum. In 1979 it stood candidates for the European Parliament election. Since 1983 it has been pro-EU. In 1988 it adopted the slogan 'Independence in Europe'. In 2000 it joined the doomed 'Britain in Europe' campaign which wanted us to scrap the pound and join the euro.

Ms Sturgeon said in 2012 that independence was not necessary to preserve 'our distinctive Scottish identity'.

Salmond wrote in the 2014 referendum's consultative document that Scotland was not oppressed and so 'had no need to be liberated'.

On the eve of the 2014 referendum, Ms Sturgeon told the *Sunday Herald*: "I don't have and never have had a [view] we should be independent regardless of what it might mean for Scotland. Existential Nationalists say, 'We're a country therefore we should be independent', end of story. I've always been more the utilitarian kind of Nationalist. I believe in it for a purpose, because I think it equips us with the powers to build the kind of country I want Scotland to be." But on 18 September 2016 she said, "The case for full self-government ultimately transcends the issues of Brexit, of oil, of national wealth and balance sheets and of passing political fads and trends."

Before the 2014 referendum, the SNP poster had said this was 'their one opportunity'. The SNP's 'White Paper' called it 'a once in generation opportunity'. As Ms Sturgeon said, "constitutional referenda are once-in-a-generation events." [92] And, "We won't stop believing in independence if that's what you're asking me. Would there be another referendum in our lifetimes? We've always said it's a once-in-a-generation thing." [93] And, "These kind [sic] of referendums are once in a generation, but if you'll forgive me, I'll concentrate on campaigning for this one." [94] On 18 September 2013 Ms Sturgeon said she hoped people would seize the 'once in a lifetime opportunity for Scotland' in 2014's vote. Alex Salmond said, "In my view this is a once in a generation, perhaps even a once in a lifetime, opportunity." But on 19 March 2017 he claimed, "The phrase was not 'once in a lifetime'."

In the referendum 2,001,926 Scots, 55.3 per cent, voted to stay in Britain. 1,617,989 people, 44.7 per cent, voted to leave Britain. Turnout was 84.59 per cent, the highest ever recorded in a UK election or referendum. Only 13 of Scotland's 59 Westminster seats backed the SNP call for secession.

The SNP's white paper had stated that "if we remain part of the UK, a referendum on future British membership of the EU could see Scotland taken out of the EU against the wishes of the people of Scotland." Yet Scots still voted to stay in Britain. In the Scottish government's paper on 'Scotland in the European Union', published to accompany its white paper, it asserted, "under the current constitutional arrangements, it is a real possibility that in less than four years' time Scotland could be forced out of the EU even if a majority of people in Scotland want to retain membership." [95] As Professor Kenneth Armstrong commented, "This was a risk that the electorate was apparently prepared to contemplate given that they also voted for Scotland to remain part of the United Kingdom in the 2014 referendum."[96]

Ms Sturgeon and Mr Salmond had both signed the agreement to respect the referendum result: "AGREEMENT between the United Kingdom Government and the Scottish Government on a referendum on independence for Scotland, 15 October 2012 ... The governments are agreed that the referendum should: ... deliver a fair test and a decisive expression of the views of people in Scotland and a result that everyone will respect. Signed by The Rt. Hon. David Cameron MP, The Rt. Hon. Alex Salmond MSP, The Rt. Hon. Michael Moore MP and Nicola Sturgeon MSP."

After the SNP lost the 2014 vote, many joined it, just as, after the Labour party and the LibDems lost in the EU referendum, many joined those parties. All three sets of new members joined too late to affect the decision, and all joined the side that opposed Britain's unity and independence. They were reacting to and joining lost causes. There could be no progress without upholding Britain's sovereignty as a united independent nation.

The SNP and the EU

The conventional claim was that the new post-2014 SNP members were mainly working class, young, active and left wing. In fact, two thirds of its new recruits were from social groups A and B and only 13 per cent were from groups D and

E. Only eight per cent were aged between 18 and 29; 53 per cent were over 50. More than half these new recruits never subsequently attended any SNP or secession-related meetings or events.

The 2013, 2014 and 2015 Scottish Social Attitudes survey found euroscepticism in well over half of Scots. The 2015 survey found that 11 per cent of Scots wanted us to stay in the EU and increase its powers. 6 per cent wanted the government to work for a single EU government. 20 per cent wanted our relationship with the EU to stay the same. 43 per cent wanted us to stay in but to reduce the EU's powers. 17 per cent wanted us to leave. So, 17 per cent (11 plus 6) wanted the pro-EU options that were on the table. 80 per cent (20 plus 43 plus 17) opposed the 'ever closer union' which was what would have happened if we had voted to stay in the EU.

The SNP wanted Britain to stay in the EU single market. But 64 per cent of Scots believed that, post-Brexit, anyone from the EU who wished to live in Britain should have to apply to do so in the same way as anyone from outside the EU. Yet we could not adopt this policy while bound by single market rules on the free movement of labour. There was little support for the SNP's idea that Scotland might have a closer relationship with the EU even while still being part of Britain. And 62 per cent said that the rules on trade between Scotland and the EU should be the same as those in the rest of Britain.

The SNP 2015 manifesto said, "we will oppose a referendum on membership of the EU." The SNP opposed the Scots having a vote on our EU membership and it also opposed the whole British people's having a vote. It had no mandate for that: no mandate from the Scots permitted the SNP to make recommendations for the whole of Britain.

Similarly, when Ms Sturgeon campaigned for Britain to stay in the EU (as she did in the national TV debate and on many other occasions) she was acting as the British citizen that she is (although she denied it), not as a citizen of Scotland. Her being a British citizen allowed her a say in Britain's future.

The SNP manifesto also said, "If an in/out EU referendum does go ahead, we will seek to amend the legislation to ensure that no constituent part of the UK can be taken out of the EU against its will. We will propose a 'double majority' rule - meaning that unless England, Scotland, Wales and Northern Ireland each vote to leave the EU, the UK would remain a member state."

This 'double majority' was really a quadruple minority lock. It would have meant that if any one of Northern Ireland, England, Scotland or Wales had voted, even by the smallest majority, to stay in the EU, this vote would have vetoed even the largest majorities in every one of the other three. A minority could have overruled the majority. In a democracy, the majority had more rights than the minority. Only opponents of democracy could want the minority to overrule the majority.

But this lock only applied if that minority was for Stay. The SNP demanded a minority veto if a majority in any one of England, Scotland, Wales or Northern Ireland, or even in three out of four, voted to leave the EU, but it did not demand a minority veto if a majority in any of the four voted to stay in the EU. If a majority voted to leave, a minority could veto, but if a majority voted to stay, a minority could not veto.

The SNP's loss in 2014 meant that Britain voted as one united country in 2016. The EU referendum vote in Scotland was not 'overwhelming and emphatic' for staying in the EU, as Ms Sturgeon claimed. Scotland's turnout was only 67.18 per cent, lower than the overall 72.2 per cent turnout. 1,661,191 Scots voted for Britain to stay in the EU. This was 340,735 fewer than had voted to stay in Britain. 1,018,322 voted for Britain to leave the EU.

The EU was increasingly unpopular, in Scotland as in the rest of Britain. The 2016 Scottish Social Attitudes survey found that 67 per cent of voters were critical of the EU: 25 per cent wanted to leave the EU while another 42 per cent wanted to reduce its powers. This was up from 2014 when 53 per cent were critical of the EU and up from 1999 when 40 per cent were critical of the EU. Most Scots believed that post-Brexit rules on trade and immigration should be the same in Scotland as in the rest of the UK. This survey also found that a minority, 46 per cent of Scots, wanted to leave Britain and that 21 per cent of those pro-separatism voters still wanted to leave the EU, while 41 per cent wanted its powers cut, so 62 per cent of these voters were unhappy with the EU's powers. Also, those Unionists who voted to stay in the EU valued the Union with the UK more than the link with the EU.

After the referendum, Ms Sturgeon threatened to veto our leaving the EU, saying on 26 June 2016 that the Scottish Parliament could block our exit from the EU. This was bluff. She knew quite well that Holyrood did not have the power to block Brexit. Scotland's 1.6 million votes to stay in the EU did not overrule Britain's 17.4 million votes for leaving. The SNP had wanted to deny the Scottish people even having a vote on whether we stayed in the EU or not, so it was rich of it to claim that the Scottish people's vote should override the vote of the whole British electorate. Even Alex Salmond said that she had no veto over leaving.

Ms Sturgeon also claimed that Scotland, even when still part of Britain, could stay in the EU. But Spanish Prime Minister Mariano Rajoy and French President François Hollande both disagreed. "If the UK leaves, Scotland leaves," Rajoy said. "Scotland has no competences to negotiate with the EU. The Spanish government rejects any negotiation with anyone other than the United Kingdom." Hollande said, "The negotiations will be conducted with the UK, not with a part of the UK." The European Parliament Research Service confirmed that a 'part' of a member state "cannot ... 'remain' in the EU if the Member State itself withdraws."[97] Nor could a part of a country apply for EU membership. Similarly, only a 'State' may accede to the European Free Trade Association. Because Scotland did not qualify for either EU or EFTA membership, it could not directly seek membership of the European Economic Area.

Further, the European Parliament Research Service said that if Scotland voted to leave Britain, it would have to reapply for EU membership. Spanish Foreign Minister Alfonso Dastis confirmed this on 14 March 2017, "If, under mutual agreement and in accordance with the applicable constitutional regime in the UK, Scotland ended up being independent, our thesis is that it cannot remain in the EU because it is only a member insofar it is part of the UK." He added that Scotland "would have to join the queue, meet the requirements for accession and enter negotiations."

So, a separate Scotland would have to apply to join the EU as a new member state, so it would lose its right to negotiate its own trade treaties, including with its most important trading partner – the rest of Britain. It would have to go through the full application procedure set out in Article 49 of the Lisbon Treaty. This would require it to join the euro. As Danish MEP Anders Vistisen said, it would take Scotland four to six years to get EU membership, it would have to pledge to join the euro and it would have to cut its huge deficit (currently higher than Greece's).

After the EU referendum, the SNP's deputy leader Angus Robertson said, "There may only be days, may only be weeks, but where all of our efforts are currently focused is trying to convince the UK government to come to a compromise agreement protecting Scotland's place in Europe," he said. It was not a 'compromise' to stay in the EU: the SNP was still demanding a minority veto over our majority decision to leave the EU.

The SNP claimed it was not bound by this decision. Ms Sturgeon claimed that the Prime Minister had a mandate to take only England and Wales out of the EU. She wrote of England and Wales, "I accept that these parts of the UK voted to leave the EU."[98] But she did not accept that the UK as a whole had voted to leave the EU. This was because she also did not accept that Scotland had voted in 2014 to stay in the UK. She lost in both referendums and she refused to accept both decisions. The

British government had a mandate to take all of Britain out of the EU.

Ms Sturgeon claimed that Mrs May's government had 'no mandate' in Scotland. Not so. Scotland voted in 2014 to stay in Britain, so in subsequent general elections Scotland voted as part of Britain. Later, in the 2017 election, the Conservative Party won enough seats across the whole of Britain to form a government, so Mrs May had as much of a mandate in Scotland as in any other part of Britain.

By contrast, the SNP had no mandate whatsoever in England, Wales and Northern Ireland, but this had not stopped it from joining the 'Britain in Europe' campaign which told all of Britain, not just Scotland, to join the euro, not stopped it from voting against the Act which enabled the whole British people to have a referendum on whether to leave the EU, and not stopped it from campaigning for the whole British people to stay in the EU.

After the 2014 referendum Ms Sturgeon said she would not call for a second referendum until support for separatism had stood at 60 per cent for at least a year. She told the SNP when she launched its election manifesto in April 2016: "setting the date for a referendum before a majority of the Scottish people have been persuaded that independence [is] the best future for our country is the wrong way round." She often said that unless voters changed their minds and decided they wanted to leave Britain, she would have no right to call for a second referendum. The Scottish Greens' 2016 manifesto likewise said that it would only support a second referendum if it came about 'by the will of the people'. No opinion poll since July 2016 has given Ms Sturgeon that majority.

Ms Sturgeon agreed with Blair when he threatened, "if the UK votes to leave Europe, Scotland will vote to leave the UK." But they were both wrong. Polls conducted after our vote to leave the EU showed no gain in support for a second referendum in Scotland and no gain in support for leaving Britain. In twelve polls conducted in the six months before the

EU referendum, an average of 53 per cent of Scots had said they would vote to stay in Britain. And in twelve polls conducted in the six months after the EU referendum, an average of 53 per cent of Scots said they would vote to stay in Britain.

For example, a BMG poll for *The Herald*, held between 29 September and 3 October 2016, found that 47 per cent opposed a second referendum, with 38 per cent in favour and 15 per cent 'don't knows'. Referring to the EU referendum, BMG research director Dr Michael Turner told *The Herald*: "It is not a game changer. The vast majority of people who think there shouldn't be an independence referendum are not going to be swayed by whether or not we leave the EU. This group are [sic] more bothered about UK identity and break-up of the UK than any perceived European identity. On the other side of the coin, those people who do want independence are much more divided about when a referendum should be called."

The YouGov poll reported in *The Times* on 1 December 2016 found support for breaking away at just 44 per cent, lower than in the 2014 referendum. The survey also found that only 31 per cent of Scots wanted the Scottish government to campaign to leave Britain in the next two years.

And the BMG poll held in 9-13 December 2016 for *The Herald* found that, when 'don't knows' were excluded, 61.5 per cent opposed a new vote in 2017, including almost a third of SNP voters. This poll showed support for Scotland staying in Britain at 54.5 per cent, when 'don't knows' were excluded.

Our vote for independence from the EU made it even harder for the SNP to win support for a second referendum in Scotland. Tom Devine, the leading historian of Scotland (who had voted to leave Britain) wrote in August 2016, "At the moment, the auguries are really pretty bad. I would say they are worse than in 2014, not least because of the instability. You could argue that the recent Brexit decision could be a symbolic trigger for another vote. But in one sense it adds to the European instability. Of course, we now know from what went on in terms of voting in 2014 that many people were concerned with risks. Instability produces risk. At the same time there has been no intellectual response to the weaknesses in the SNP economic programmes, not simply in relation to the currency, but elsewhere."[99] And the former SNP leader Gordon Wilson wrote in September 2016, "A second referendum is no longer on the cards. It is a dead duck."[100]

On 6 January 2017 Ms Sturgeon offered to drop her demand for a second referendum, which all the evidence suggested she would lose. All she wanted in return was the power to overrule the referendum decision made by the majority of the British people.

Polls continued to forecast that another once-in-a-lifetime referendum would see an even bigger defeat for the separatists. The poll by Kantar Scottish Opinion Monitor of 25 April 2017 found that only a quarter of Scots backed the SNP call for a referendum before 2019 and that 60 per cent of Scots backed union. Only 40 per cent said there should be another referendum on breaking away from Britain. There was a staunch Unionist majority in Scotland; Union was the settled will of the Scottish people.

It was also the settled will of the British people. The Future of England Survey of 19 August 2014 found that people south of the border were overwhelmingly against Scotland leaving the UK, with 59 per cent saying they would like the Union to stay intact and only 19 per cent favouring separation. A 14 June 2017 British Future poll by ICM found that 57 per cent opposed Scotland breaking away, 18 per cent supported it and 25 per cent didn't know.

Ms Sturgeon kept claiming she had a mandate for a second referendum. She said in 2016, "We got a mandate for a referendum in the election last year ..." But the SNP 2015 manifesto had said, "The SNP will always support independence - but that is not what this election is about." In election campaigns the SNP always played down leaving Britain because they knew it was unpopular.

On 14 March 2017 Ms Sturgeon said she had a 'cast-iron mandate' for another referendum. This was not the case. Firstly, her 2016 manifesto said only that the SNP "believe that the Scottish Parliament should have the right to hold another referendum ...." A belief was not a pledge. The manifesto did not say, 'if elected we will call another referendum' or 'if elected we will request the legal power from Westminster to call a referendum'. There was no manifesto promise to call for, never mind to hold, a referendum. Secondly, Holyrood's five parties were split on the issue. In 2012 all five parties had agreed on holding the 2014 referendum. But in 2017 there was no agreement. So, she had no mandate for a referendum.

Ms Sturgeon said on 16 March 2017, "Westminster thinks it has got the right to block the democratically elected mandate of the Scottish Government and the majority in the Scottish Parliament." Yes indeed, the British government, representing the majority of the people of Britain, had the right to overrule the wishes of any minority. But Ms Sturgeon had no right to block the democratically elected mandate of the British government and the majority in the British Parliament.

Since constitutional affairs were legally reserved to Westminster, it was for the British government not the Scottish parliament to decide about any referendum on any constitutional matter. The Scottish parliament had no legal right to hold a referendum, nor was the British parliament obliged to comply with any request from the Scottish parliament to hold a referendum. But Ms Sturgeon said on 17 March, "If the Prime Minister refuses to engage on the terms of a referendum before Brexit takes place then she is effectively trying to block the people of Scotland having a choice over their future. That would be a democratic outrage. It is for the Scottish Parliament not Downing Street to determine the timing of a referendum, and the decision of the Scottish Parliament must be respected."

The people of Scotland had had a choice over their future in 2014 and they chose to stay in Britain and chose therefore to accept the decisions of the British people. The people of

Scotland had also had a choice over their future in 2016. And in 2016 they voted as part of a Britain whose majority voted to leave the EU. Britain decided to leave the EU, so Scotland, as part of Britain, left too. We voted as one Britain, so we left as one Britain.

Ms Sturgeon said it was a 'democratic outrage' that Mrs May said no to her demand for a second referendum in Scotland before March 2019. Not so. It was a democratic outrage for the SNP to reject the result of the 2014 referendum. It was a democratic outrage for the SNP to demand less than three years later that a once-in-a-lifetime referendum be repeated within five years. It was a democratic outrage for the SNP to demand the right to determine the timing of any referendum. It was a democratic outrage for the SNP to demand a minority veto over our decision in the 2016 referendum.

Ms Sturgeon had said on 6 May 2016, "We will always respect the opinion of the people now and in the future ..." But the SNP did not respect the 2014 decision of the Scottish people to stay in Britain. The SNP did not respect the 2016 decision of the British people, of whom the Scottish people are a part, to leave the EU. Nearly 40 per cent of Scots voters voted to leave, yet no SNP MP voted to trigger Article 50. The SNP rejected, at Westminster anyway, the duties of a member of any legislature, because Parliament, in Edmund Burke's words, "is not a *congress* of ambassadors from different and hostile interests, which interests each must maintain, as an agent and advocate; but parliament is a *deliberative* assembly of *one* nation, with *one* interest, that of the whole; where, not local purposes, not local prejudices ought to guide, but the general good, resulting from the general reason of the whole. You choose a member indeed, but when you have chosen him, he is not member of Bristol, but he is a member of *Parliament*."[101] So SNP MPs at Westminster are obliged not to act as members of, say, Banffshire, but as members of the parliament to which they were elected.

Ms Sturgeon claimed that our vote to leave the EU showed that 'Scotland isn't listened to'. But we did listen to Scotland when we asked Scotland whether it wanted to break away from Britain, and we respected Scotland's decision to stay in a united Britain. We listened to Scotland in the 2016 referendum. Everyone in Scotland got a vote. Every Scottish vote was counted, just as in 2014 when Scots voted to stay in Britain.

Ms Sturgeon's 'flagship policy' was for Scotland to join the EU. Will the EU listen to Scotland? Did the EU listen to Ireland when it forced them to vote twice on the Lisbon Treaty, after they got it 'wrong' the first time? Did the EU listen to Greece when they voted 'No' to more austerity?

Was Scotland's voice heard louder in Britain or in the EU? Scotland had 9 per cent of MPs in the UK Parliament (59 out of 650) but only 0.7 per cent of Members of the European Parliament (6 out of 766). Parliament was the sovereign legislative body of the UK and was entirely elected. The European Parliament could not initiate or repeal legislation; only the unelected Commission could do so. It was clear in which union Scotland had more influence and which union was more democratic. Yet the SNP wanted Scotland to leave Britain to merge into a much larger political union where Scotland would have less influence, less wealth and would have to join the disastrous euro.

The SNP continued to try to break up Britain. Along with the Welsh and Northern Irish governments, it claimed that the 'legislative consent' of all three parliaments was needed before Article 50 could be triggered. They claimed that they had a veto over our decision to leave the EU. This claim, if accepted and implemented, would have meant the break-up of Britain.

On 24 January 2017, the Supreme Court unanimously rejected this claim. The President of the Court, Lord Neuberger, said, "On the devolution issues, the court unanimously rules that UK ministers are not legally compelled to consult the devolved legislatures before triggering Article 50. The devolution statutes were enacted on the assumption that the UK would be a member of the EU, but they do not require it. Relations with the EU are a matter for the UK government."

The Press Summary of the Court's judgement stated: "Relations with the EU and other foreign affairs matters are reserved to UK Government and parliament, not to the devolved institutions." The judges concluded: "The devolved legislatures do not have a veto on the UK's decision to withdraw from the EU."

But the SNP's leaders dismissed the Court's rejection of their claim. The SNP's international affairs spokesman Alex Salmond said he would introduce fifty 'serious and substantive' amendments to Article 50 legislation, including a demand that the British government had to get the agreement of all three devolved governments before it could trigger article 50. So, despite the Court's ruling, he still claimed a veto over our decision. The SNP rejected the Court's judgement and the rule of law.

Ms Sturgeon said that the SNP still believed that Scotland's best interests lay in full EU membership. An SNP spokesman said on 14 March, "our longstanding position is EU membership, and that remains the case." John Swinney, Scotland's deputy first minister, said on 17 March that the 'policy position' of the SNP was that "Scotland should be an independent member of the EU".

On 20 May 2018 on ITV's Peston on Sunday, the presenter asked Nicola Sturgeon, "Would you support a call for another vote another referendum once we've got the Brexit terms?" She replied, "Well look the SNP will be the block to that ... So you know the SNP is not a block to this ..."

In a poll taken on 29-31 May 2018, 44 per cent in Great Britain said that Scotland should remain part of the UK. 39 per cent said that they did not have a view as to whether Scotland should be part of the UK, as it was for the people of Scotland to decide. By comparison, only 28 per cent said that Northern Ireland should remain part of the UK. 57 per cent said they did not have a view as to whether Northern Ireland should be part of the UK, as it was for the people of Northern Ireland to decide.[102]

Ms Sturgeon was a serial loser. She lost in the 2011 referendum, when she backed AV. She lost the 2014 referendum. She lost in her attempt to deny Scots – and the rest of us - a vote on the EU. She failed in her attempt to ensure that minorities could veto our majority decision, and of course she failed in the 2016 referendum. In May 2016 the SNP lost its overall majority and in the 2017 election it lost 21 seats; its vote share fell from 50 per cent to 36.9 per cent.

The EU not Brexit fostered disunion, secession. The SNP were the true little Englanders because they wanted a separate little Scotland, which would mean a separate little England. Ms Sturgeon's youthful inspiration was Nelson Mandela. She liked to think she was Scotland's Mandela, but she was only Britain's Chief Buthelezi.

'Economic suicide'

Scotland's budget deficit, including a geographical share of oil revenues, was 9.7 per cent of GDP in 2014/15. This was in the same range that Greece experienced in the worst years of its EU-inspired crisis. The Treasury estimated that Scotland's spending per person in that year was £10,374, a fifth higher than England's £8,638. Britain covered the cost. Without the UK contribution, Scotland could not sustain this level of public spending.

As the SNP MP and economist George Kerevan wrote in March 2015, "We all know that in present UK economic circumstances a fiscally autonomous Scotland would face a significant budget deficit. For Scotland to accept fiscal autonomy without inbuilt UK-wide fiscal balancing would be tantamount to economic suicide."

The oil price has crashed. The Scottish government's 2014 blueprint for independence had forecast that the oil price would not fall below $113 a barrel. In 2017 it was around $53. Oil revenues for 2015/16 were £130 million, down from £2.2 billion the previous year and far from the £7.5 billion that the SNP had forecast.

The Scottish government's 'Government Expenditure and Revenue Scotland' showed that in 2015/16 Scotland spent £15 billion more than it collected in tax, causing a budget deficit of 9.5 per cent of its GDP (three times Britain's). Yet the collapse in Scotland's tax revenues did not lead to a collapse in public spending because the British state filled the gap. If Scotland left Britain it would lose this £15 billion. A separate Scotland would also have to pay around £1.5 billion a year to the EU (its share of the British contribution minus the rebate, which would vanish together with Britain's membership). So the SNP call would be - leave Britain and be £16.5 billion year worse off.

This Britain-wide sharing of resources, which was more than a fifth of Scotland's annual government spending, meant that Scotland could weather economic downturns without slashing vital public services. By contrast, the EU punished member states that ran budget deficits of more than 3 per cent by fining them hundreds of millions of euros and by enforcing huge cuts in wages, pensions and benefits. To join the EU, Scotland would have to cut its budget deficit to 3 per cent, which would mean cutting spending, or raising taxes, by about £7.5 billion. It would have to double the basic rate of income tax to balance the books. But the SNP wanted to leave Britain and join the EU.

In 2015, 63 per cent of Scotland's exports went to the rest of Britain, and just 16 per cent to the EU. Its exports to the rest of Britain had grown since 2002 by 69 per cent to £49.8 billion in 2015.[103] Scotland's exports to the EU had grown by just 6 per cent to £12.3 billion.

The SNP claimed that trading with the EU from outside the single market would be a disaster, yet that trading with Britain from outside our single market would be fine. Ms Sturgeon said that "losing our place in the [EU] Single Market would be potentially devastating to our long-term prosperity." But if leaving the EU single market, with its £12.3 billion export sales, would be 'devastating', surely her aim of leaving the UK single market, with its £49.8 billion export sales, would be even more so? If leaving the EU, a political union with no currency or fiscal union, to which Britain was a net contributor, would result in disaster, then what would result from Scotland leaving Britain, a currency and fiscal union whereby Scotland got £15 billion a year? And yet the SNP wanted to build an economic wall between Scotland and the rest of Britain, in order to stay in the EU's single market.

Even Charles Grant, a member of the First Minister's Standing Council on Europe, admitted that "legally, politically, technically, it's extremely difficult for Scotland to stay in the single market if the UK as a whole does not, the basic point being that there would have to be one set of business regulations applying to England and another set applying to Scotland."[104]

The SNP wanted to take powers from Britain only to give them to the EU. By contrast we voted to take powers from the EU and give them to Britain. The SNP wanted all the powers that came back from the EU, especially fishing and farming, to go back to the EU. Devolution of powers over fishing would mean that the Scottish and Welsh governments could continue to allow EU vessels to fish in Scottish and Welsh waters, while the British government would only be able to stop EU vessels fishing in the waters off England. We needed a common framework establishing the core principles of farm support policy across Britain. So, for example, the Scottish Parliament would not be allowed to give significant subsidies to sheep farmers in Scotland which would not be available to sheep farmers in England or Wales.

Alex Salmond's pledge to keep the pound had played a key role in getting support for the SNP in the 2014 referendum. But a separate Scotland would not be able to keep the pound, because the EU would never allow a new member state to be in an economic union with a state that was not an EU member. The SNP claimed that it did not know what currency a separate Scotland would have inside the EU, because it knew that if it admitted that the currency would be the euro, it would not have a chance of winning a vote for secession. Inside the EU's eurozone, without its own currency, a separate Scotland would not be able to set its own interest rates, print money or devalue.

In 2014 the SNP had not been able to give good answers about the currency, the economy and joining the EU. Asked in 2017 whether a separate Scotland would use sterling or the euro, SNP spokesman Angus Robertson said the party would set out its plans about currency and the economy sometime in the future. So it could not or would not make public any plans about currency and the economy, even three years after its 2014 failure.

For Scots to vote to leave Britain would be a true act of self-harm. A Scotland outside Britain would have to join the euro and it would have no single market and no banking union with the rest of Britain. It would have a very big deficit, with no control of the currency in which it issued its debt. It would have little revenue, no rebate, no independent currency, and no veto.

By contrast, outside the EU as part of an independent Britain, Scotland had a bright future. For example, Svea Miesch of ScotlandIS, the trade body for Scotland's digital technologies industry, has pointed out some of the opportunities provided by Brexit: "Digital technologies can help all sectors of the economy to increase productivity through, for example, business and process transformation, ecommerce and the increased use of data analytics to inform decision-making. This represents an exceptional commercial opportunity for the digital technologies industry …

"Brexit and the associated changes to immigration rules represent an opportunity to refocus efforts to ensure that we have enough home-grown digital professionals in the years to come. Increased spend and commitment to digital technology skills education, both upskilling those already in the workforce and giving young people the ability to thrive in the digital world, would help addressing the skills gap which is holding the digital technologies industries back. To seize both these opportunities fully, adequate government funding and policy reforms are required to incentivise investments and commitment by both the public and private sectors."[105]

The devolution of powers to Scotland, Wales and Northern Ireland was very ad hoc, without counter-balancing efforts to integrate the Union. Our leaving the EU gave us the opportunity to put this right and to strengthen our union by investing in skills and industry. We will get back powers over fishing, farming, environmental and employment policy among others. Instead of passing these powers onto the devolved legislatures and adding to the fragmentation of Britain, we must use them to strengthen the integration and effectiveness of our country and to bring us all closer together.

Chapter 4 The 2016 referendum

1975 and other referendums

In 1975 the question was, "Do you think the UK should stay in the European Community (Common Market)?" Some said that this question was rigged. The 2015 EU Referendum Bill proposed this question - "Should the United Kingdom remain a member of the European Union?" The Electoral Commission said this question was doubly unbalanced, since only the Remain option was in the question and the Yes response was for the status quo. So the Commission changed the question to "Should the United Kingdom remain a member of the European Union or leave the European Union?" In effect then, the Electoral Commission agreed that the 1975 question was indeed rigged. It follows that the question in the 2014 referendum - 'Should Scotland be an independent country?' – was also rigged since only the leave option was in the question.

The EU Referendum Act said that the majority would decide, as in the 1975 referendum on the EEC that Prime Minister Harold Wilson called. This referendum was decided by a simple majority vote, with no condition that there had to be an absolute majority. No threshold was stipulated, no minimum margin. The majority backed staying in the EEC: 67.2 per cent to 32.8 per cent on a 64.5 per cent turnout. The vote of 43 per cent of the electorate was deemed enough. So it was only fair that a majority vote was enough to leave.

The pro-EEC campaign was a shot in the counter-revolution. Our vote to stay in the EEC showed weakness and a lack of self-confidence: it opened the way for Thatcher. In 1975 those on the losing side did not challenge the legitimacy of the outcome, just the wisdom of the decision.

Subsequently referendums across Europe showed that the EU was increasingly unpopular. In 2005 French voters rejected the European Constitution by 55 per cent to 45. Enthusiasm for the EU was confined to the wealthiest suburbs and quarters of Paris, and the only groups that voted Yes were big business, the liberal professions and academics. [106] Dutch voters rejected the Constitution by 61.6 per cent to 38.4. Yet President Juncker told MEPs, "the French and Dutch did not really vote 'No' to the European Constitution."

In the 2004 referendum on Labour's EU-style regional scheme to break up Britain, the people of the North-East voted 77.9 per cent No, 22.1 per cent Yes, on a turnout of 47.1 per cent. In the 2011 referendum on the EU-style Alternative Vote scheme 67.9 per cent voted No, 32.1 per cent Yes, on a turnout of 41 per cent. And in 2014 the people of Scotland voted against breaking up Britain. All these decisions paved the way up to our vote in 2016.

In November 2012 David Cameron told Chancellor Merkel that "The British people never got a choice to vote on Lisbon. It spread much unhappiness towards the political establishment. ... if I don't listen to British public opinion, then Britain will depart from Europe. ... I have a problem with my party, even though elements in the Conservative Party are more pro-Europe than the country, which is even more sceptical."[107]

In the EU Parliament elections of 2014 only 34 per cent of people in the UK voted. That is, huge numbers of those who voted remain in 2016 could not even be bothered to vote for an MEP in 2014. At most only about a fifth of people were strongly committed to the EU.

The 2016 campaign

The EU lost the campaign, not Cameron or Corbyn or the media. Some pro-EU politicians and commentators claimed that 40 years of anti-EU propaganda swung the referendum. No, rather 40 years' experience of being in the EU showed us that it was not good for us. Our positive desire for freedom and independence, not the Stay campaign's mistakes, achieved the decision to leave.

Britain was the country most resistant to ceding greater powers to the EU. A Eurobarometer poll in 2013 showed that Britain was the only EU member state in which most people felt that they could face the future better outside the EU. Opinion polls showed that only 6 per cent of people in the UK (compared to 34 per cent in France, for instance, and 26 per cent in Germany) favoured increased centralisation. Two-thirds wanted powers returned from the EU to the British government, with a majority even among the young. Half even of Remain voters opposed greater powers being given to the EU. This suggested much more opposition to EU centralisation than was shown by the 52 per cent vote for Brexit.[108]

The NatCen Social Research's 2015 British Election Study found that 8 per cent wanted us to stay in and add to the EU's powers. 3 per cent wanted the government to work for a single EU government. 19 per cent wanted the relationship with the EU to stay the same. 43 per cent wanted us to stay in but reduce the EU's powers. 22 per cent wanted us to leave. So, just 11 per cent wanted the pro-EU options that were on the table. 84 per cent opposed the 'ever closer union' which is what would have happened if we had voted to stay in the EU.

But the parliamentary parties did not want to let us have a say on the matter. For years, they opposed holding a referendum on our membership of the EU. They opposed holding a referendum because, as George Osborne said, in a referendum, "you can't control what people do."[109] They had no right to deny us a vote. They told us we had no right to a vote (then they turned around and told us how to vote in the referendum they fought to deny us). But public opinion was more and more in favour of holding a referendum, which pushed the parliamentary parties into accepting the idea. So, by the 2015 general election all three major parties were promising an in/out referendum.

The 2015 Conservative election manifesto said, "We believe in letting the people decide: so we will hold an in-out referendum on our membership of the EU before the end of 2017." And, "We will hold that in-out referendum before the end of 2017 and respect the outcome." "We will honour the result of the referendum, whatever the outcome." Labour's election manifesto gave a 'guarantee no powers will be transferred to Brussels without an in/out referendum'. The LibDem election manifesto promised to 'Hold an In/Out referendum when there is next any Treaty change involving a material transfer of sovereignty from the UK to the EU'.

Then the Labour party and the LibDems campaigned to stay in the EU. Shadow Chancellor John McDonnell told the House of Commons on 15 June 2016, "Polling suggests that many of our own Labour supporters are unclear about Labour's position. So let people be absolutely clear: as the motion before us today unambiguously states, Labour is for remain." He also complained, "The Brexit campaign has done more damage to capitalism in four days than the Socialist Workers Party did in 40 years."

Most MPs, including most Labour MPs, including Messrs Corbyn and McDonnell, campaigned to stay in the undemocratic, privatisation-enforcing, austerity-enforcing EU. Those who backed Jeremy Corbyn should ask themselves, are you backing the Jeremy Corbyn who opposed the EU from 1968 to 2015? Or the Jeremy Corbyn who urged us in 2016 to back the EU? Or the Jeremy Corbyn who in the 2017 general election backed leaving the EU single market? Or the Jeremy Corbyn who in September 2017 backed staying in the EU single market?

The Leave campaign was in tune with majority sentiment on many key economic and political issues. Surveys found "large majorities (ranging from 62 per cent to 79 per cent) of UKIP members agreeing that excessive profits by banks, corporate greed, economic inequality and social injustice are major problems. It is striking that similarly large majorities in the electorate as a whole share these sentiments; 79 per cent believe that corporate greed is a major problem and 77 per cent judge that banks are making excessive profits. Solid majorities of people at large also think that economic inequality and social injustice are major problems. Overall, the average difference between UKIP-ers and the wider electorate in responses to these four questions is less than 4 per cent."[110]

By contrast, the pro-EU campaign was not in tune with popular sentiment. As Dominic Cummings wrote, "It doesn't occur to SW1 and the media that outside London, *their* general outlook is seen as extreme. Have an immigration policy that guarantees free movement rights even for murderers, so we cannot deport them or keep them locked up after they are released? Extreme. Have open doors to the EU and don't build the infrastructure needed? Extreme. Take violent thugs who kick women down stairs on CCTV, there is no doubt about their identity, and either don't send them to jail or they're out in a few months? Extreme. Have a set of policies that stops you dealing with the likes of 'the guy with the hook' for over a decade while still giving benefits to his family? Extreme. Ignore warnings about the dangers of financial derivatives, including from the most successful investor in the history of the world, and just keep pocketing the taxes from the banks and spending your time on trivia rather than possible disasters? Extreme. Make us – living on average wages without all your lucky advantages – pay for your bailouts while you keep getting raises and bonuses? Extreme. These views are held across educational lines, across party lines, and across class lines."

Pro-EU campaigners and much of the media tried to frame the entire Leave campaign as right wing. But to see leaving the EU as an innately right-wing enterprise was to assume that the EU was an innately left-wing enterprise. It was no such thing. Its treaty-bound four freedoms defined it as innately right-wing, pro-capitalist, anti-democratic.

And most Tory MPs and all of UKIP opposed the Vote Leave campaign when it championed the NHS and when it attacked the indefensibly high pay of top businessmen. Most people agreed with the Leave campaign on the NHS and executive pay and also agreed with it on the need to control immigration policy.

The pro-EU camp claimed that nobody on the leave side had any plan for the future of Britain. Business for Britain (the forerunner of the Vote Leave campaign) published in 2015 its plan, 'Change Or Go', available for free on the internet. By contrast, the pro-EU Cameron did not allow any government department to plan for leaving. The House of Commons Foreign Affairs Committee judged that "The previous Government's considered view not to instruct key Departments including the FCO [Foreign and Commonwealth Office] to plan for the possibility that the electorate would vote to leave the EU amounted to gross negligence. It has exacerbated post-referendum uncertainty both within the UK and amongst key international partners, and made the task now facing the new Government substantially more difficult."[111]

Osborne said that there would be a recession the day after a vote to leave and he said that there would be a recession after we left. His first claim has already been proven wrong. So why believe his second claim? Until the referendum campaign, hardly anyone, especially Labour and LibDem supporters, believed a word that Osborne said. After the campaign started, some seem to have believed everything he said.

There were many scare stories about what would happen if we voted to leave. Some pro-EU people said that Wales would vote to leave Britain. A poll on 18 July 2016 found that 53 per cent would not back leaving Britain. Only 28 per cent of Welsh voters would back leaving Britain if it allowed Wales to 'remain a member of the European Union' upon becoming an independent country. Wales raised only £23 billion of the £38 billion it spent every year. Some pro-EU people said that Northern Ireland would leave the UK. Northern Ireland's largest political party was on board with Brexit and the government's plans. Some pro-EU people said that Gibraltar would have to be given away to get a Brexit deal. Spain has said it will not veto a Brexit deal over Gibraltar.

Some wrongly assumed that a vote to leave would also be a vote for hard-right policies. For example, *Jacobin* journalist Ed Rooksby wrote just before the referendum, "a Brexit victory would probably facilitate the promotion of key figures from the Leave camp to top positions in a reformulated government dominated by the Tory hard right. It seems unlikely that Cameron would survive the referendum's defeat, and the figure poised to replace him as prime minister, many commentators agree, is Boris Johnson. ... Johnson - or one of his cronies - would likely introduce draconian anti-migrant measures in response to the xenophobic feelings that the Leave camp is now doing its best to ramp up."[112] These doom-laden forecasts were all wrong.

Some seemed to believe that the British right was so strong that only EU membership could contain it. But despite the forecasts of a hard-right takeover after Brexit, the British National Party got just 4,850 votes in the 2017 General Election, while UKIP (absurdly branded 'fascist' by some) imploded, winning just 1.8 per cent of votes cast.

The fears of what would happen when we leave the EU have already been realised, under the EU's reign. Formerly well-paying working-class jobs were destroyed as imported cheap labour led to a dog-eat-dog job market. Sickness pay and holiday pay were stripped from the million workers forced into zero-hours contracts. Food banks became common. Workers got poorer while the rich got even richer. Public assets were sold off to the highest bidder. Housing was priced out of the reach of ordinary people and private landlords got billions from the taxpayer in housing benefits, so a quarter of 21-34-year-olds still lived with their parents. More homeless people live, somehow, on the streets. Public services like libraries were decimated. People struggled to get a GP appointment in increasingly overstretched clinics. The elderly care system was near collapse. Global corporations could make billions in profit here and pay not a penny in tax; and greedy bankers, freed by deregulation to run riot, bring the entire banking system to the edge of ruin and the government makes the taxpayer refloat the bankers with hundreds of billions of pounds.

Guardian columnist Paul Mason wrote, "The left wing case for Brexit is strategic and clear. The EU is not – and cannot become - a democracy. Instead, it provides the most hospitable ecosystem in the developed world for rentier monopoly corporations, tax-dodging elites and organised crime. It has an executive so powerful it could crush the leftwing government of Greece; a legislature so weak that it cannot effectively determine laws or control its own civil service. A judiciary that, in the Laval and Viking judgments, subordinated workers' right to strike to an employer's right do business freely.

"Its central bank is committed, by treaty, to favour deflation and stagnation over growth. State aid to stricken industries is prohibited. The austerity we deride in Britain as a political choice is, in fact, written into the EU treaty as a non-negotiable obligation. So are the economic principles of the Thatcher era. A Corbyn-led Labour government would have to implement its manifesto in defiance of EU law."[113]

He claimed that, "Johnson and the Tory right are seeking a mandate via the referendum for a return to full-blown Thatcherism: less employment regulation, lower wages, fewer constraints on business. If Britain votes Brexit, then Johnson and Gove stand ready to seize control of the Tory party and turn Britain into a neoliberal fantasy island." But within the EU we were already suffering employment regulation that did nothing to defend workers, we were already suffering lower wages, and business already had fewer constraints.

Mr Mason rejected his own fact-based appraisal of the EU in favour of flawed forecasts and hypothetical events. He used his imagined scenario to claim it was necessary to embrace the reality of the EU in all its undemocratic, pro-corporation, anti-worker, pro-austerity glory. He rejected the actual present chance to evict the EU instead imagining a future referendum when all his reasons for not voting now to leave would miraculously vanish.

Likewise, none of these scare stories came to pass:

1) Farming could disappear altogether from Britain [Patrick McLoughlin]
2) The global environment would be under threat if the UK voted to leave [Ed Miliband]
3) Leaving the EU would risk bringing war to Europe [Cameron]
4) Brexit could lead to the downfall of Western political civilisation [Donald Tusk]
5) Brexit risked the destruction of the international order [David Miliband]
6) The UK could not enforce workers' rights without the help of the EU [Gordon Brown]
7) Brexit could derail the fight for women's rights [Harriet Harman]

During the referendum campaign, Defence Secretary Michael Fallon repeatedly warned that leaving the EU would undermine our security. After the vote, he said that leaving "doesn't affect the security that our Armed Forces help to deliver."

The government campaigned for us to stay in the EU. Juncker said that Cameron told him that he aimed to use the referendum 'to dock Britain permanently in the EU'.[114] David Lidington, the Europe minister, said on 9 June 2015, "The government will be restrained in their use of public money and have no wish to compete with the umbrella campaign organisations whose job it will be to lead the yes and no campaigns." On 7 September, when the EU referendum legislation went through parliament, Lidington said, "Let me repeat that we have no intention of legislating to allow the government to do things such as mailshots, paid advertising or leafleting." But on 6 April 2016 the government announced that it would spend £9.3 million of public money on producing and sending a pro-EU leaflet to all 27 million homes in the country.

The leave campaign spent £13,436,241; the pro-EU camp spent £19,070,566, according to the Electoral Commission. The Labour party spent £4.8 million. Some US banks also funded the Remain campaign – half a million from Goldman Sachs, half a million from Morgan Stanley. The US bank JP Morgan backed the EU to undermine nations' constitutions, because, as it complained, "Constitutions tend to show a strong socialist influence, reflecting the political strength that left wing parties gained after the defeat of fascism." The company deplored 'constitutional protection of labor rights; consensus building systems which foster political clientalism; and the right to protest if unwelcome changes are made to the political status quo'.

Some claimed that those who opposed the EU opposed its ideals. All too many in the pro-EU camp assumed that the EU was all about Enlightenment ideals, so they then also assumed that leaving meant undermining those ideals. In fact, many opposed the EU because it had failed to carry out those ideals.

Claims that people were persuaded by propaganda assumed that people still listened to politicians and could not make up their own minds based on their own experience.[115] Many pro-EU people seemed to be in thrall to the old undemocratic model of politics of leaders and led and assumed that everyone else was too. "Put not your trust in princes", as the psalmist wrote.[116] Many pro-EU people focused on the process – the campaigns, the leaders, the other side's rhetoric – not on the issue, the substance.

The BBC has consistently backed our membership of the EU. In its coverage of the 1999 EU election campaign, despite polls recording majority support for leaving the EU, there was only one interview on that theme, with Nigel Farage. In the exchange, John Humphrys bracketed UKIP with the fascist British National Party and said that leaving the EU was 'literally unthinkable'. Between 2005 and 2015, only 132 of 4,275 guests talking about the EU on BBC Radio 4's flagship *Today* programme were supporters of our leaving the EU.

In 274 hours of BBC coverage of EU issues between 2002 and 2017, only 14 speakers of the total 6,882 were non-Conservative advocates of leaving the EU. These 14 delivered a total 1,680 words. In the same period, pro-EU Conservatives Kenneth Clarke and Michael Heseltine appeared 28 times and delivered a total of 11,208 words. So, BBC audiences were made familiar with Conservative reasons for Remain. They heard very little about non-Conservative reasons for leaving, for example the EU's ban on state aid to protect jobs, the threat to the NHS from TTIP, the EU's treatment of the Greek government and people, the high unemployment in the eurozone, the EU's import tariffs against developing countries, and the belief that the EU had become a 'neoliberal marketplace'.

The BBC presented a far greater breadth of opinion in Remain contributions – from Conservatives, Labour, the Liberal Democrats and the Green party. Conversely, the BBC featured only Conservatives and UKIP from the Leave side, never any pro-leave people from Labour, the LibDems or the Greens.

The BBC nearly always linked the case for leaving to the referendum's presumed effect of dividing the Conservative party or on its likely effect on the prospects of its present and possible future leaders. When the BBC mentioned UKIP, it almost always linked it to the BNP. If people wanted to make links, it should be noted that the first party in Britain to call for European unity was the British Union of Fascists.

During the referendum campaign, despite BBC editorial guidelines requiring strict balance, BBC Radio 1 *Newsbeat* (the

BBC's leading news programme for young listeners) heard 1.5 times more Remain supporters than Leave supporters. On the BBC's two leading political discussion programmes – *Question Time* and Radio 4's *Any Questions?* - from June 2016 until the end of December 2017, 68 per cent of the panellists were Remain voters, 32 per cent were Leave voters. Just 0.04 per cent of the BBC's coverage of the EU was devoted to the potential benefits of leaving the EU.

But all the media most probably had little effect. As Kenneth Newton explained, "The idea that the modern mass media have a strong and malign effect on many aspects of social and political life is widely and strongly held. Television is often said to undermine democratic government and popular support for leaders and institutions. In spite of all that has been written about media malaise, however, both theory and evidence suggests {sic} that the media are a comparatively weak force whose effects can be deflected, diluted and diffused by stronger forces. These include bedrock political values associated with class, religion, age, gender and education, as well as social networks and discussions, distrust of the mass media, and personal knowledge and experience. Equally, the variables that mediate the media may also magnify its effects so that what appears to be a large media effect is, in fact, the result of an interaction between the media and other forces."[117]

Some complained that Nigel Farage got too much media attention. In fact, Cameron was the most quoted politician, then Boris Johnson, then George Osborne, then Michael Gove and only then Farage. Farage got so much media attention partly because in 1997 the Labour government decided that the 1999 European Parliament elections would be held using a form of proportional representation. This made it easier for smaller parties to gain representation so in 1999 UKIP, Plaid Cymru and the Greens got their first MEPs, which obliged broadcasters to allow them airtime.

But he also got so much attention because the pro-EU campaign saw him as an asset to their side because far more people disliked Farage than liked him. In a YouGov poll of 27 November 2016, 48,848 said they disliked or really disliked him, and more than half of these responses were the most negative, the 'Really don't like' option. 18,718 respondents said they liked or really liked him. So the pro-EU campaign did all it could to identify Farage as the key leave campaigner. The media also focused on Farage as if he led the whole leave campaign.

But Farage fronted only the minority, unofficial wing of the leave campaign, Grassroots Out. Grassroots Out was quite separate from the official Vote Leave campaign, led by Johnson and Gove, which the Electoral Commission designated as the official campaign. And even though Farage was not the leader of the Vote Leave campaign, ITV chose to pair him with Cameron in debate, shutting out the official leave campaign. Farage had no government position, he held no position of power; he was, famously, never elected as an MP despite standing seven times.

But by voting to leave the EU we did not endorse Farage. Many pro-EU campaigners claimed that a vote for leave was a vote for Farage, but the referendum was never a vote about Farage. Farage wanted it to be about Farage. Cameron and Osborne tried to make it about Farage. Farage did not speak for the leave campaign on policy towards refugees or migration or anything else. When UKIP won the 2014 Euro-elections, it got 4.376 million votes, its peak. But 17.4 million of us voted for independence. So, 13 million people never voted UKIP but did vote leave. So, the vast majority of those who voted to leave did not do so because they backed Farage. So most probably the vast majority of those who voted to leave the EU did so despite Farage, not because of him. And those who voted Remain in order to vote against Farage were taking the part for the whole.

When the Conservatives won the 2015 general election, 11.3 million people voted for them. So, 6 million people did not vote Conservative then but did vote leave a year later.

17.4 million people did not vote to leave because they were Tories or Ukippers but because they preferred Britain to be independent rather than a province of the United States of Europe. By contrast, many of those who voted Remain voted not so much for the EU as against Farage or against the Conservatives, particularly against Johnson and Gove.

Some claimed that foreign interference swung the referendum result. But, as Boris Johnson declared, "We have no evidence the Russians are actually involved in trying to undermine our democratic processes at the moment. We don't actually have that evidence."[118] Similarly, the 2016 FBI/CIA report on alleged Russian interference in the US election admitted: "Judgments are not intended to imply that we have proof that shows something to be a fact." *The New York Times* noted that: "What is missing from the public report is what many Americans most eagerly anticipated: hard evidence to back up the agencies' claims that the Russian government engineered the election attack." An indictment issued by special counsel Robert Mueller's investigating committee named the Internet Research Agency of St. Petersburg, but, as the *Washington Post* reported, "The indictment does not accuse the Russian government of any involvement in the scheme, nor does it claim that it succeeded in swaying any votes."[119]

The decision

The referendum was not a choice about what laws to have but about who wrote the laws. When we entered the polling booth the question in front of us was not about any of the EU's policies. It was about how, where and by whom our laws would be made.

The referendum was not about hope as against fear, or love as against hate, or reason as against emotion. It was not about who we were. It was not asking us about our values or our identity. It was not about you or me, not about whether we were nationalist or internationalist. It was not about race or nationalism. There were no names on the ballot paper, no political parties, no isms, because it was not about politicians or political parties. It was not an opinion poll, or a popularity poll, or a general election, or a vote for a different government.

It was not about the merits or otherwise of the campaigns. The campaign was not about the campaign. The question was not, "Do you approve of the leave campaign or not?" Yet some were still, after the decision, commenting on comments made by the national leaders of the campaigns. We did not vote to leave the EU because of the campaigns. We were asked whether we wanted to stay in the EU or not, and we decided, fairly, democratically, to leave.

What question was on the ballot paper? Leave or not – all the rest was interpretation. Voting 'against Farage' or 'against racism' was also voting against the progressive case for leaving the EU, was voting to block the path to independence. The question was, 'Should the United Kingdom remain a member of the European Union or leave the European Union?'

It was too little remarked that media coverage of sovereignty as an issue more than tripled through the campaign – 132 articles in the first week, 157 in the seventh week, 277 in the eighth week, 323 in the ninth week and 454 in the tenth.[120]

When we decided to leave the EU, we decided to make our own decisions, as grown-ups should. We voted to make our own decisions without the EU telling us what to do. We voted to take responsibility, to take control, challenging, but a great opportunity. We now have the duty to address the country's problems. We cannot blame anybody else.

The debate would have been better if more people had discussed the issue at work, in their trade union meetings and elsewhere. There were bubbles of the like-minded. We never heard a leave voter saying that he had never met a pro-EU voter, but all too many pro-EU voters claimed never to have met a Leave voter.

17,410,742 people voted for leave, more people than have ever voted for anything in British history. This was 51.9 per cent of those who voted, on a 72.2 per cent turnout, the highest turnout in a UK-wide vote since the 1992 general election. This was far more than voted for Thatcher in her 1979 victory - 13.7 million, or for Blair in his 1997 victory - 13.5 million, far more than voted for the Conservatives in the 2015 general election - 11.3 million, far more than voted for the Conservatives in the 2017 general election – 13.7 million.

As election experts Robert Worcester and Roger Mortimore pointed out, the referendum decision "has greater weight as a democratic mandate than any recent general election: 33.6 million people voted in it. Only once in history (in the general election of 1992) have more – fractionally more – British voters gone to the polls in any national vote; and less than half that number voted in the last election of British MEPs to the European Parliament. Never have as many voters supported any party in a British general election as voted to leave the EU in 2016."[121]

The Electoral Commission called the vote 'a great exercise in democratic participation'. It found that 62 per cent of voters 'felt they had enough information to make an informed decision on how to vote' and that 77 per cent of voters were 'very or fairly confident' that the referendum was well run. It stated that in elections, "national campaign limits are quite flexible. But the very strict rules and caps on referendum campaign spending meant that this one couldn't be bought."

Some said the majority was not big enough to be decisive. But leave voters outvoted stay voters by a majority of 3.8 per cent. This was a bigger margin of victory than in nine of the 20 postwar general elections: 1950, 1951, 1955, 1964, 1970, February 1974, October 1974, 2005 and 2017. Were those nine elections not decisive? In a democracy, the majority gets its way. If we had voted to leave by just one vote, we would leave. Just as in football, you win by one goal, you win. The majority was 1,269,501 votes. To oppose the referendum vote was to endorse the EU's usual anti-democratic practice of making people vote until they obeyed the EU.

Some said the turnout was not high enough for the result to be valid. But the turnout, 72.2 per cent of the electorate, was higher than in seven postwar general elections - 1970, 1997, 2001, 2005, 2010, 2015 and 2017. In 1970 it was 72 per cent, in 1997 it was 71.4 per cent, in 2001 it was 59.4 per cent, in 2005 61.4 per cent, in 2010 65.1 per cent, in 2015 66.1 per cent, and in 2017 68.7 per cent. Were those seven elections not valid?

The total electorate was 46,500,001. The total number of those who voted was 33,568,184. So, 37.44 per cent of the electorate voted to leave, 34.71 per cent to stay. Some said 37.44 per cent was not enough, that this meant that the majority, 62.56 per cent, had not voted to leave, so there was no majority for leaving. But if you did not vote, your abstention should not to be added to the minority vote. Abstentions do not get added to either side. And 37.44 per cent is a majority over 34.71 per cent.

Lord Ashcroft's poll of 24 June 2016 found that the only income group to back staying in the EU was AB, households with an income of more than £60,000, by 57 per cent to 43. C1 was 51 per cent for leave; C2, D and E were all 64 per cent for leave. Class, not education or age, was the decisive factor. As David Goodhart pointed out, "the Brexit vote was probably the most directly class-correlated political choice of my lifetime ..."[122]

Local authority areas where average annual earnings were above £23,000 were 35 per cent for leave. Local authority areas where average annual earnings were below £23,000 were 77 per cent for leave. Local authority areas with relatively high-priced housing were 28 per cent for leave. Local authority areas with relatively low-priced housing were 79 per cent for leave. Industrial areas were more pro-leave. 232 local authority areas with relatively high levels of manufacturing were 86 per cent for leave. 148 local authority areas with relatively low levels of manufacturing were 42 per cent for leave.

Many thought that the vote for Trump and the vote for Brexit were parts of the same movement. One key difference demolished this claim. In the US election, the richer you were, the more likely you were to vote for Trump. In the referendum, the richer you were, the more likely you were to vote against Brexit. Trump won in all income groups whose income was more than $50,000 a year: the US rich largely voted for Trump. By contrast, the leave side won in all income groups except the richest: the British rich largely voted against Brexit.

Professor Richard Tuck argued, "Brexit was in fact an inoculation against Trump and the politics of the radical right. Leaving the EU would not only kill Scottish independence, it would also kill the kind of right-wing politics in England which UKIP represented, since it was largely driven by a sense of powerlessness. The feeling – and it need be no more than that – that the political process could after all be responsive to what people wanted even on fundamental matters would immediately remove the emotional force from the radical right's message, and that too duly seems to have happened. Compare UKIP's performance in the election with Trump's, or with Marine Le Pen's, or the radical right's performance in almost any Western country today."[123]

Federica Liberini, Andrew Oswald, Eugenio Proto and Michela Redoano concluded that, "despite many commentators' guesses, Brexit was apparently not caused by the attitudes of old people. Only the very young were disproportionately pro-Remain. On our estimates, for example, there was little difference between being aged 35, 55 or 75. This was not what we had expected to observe in the data."[124]

Harold Clarke, Matthew Goodwin and Paul Whiteley concluded, "Although Leave voting was greater among older, less well-educated 'white English' people in lower social grades, it would be an error to conclude that Brexit lacked broad-based support: public support for leaving the EU was relatively widespread. In the end only London, Northern Ireland, Scotland and the university towns were bastions of support for Remain. Elsewhere across the UK Brexit was the preferred option in most locales."[125] By contrast, 73 per cent of MPs voted to stay in the EU, as did 58 per cent of the House of Lords.

22 per cent of graduates voted for leave. 33 per cent who described themselves as Asian voted for leave, as did 27 per cent of black people and 30 per cent of Muslims. Also for leave were 37 per cent of those who had voted Labour in 2015, 36 per cent of those who had voted SNP, 30 per cent of those who had voted LibDem and 25 per cent of those who had voted Green.

Some complained that UK citizens living in EU member countries were not allowed to vote, but the franchise was based on eligibility to vote in a general election. So it excluded UK citizens who had been resident abroad for more than fifteen years: the Divisional Court upheld this decision as legal.[126]

Some complained that 16- and 17-year-olds were not allowed to vote. But there are about 1.5 million 16- and 17-year-olds in Britain and it would have been difficult to register them all in time for the referendum. It was not certain how they would have voted, nonetheless Professor Kenneth Armstrong concluded, reasonably enough, that "The Leave margin of victory would have narrowed very considerably had under 18s been allowed to vote, but it may not have changed the result in June 2016."[127]

As Worcester and Mortimore pointed out, "Even if the turnout of 18-24 year olds had been as high as the 78% turnout of 65-74 year olds – and assuming that all those youngsters who didn't vote would have voted the same way as those that did (which is a big assumption in itself) – that would not have been enough to put Remain ahead; there are simply not enough of them. And even if we bring the 25-34 year olds and 35-44 year olds into the equation, both groups that had a Remain majority, and calculate what would have happened if there had been an equal turnout across all age groups, Leave still wins. The outcome of the referendum cannot be blamed on too few young people voting."[128]

To overturn the result, an impossible 120 per cent of the 18-24-year olds would have had to have voted, rather than the 64 per cent who did. To overturn the result, 97 per cent of all those aged 18-45 would have had to have voted, rather than the 65 per cent who did.[129] The youth of tomorrow will realise, as did the youth of 1975, the folly of giving up our independence.

Some complained that the referendum was won by fraud. But when the Electoral Commission investigated allegations made against Vote Leave, the Commission refused even to meet Vote Leave officials. These officials frequently tried to meet the Commission to defend themselves, but the Commission failed to interview a single senior Vote Leave staff member during its investigation. This was a breach of natural justice.

The Commission's central finding was reached because the Commission wrongly claimed that an email from Dominic Cummings to donor Anthony Clake proved that Vote Leave was raising donations for BeLeave to make BeLeave spend that money on the data analytics firm Aggregate IQ. The Commission missed the evidence from other emails that BeLeave had requested money to spend on AIQ weeks before.

The Commission claimed that Vote Leave controlled BeLeave's messaging, yet the Commission ignored evidence from the whistleblowers themselves that BeLeave controlled the messaging. The Commission claimed BeLeave was set up in May 2016. It was set up many months before. The Commission's own former retained barrister, Tim Straker QC, pointed out that all its mistakes amounted to 'an error in law'.

The Commission refused to investigate the evidence against the Remain campaign. In the month before the vote, the official Remain campaign set up five new campaigns and funnelled a total of a million pounds into them so that it could stay under the spending limit. DDB UK Ltd registered as an independent campaign on 25 May. It received £191,000 in donations. Best For Our Future registered as a permitted participant on 27 May. It received £424,000 in donations. The In Crowd registered on 10 June. It received £76,000 in donations. Virgin Management Ltd registered as a permitted participant on 3 June. It received £210,000 in donations. Wake Up And Vote registered as a permitted participant on 24 May. It received £100,000 in donations.

Britain's struggle was unique, our political culture was unique, and our decision was unique. This was the biggest peace time change in Britain for centuries. Gordon Brown wrote that the decision was "the largest popular revolt against political, business and financial elites, the nearest Britain has come in centuries to a revolution."[130] Michael Mosbacher and Oliver Wiseman wrote that it was 'the single most revolutionary democratic act since the extension of the franchise'.[131] The BBC's political editor Laura Kuenssberg said that it was 'an orderly revolution ... when the leave campaign outfoxed and outfought the political establishment'. 2016 was the first referendum in Britain when the government and the state did not get the result they wanted.

The key issue was democracy. Lord Ashcroft's poll of 12,369 people, taken on the day of the referendum after they had voted, found that the biggest single reason for their decision, cited by 49 per cent of those who had voted leave, was 'the principle that decisions about the UK should be taken in the UK'. The vote for Brexit was a vote for national democracy.

The 2016 British Social Attitudes survey found that the vote to leave the EU was not 'a backlash against social liberalism'. It reported, "Britain emerged from the referendum far more sceptical about the EU than it had ever been previously. By the time the referendum was over, as many as three in four voters (75%) felt that Britain should either leave the EU or that if it stayed the institution's powers should be reduced. This represented an increase of 11 points in the proportion feeling that way as compared with 12 months earlier, and a 9 point increase on the previous all-time high recorded by the BSA survey, of two-thirds (67%) in 2012. More importantly, however, whereas previously most Eurosceptics said that Britain should stay in the EU while endeavouring to reduce its powers, by the time that the referendum was over the majority felt that we should leave – and as a result the proportion who took that view (41%) was nearly double the proportion recorded in the previous year (22%)."[132]

We were told that it was a symbolic vote, a proxy vote, a protest vote, an anti-austerity vote (the UCU executive), 'a vote against something not a vote for something' (Jonathan Powell, Blair's chief of staff), anything other than a vote to leave the EU. Some called the referendum and our decision 'divisive'. Would they have said this if we had voted to stay? It was not sensible to object that the referendum was divisive; of course it was, so were elections, when majorities told minorities that they could not get what they wanted. The only alternative was for minorities to tell majorities that they could not get what they wanted.

Binding?

Cameron said to Parliament on 24 June 2016, "The British people have voted to leave the European Union and their will must be respected. ... The British people have made a very clear decision ... There can be no doubt about the result. I'm clear and the Cabinet agreed this morning that the decision must be accepted and the process of implementing the decision in the best possible way must now begin. ... The will of the British people is an instruction that must be delivered."

Mayor of London Sadiq Khan said on 24 June, "The British people have clearly spoken today, and their democratic will must now be fulfilled. ... We all have a responsibility to now seek to heal the divisions that have emerged throughout this campaign - and to focus on that which unites us, rather than that which divides us." On 24 June Corbyn said, "The British people have made their decision. We must respect that result and Article 50 has to be invoked now so that we negotiate an exit from the European Union." John McDonnell said, "The people have spoken and their decision must be respected."

The new Prime Minster Theresa May said on 30 June, "First, Brexit means Brexit. The campaign was fought, the vote was held, turnout was high, and the public gave their verdict. There must be no attempts to remain inside the EU, no attempts to rejoin it through the back door, and no second referendum. The country voted to leave the European Union, and it is the duty of the Government and of Parliament to make sure we do just that. ... the task in front of us is no longer about deciding whether we should leave or remain. The country has spoken, and the United Kingdom will leave the EU. The job now is about uniting the Party, uniting the country – securing the Union – and negotiating the best possible deal for Britain."

May said on 11 July, "make no mistake, the referendum was a vote to leave the European Union, but it was also a vote for serious change. Yet so many of our political and business leaders have responded by showing that they still don't get it. There are politicians – democratically-elected politicians – who seriously suggest that the Government should find a way of ignoring the referendum result and keeping Britain inside the European Union. And there are business leaders whose response has not been to plan for Britain's departure or to think of the opportunities withdrawal presents – but to complain about the result and criticise the electorate." May realised, as some did not, that the referendum decision mattered deeply, and that to let a minority overrule our majority decision would be a disaster for democracy.

McDonnell said on 15 November 2016, "Labour accepts the referendum result as the voice of the majority and we must embrace the enormous opportunities to reshape our country that Brexit has opened for us." On 19 January 2017, Corbyn said, "It is very clear. The referendum made a decision that Britain was to leave the European Union. ... I've made it very clear the Labour party accepts and respects the decision of the British people. We will not block article 50." A Labour spokesperson said on 24 January, "Labour respects the result of the referendum and the will of the British people and will not frustrate the process for invoking Article 50."

But Corbyn had also said, on 15 January, "A decision was made and we have to work around that." Not make it work, but work around it. He referred to 'the chaos of Brexit'. He said, "The Brexit vote isn't a one-off thing, it has got to be agreed by 27 national parliaments, it has got to be agreed by the European parliament." No, it did not. Under Article 50 (1), only notice to leave was necessary: "Any member state may decide to withdraw from the Union in accordance with its own constitutional requirements." We had the right to leave, the EU had no right to stop our leaving at once and it had no right to impose any conditions. But Article 50 had been drafted (by Lord Kerr) to give the EU, not the departing state, all the negotiating leverage.

Adam Tomkins, a Conservative MSP for Glasgow, wrote, "Referendums, however, are not opinion polls whose verdicts we can celebrate or ignore as the case befits. They are formal, binding, decision-making devices. They represent not advice to government, but instructions to government. Had Scotland voted 'Yes' in 2014 the United Kingdom would not have been free to ignore or to seek to overturn the result. Likewise, in 2016: having asked the people for their decision we are now duty bound to give effect to it. The UK is leaving the EU not because the Tories have willed it – both the current Prime

Minister and her predecessor campaigned and voted to remain, as did Sir John Major – but because parliament decided in the European Union Referendum Act 2015 to ask the people whether we should leave or remain, and the people gave their answer, calmly and clearly, just as the Scottish people gave their answer on the independence question in 2014."[133]

The pro-EU Labour MP for Ilford North, Wes Streeting, said in the House of Commons on 31 January 2017, "... it is hard to overstate the damage that this Parliament would inflict on our democracy were we to reject the outcome of a referendum in which 33.5 million people voted. This was not an advisory referendum. None of us went to the door asking for advice. We warned of the consequences of leaving, and the majority of voters and the majority of constituencies voted leave with the clear expectation that that would actually happen."

Mr Streeting and the pro-EU Labour MP Chuka Umunna wrote in the *i* on 2 February 2017, "Those who voted to leave were not duped by the right-wing media. They were not any more or less ignorant of the technical issues of the EU debate than were Remainers. They were no more or less bigoted in their views than Remainers. In fact, the division between Remainers and Leavers in the country is much less pronounced than people think. There exists a shared desire for national renewal and for Britain to be great again. People want a more equal, more decent Britain that is a moral leader, a creator, a trader, a connector, and an ideas maker in the world. A European country, if not a member of the EU. Neither Leavers nor Remainers want Britain turned into a bolt hole for the super-rich, a tax haven for monopoly capitalism, a sweatshop for Europe. Brexit demands that we construct an enduring social and economic settlement at home in the interest of working people, and a new strategic security and foreign policy for Britain in the world."

The consequences

The consequences of Brexit included ousting the unpopular Cameron; ousting Osborne the architect of austerity; the new government's dropping the previous government's key policy of prioritising cutting the debt by 2020; and crucially, the restoration of our sovereignty over decisions affecting our country.

We voted against the EU's unelected European Central Bank, its unelected European Commission, its European Court of Justice, its Common Agricultural Policy and its Common Fisheries Policy. We voted against its undemocratic trilogue procedure and its pro-austerity Semester programme. We voted against its treaty-enshrined 'austerity' (depression) policies, which have impoverished Greece, Spain, Portugal and Italy. We voted against the EU/US Transatlantic Trade and Investment Partnership, which threatened to privatise our public services and to discriminate against the countries of Africa, Asia and Latin America. We voted against the EU's tariffs against African farmers' cheaper produce.

We voted against the three most recent Conservative Party Prime Ministers, Major, Cameron and May, and against the Labour Party, the LibDems, the SNP and Plaid Cymru. We voted against the City of London Corporation, the Institute of Directors, the CBI, the IMF, Goldman Sachs, JP Morgan, Citigroup and Morgan Stanley, which all campaigned for us to stay in the EU.

We voted to stop paying billions to the EU. We voted to withdraw our MEPs from the European parliament. We voted to trade with other countries, including with EU members, as other countries do. We voted to end the free movement of EU nationals into Britain. We voted to control our laws and our borders. We voted to leave a political union, an ever more centralised and undemocratic state.

Voting to leave was an assertion of sovereignty, of national independence and of democracy, as inspiring to our fellow workers across the world as the Cuban people's assertion of sovereignty and national independence against the US empire. Independence is good for countries. Countries that run their own affairs do better than those that do not.

Inside the EU we were trapped in a failing, unstable, unsafe, unfree, undemocratic, stifling bloc, where we were not free to change policies we opposed, where we were not free to vote out leaders we opposed. If we had stayed in, we would have stayed on the conveyor belt towards ever closer union, a single EU state.

The great economist John Maynard Keynes famously asked, "When the facts change, I change my mind. What do you do, sir?" Our referendum decision was just such a change of the facts. It was not a majority overriding minority rights. Minority rights did not include the right to overrule the majority. When a minority of EU enthusiasts refused to change their minds just because the majority voted for independence, they were not defending minority rights against majority tyranny; they were demanding the minority's right to overrule the majority.

Whichever party ran the government, it had the duty to carry out our democratic decision to leave the EU. Any government which tried to override the majority decision and impose instead the wishes of the minority would stand condemned as an enemy of democracy. Craig Oliver, Cameron's director of communications, drafted this for Cameron's Commons statement of 22 February 2016: "For the Prime Minster to ignore the express will of the British people who had voted to leave would not just be wrong. It would be undemocratic." Oliver wrote, "I cannot see the circumstances in which any politician could or should amass the political capital to go against the democratic will of the British people, or take on the sheer intensity of the campaign they would face." We should all respect the legitimacy of the outcome of the 2016 referendum, whatever we think of its wisdom.

Chapter 5 Rights and immigration

The EU Charter of Fundamental Rights

The EU Charter of Fundamental Rights of 2000 was not what it seemed. It was not about giving us rights that we had never had before. It was not about confirming rights that we already had.

In fact, as the EU commissioner for Justice and Home Affairs stated in 2000, the Charter marked "a definitive change in the Community, which will move away from the essentially economic raison d'être of its origins to become a full political union."[134] So the Charter was a way to advance the interests of the EU, not a way to advance the rights of EU citizens.

And further, as Anthony Coughlan pointed out, "A basic objection to the conferral of a human rights competence on the EU, whatever one's view as to the content of human rights, is that such a development is quite unnecessary as all the Member states are already bound by the provisions of the European Convention on Human Rights, which they acceded to well before the EU Charter of Fundamental Rights was thought of. Moreover, there are already human rights provisions in the national Constitutions of each Member state. The only reason for the EU arrogating to itself a human rights competence would seem to be the desire to build itself up further as a quasi-federal state."[135]

A team of British lawyers originally drafted the European Convention on Human Rights and Britain was the first to ratify it, on 8 March 1951. (France did not ratify it until 1974.) So, Britain in effect gave Europe human rights, not vice versa.

Prime Minister Blair told the House of Commons in 2007 that "it is absolutely clear that we have an opt-out from … the Charter." [136] He claimed that the Charter was only a 'declaration' with no legal status.[137] Keith Vaz, Blair's Minister for Europe, told us the Charter would have all the force in law of 'the *Beano* or the *Sun*'.[138] When the Lisbon Treaty gave the

Charter legal effect, Blair told the House of Commons' Liaison Committee that "we will not accept a treaty that allows the Charter of Fundamental Rights to change UK law in any way."[139]

The European Court of Justice then told us that our opt-out was worthless and started to make judgments using the Charter to change our law.[140] The Court stated that the relevant Protocol 'does not intend to exempt ... the United Kingdom from the obligation to comply with the provisions of the Charter or to prevent a [UK] court ... from ensuring compliance with those provisions'.[141] The UK Supreme Court confirmed "the Charter thus has direct effect in national law."[142]

Workers' rights

The EU did not promote or protect collective bargaining. It did not protect the right to strike. EU law gave trade unions no extra protection. In 1981 the European Court of Justice ruled against the closed shop, drastically weakening trade unions in their struggle against Thatcher.

EU law banned industrial action which 'disproportionately' obstructed the EU's founding principle of the free movement of goods, services, capital and labour. Successive rulings of the European Court of Justice made it clear that in the EU these rights to free movement came way ahead of workers' rights. ECJ Advocate General Poiares Maduro explained why: "the possibility for a company to relocate to a Member State where its operating costs will be lower is pivotal to the pursuit of effective intra Community trade." The EU's economic policy strengthened the market through liberalisation and privatisation, at the expense of employment and social protection.

The EU's fundamental rights were all about the market. In effect, it acted as a state whose constitution embodied the freedom of capital and capitalists in a way unheard of in any other country. These freedoms trumped workers' rights. Workers were forbidden to act to prevent work being outsourced to a cheaper country or to stop the privatisation of national industries and services. And they were supposed to stand by while the free movement of labour eroded pay.

The 2007 Treaty on the Functioning of the European Union said that its Article 151, 'employment, improved living and working conditions', did not apply to pay, the right of association, the right to strike or the right to impose lock-outs. In the cases of the Viking Line (2007) and Laval (2008), the European Court of Justice found for the employers and against the workers.

All Thatcher's anti-trade union laws were legal under EU law. The EU did nothing for the miners in 1984-85. The EU, far from protecting Greek workers, instead demanded the destruction of their trade union rights as a condition of its bailouts. France's President Hollande used emergency powers to impose cuts on workers' rights and to attack trade unions – the EU did nothing to counter this.

As the leading labour lawyer John Hendy summed up, "The EU has become a disaster for the collective rights of workers and their unions." Bob Crow of the RMT wrote, "The Social Europe agenda was always a smoke screen to fool the organised working class that we had something in common with big business. We didn't then and we don't today when unelected EU institutions, directly representing Europe's biggest banks, are removing elected governments and imposing mass unemployment, social dumping and unending austerity ..." [143] Capitalism abused the doctrine of rights to defend exploitation.

In 2015 the TUC noted 'the increasing domination of neo-liberal ideology within the European Union'. Yet Frances O'Grady of the TUC wrote in *The Times* on 16 January 2018 that the EU's "single market is the only realistic option that guarantees rights at work long-term." If the EU guaranteed workers' rights, what need was there for the TUC or indeed for trade unions? Likewise, the Labour Party kept Thatcher's anti-trade union laws and then claimed that we must stay in the EU to defend trade union rights.

EU rights for workers did not exist in practice. Nearly two million workers did not get their legally entitled paid holidays. There was a minimum wage, but millions got far less. There was a working hours directive, yet people worked longer and longer hours. There was no EU maternity benefit, not a penny. There was no EU minimum wage, not a penny.

The laws against discrimination, the laws on paid maternity and paternity leave, equal pay, minimum paid holiday, the 48-hour working week and TUPE [Transfer of Undertakings (Protection of Employment)] rules were all national laws. When we leave the EU, the laws will still stand. They did not come from the EU; they did not depend on our being in the EU.

Britain has often gone much further than required by EU law. For example, we gave 52 weeks of maternity leave and 39 weeks of pay while the EU gave only 14 weeks. Britain also provided greater flexibility around shared parental leave, where, subject to certain conditions, parental leave could be shared by the father, giving families choices about how they balanced their home and work responsibilities. In addition, the UK offered 18 weeks' parental leave, and that provision went beyond the EU's 1996 Parental Leave Directive because it was available until the child's 18th birthday. In fact, in most EU member countries, entitlement to leave was at a higher standard than in the EU Directive.[144]

"Europe is responsible for making sure you get 28 days paid leave a year," said Unite the Union. Not so. The UK Working Time Regulations were a UK law. The European Working Time Directive of 1998 specified a minimum of four weeks' holiday including statutory public holidays - 20 days. But workers could sign a written opt-out, if they wanted to, or were pressured to do so. And most collective agreements gave workers a better deal, including a maximum 40-hour week. Our domestic law already had a minimum of four weeks plus statutory public holidays - 28 days. As Liam Halligan and Gerald Lyons summed up, "Britain has a track record on working conditions and labour standards that, in many respects, is more progressive than much of the EU."[145]

Some cited the Temporary Agency Workers Directive 2008 as a fine example of the EU's giving workers rights. It stated that agency workers should receive the same treatment as workers employed directly by a company. But if this worked so well, how come there were so many people working in the gig economy and on zero-hours contracts?

The 1970 Equal Pay Act was passed before we joined the EU, before the EU's Equal Pay Directive of 1975 and its Employment Equality Directive of 2000. Equal pay did not come from the EU or from Parliament but from the struggle by the Ford Dagenham women workers in 1968. Strong workplace-based trade unions, not reliance on EU law, improved workers' rights.

On equality rights, Angela O'Hagan, Convenor of the Scottish Women's Budget Group, wrote, "In the face of withdrawal from the EU arguably none of these rights and protections are threatened. Legal protection from discrimination on a number of specified protected characteristics is provided under the Equality Act 2010: an act of the Westminster parliament ... with its 'very good protections' (SP OR EHRIC [Scottish Parliament Official Report, Equality and Human Rights Committee], 3 November 2016) that include provisions beyond the European minima."[146]

Johanna Kantola pointed out in the definitive study of discrimination in the EU, "The European gender gap has remained at about 15-20 per cent despite 50 years of legislation and policy in the field."[147] Development expert Karin Arts wrote: "Gender mainstreaming of EU development cooperation has largely remained an exercise of expressing policy priorities and intentions, which have not been followed up by active and well-supported implementation efforts."[148] On disability mainstreaming Kantola noted, "Again, as with gender mainstreaming, the implementation of mainstreaming has not been successful and member states have accepted it only on a rhetorical level."[149]

Kantola observed that "The European need for migrant labour, the lack of rights for migrant workers and the structural conditions of women in the labour market fuel illegal migration and trafficking." [150] She pointed out that "Trafficking in women and domestic violence are issues that feminists have argued are a key to Gender equality, but that have long been either ignored or ridiculed at EU level."[151]

As she observed, "In the EU, social policy, equal opportunities policy and the reconciliation of work and family have to operate within the hegemonic aims of competition, growth and efficiency."[152] This was the US model of market primacy backed by anti-discrimination measures encouraging access to the labour market. The aim was not equality but getting more women into the labour market, cutting wages. Unhelpfully, EU law did not even recognise caring as work.

On 14 April 2016 Jeremy Corbyn warned, "Just imagine what the Tories would do to workers' rights here in Britain if we voted to leave the EU in June. They'd dump rights on equal pay, working time, annual leave, for agency workers, and on maternity pay as fast as they could get away with it. It would be a bonfire of rights that Labour governments secured within the EU."

Two days before the referendum he said, "On 23rd June we are faced with a choice: Do we remain to protect jobs and prosperity in Britain? Or do we step into an unknown future with Leave where a Tory-negotiated Brexit risks economic recovery and threatens a bonfire of employment rights?"

The law firm Linklaters did a study, *Corbyn's Brexit 'bonfire' of workers' rights - is it likely?* It concluded, "We believe that it is highly unlikely that Parliament would want (and the public would allow it) to repeal existing equal pay measures. This is particularly true bearing in mind recent government initiatives to stamp out the gender pay gap. ... Although Parliament would be able to amend UK discrimination legislation following a Brexit so as to deprive UK workers of certain protections imposed by EU Directives, we suggest that it would be unlikely to make retrospective changes. ...

"as things currently stand, UK maternity laws exceed minimum EU requirements. ... as regards maternity pay, this right is now engrained in the UK's work culture and we question whether there will be much political will (and power) to attack it, as suggested. The right to unpaid parental leave originates from the EU and is enshrined in UK Regulations. As such, it is, in principle, susceptible to abolition. However, few major employers object to this right and, bearing in mind government's efforts to encourage women to return to work after maternity leave and to have both parents share childcare more equally, we suggest that the abolition of this right is unlikely to be a priority following a Brexit. ... As for the right to request flexible work, it has UK origins and a Brexit would not impact on it in any way. ...

"Employee's [sic] rights on business transfers and outsourcing (under TUPE) and for collective consultation are now enshrined in UK law and it is telling that Mr Corbyn has not suggested that they would be lost. In our opinion these rights (although originating in the EU) are now so enshrined in UK law and UK labour culture that no significant changes would be expected. It is also interesting to note that Parliament chose to introduce wider TUPE protections for employees than was strictly necessary under the EU Directive, which further supports the belief that there would be little interest in weakening or removing such protections post Brexit."[153]

But in 2013 the European Court nullified TUPE. In 2013 it backed the employer in the Alemo-Herron case. The claimants' employment contracts with the London Borough of Lewisham had said that they were entitled to the terms and conditions negotiated from time to time by the National Joint Council for local government. Under TUPE, these workers had the right to pay awards agreed by the National Joint Council. Due to takeovers, their employment then transferred twice and their ultimate employer, Parkwood Leisure, refused to respect this right. The ECJ called in aid Article 16 of the EU's Charter of Fundamental Rights, which guaranteed employers' rights to conduct a business and not be bound by any agreement to which they were not a party.

In 2016, the Norwegian Supreme Court, acting under the rules of the EEA, ended the country's 1976 collective agreement for dock workers which, like the pre-Thatcher dock labour arrangements in Britain, had granted the Norwegian dock labourers' union the sole right to unload cargo. This showed that there was little difference between the EEA and the EU and that no member states had any power over these rulings.

Even the pro-EU European Trade Union Confederation said that recent ECJ judgements confirmed 'a hierarchy of norms, with market freedoms highest in the hierarchy, and collective bargaining and action in second place'.

Workers' rights were in more danger inside the EU. The EU prevented rebuilding its members' economies, so its only alternative was to cut wages and public spending, in a race to the bottom. As Halligan and Lyons wrote, "there is the overwhelming need to uphold workers' rights. Some might view leaving the EU as an opportunity to pursue a race to the bottom on labour standards. This is precisely the kind of Brexit that, overwhelmingly, voters do not want. It is not highlighted enough that by returning sovereignty to Parliament, we empower the UK public to get the policies it chooses."[154]

Those worried that leaving the EU will threaten workers' rights and social protections should recognise that staying in the EU would be no safeguard of these rights and protections and that the EU's big-business backers are no friends of these rights and protections. Focusing exclusively on the hypothetical, though admittedly plausible, threat to workers' rights from some Brexiteers is to ignore the very real and present threat to workers' rights and social protections from the EU, especially its Court, and from its big-business supporters.

The government's Repeal Act transposed all existing EU law including workplace laws, consumer rights and all EU environmental law into our law, and the government pledged to preserve all the rights granted by EU law. So, workers' rights in EU employment law will all be saved into our domestic law. Fine, but workers should never rely on rights in law. Our rights were not handed down to us from courts or parliament or government or the EU. Organised workers won our rights.

Britain led the world in developing LGBT rights, starting with the decriminalisation of homosexuality in 1967. The International Lesbian, Gay, Bisexual, Trans & Intersex Association's 2017 Rainbow Index placed Britain as the second best EU member state to be LGBT. We could marry whoever we loved (Marriage (Same Sex Couples) Act 2013), start a family (Adoption and Children Act 2002) and were protected from discrimination in society and at work (Equality Act 2010). None of these rights came from the EU.

The 1999 Treaty of Amsterdam only required EU member states to ban anti-gay laws in employment. It did not protect LGBT people from discrimination in other areas such as the right to equal access to medical treatment, protection against being refused a double room in a hotel, or protection from homophobic bullying in schools. Only 13 of the 27 EU member states allowed same-sex marriage; seven countries' constitutions banned it. Adoption by same-sex couples was illegal in 13 EU member states. One state, Cyprus, still banned LGBT people from serving openly in the military. 13 member states had laws which insisted on forced sterilisation for trans people who wished to change gender.

Nicola Sturgeon claimed in the 9 June 2016 debate that the EU gave the 'freedom for all of us to travel freely in Europe'. But we did not have to be in the EU to travel to, work in, live in, study in, holiday in or retire to Europe. Did pro-EU people really believe that the EU was so illiberal that it would forbid us to travel, work, live or study there? Nobody proposed to end these freedoms, which we had before the EU ever existed. Our freedoms had not come from the EU and they did not depend on our being in the EU. Leaving the EU did not threaten any of them.

Parliament, or any sovereign body, could repeal Habeas Corpus or trial by jury or freedom of speech, but it should never do so, because Habeas Corpus, trial by jury and freedom of speech are in the interests of the people. The European Parliament was far more likely to abolish trial by jury and free speech. In case c-274/99 the EU's Advocate General stated, "Criticism of the EU is akin to blasphemy and can be restricted without affecting freedom of speech." The EU was on a path to classing 'eurosceptic sentiment' (that meant the British people in particular) as a 'threat to the union' enforceable by internal security action via Federica Mogherini's Security and Defence Implementation Plan published on 14 November 2016 and approved the same day at EU Council.

EU citizens' rights

During the referendum campaign the pro-EU camp, not the leave camp, raised the spectre of deporting EU citizens living here. Ministers were asked in the House of Lords "whether it is their intention that, in the event of the UK leaving the EU, citizens of EU member states who had previously settled in the UK would be entitled automatically to remain?"

Lord Keen of Elie, a Home Office minister, replied, "UK citizens get the right to live and work in the other 27 member states from our membership of the EU. If the UK voted to leave the EU, the Government would do all it could to secure a positive outcome for the country, but there would be no requirement under EU law for these rights to be maintained."[155] This implied that EU citizens living here would similarly have no right to remain. The pro-EU Mayor of

London Sadiq Khan claimed that if Britain left the EU, London's EU citizens would 'face massive uncertainty and even the prospect of having to leave London altogether'.[156]

Some claimed that the leave campaign backed deportation. Not so. Throughout the campaign, Vote Leave said on its website, "There will be no change for EU citizens already lawfully resident in the UK ... These EU citizens will automatically be granted indefinite leave to remain in the UK and will be treated no less favourably than they are at present."

Leading Leave campaigners explicitly rejected deportation. Philip Davies MP asserted, "Nobody would ever suggest that anybody who has arrived here legally would be evicted from the country. For the Government not to make that abundantly clear is ludicrous." He added, "They must know full well that they wouldn't and couldn't deport people who previously arrived here legally."

Jacob Rees-Mogg MP added that it was 'really grubby politics' to worry people who had established "a legitimate right to be here. It would be straightforwardly immoral to deport people who have come here legally and who have established their lives here." Peter Bone MP said, "Clearly any EU citizen that is legally here if we come out of the EU would absolutely have the right to remain here. Any other suggestion is just absurd. It is a scare story, full stop. It just shows how desperate the Government and the Remain campaign are."

Some in the pro-EU camp said that leaving the EU would break up hundreds of thousands of couples. But pro-EU government leaders said that this was not so. On 21 July Hollande said, "there is no doubt that the French people who reside in the UK will be able to continue to work there and that the British people in France will be able to continue to work there and spend as much time as they wish." Prime Minister May said on 28 July, "I want to be clear that Poles living in the UK continue to be welcome and we value the contribution that they make to our country."

EU nationals living here had their rights protected. The 1969 Vienna Convention on the Law of Treaties stated in article 70.1.b that leaving a treaty "Does not affect any right, obligation or legal situation of the parties created through the execution of the treaty prior to its termination." This long-recognised principle of respect for acquired rights safeguarded the rights of all EU citizens living in Britain. They had nothing to fear. Further, there was no political will in Britain to remove their rights. The overwhelming majority of British people supported the rights of EU nationals to stay here. An ICM study of 3 July 2016 found that 84 per cent, including majorities among UKIP voters, thought that resident EU nationals should stay. 77 per cent of Leave voters agreed.

As the May government stated on 16 July 2016: "There has been no change to the right of EU nationals to reside in the UK and therefore no change to the circumstances in which someone could be removed from the UK. As was the case before the referendum, EU nationals can only be removed from the UK if they are considered to pose a genuine, present and sufficiently serious threat to the public, if they are not lawfully resident or are abusing their free movement rights."

The Prime Minister said on 17 January 2017, "We want to guarantee the rights of EU citizens who are already living in Britain, and the rights of British nationals in other member states, as early as we can. I have told other EU leaders that we could give people the certainty they want straight away, and reach such a deal now." The Prime Minister made numerous offers to settle this issue, but Chancellor Merkel and other EU leaders always refused, saying 'no negotiation before notification'.

Hate crimes

The Operational Guidance for police forces dealing with hate crimes was: "For recording purposes, the perception of the victim, or any other person, is the defining factor in determining whether an incident is a hate incident... The victim does not have to justify or provide evidence of their belief, and police officers or staff should not directly challenge this perception. Evidence of hostility is not required for an incident or crime to be recorded as a hate crime or hate incident." So, for any alleged incident to be recorded as a hate crime, the victim or any other person simply had to say that it was a hate crime. Hate crime, unlike any other crime, was based entirely on say-so. Every phone call alleging a hate crime was instantly recorded as a hate crime.

Various bodies increased their trawling for such crimes immediately after the referendum. Pro-EU Sadiq Khan, the Mayor of London, put up a special webpage imploring people to phone or email about 'hate crimes following the referendum result'. Many people Twitter-shared the police's hate-crime hotline.

There were significant increases in hate crimes against Asians and Arabs almost immediately after the 7/7 terror attack in London in July 2005 and the 9/11 terror attack in New York in September 2001. The increases subsequently declined, but offences were still at higher than pre-attack levels a year later.

There was also a sudden increase in hate crime soon after the referendum and lasting for some time before falling back to (and below) pre-referendum levels. Hate crimes increased again, to even higher levels, after the 2017 terror attacks in Westminster (22 March), Manchester (22 May), London Bridge (3 June) and on the Finsbury Park mosque (19 June). Again, the crimes declined soon after.

In the month after the referendum, there were an extra 638 hate crimes. In the month after the Westminster attack, there were an extra 831 hate crimes. In the month after the Finsbury Park and London Bridge attacks, there were an extra 740 hate crimes.

Hate crimes have been on an upward trend since 2013, and they always increase in June and July. In 2015-16, hate crime was up by 20 per cent on the previous year. In 2014-15, it rose by 18 per cent. In 2016-17, hate crime was up by 29 per cent on the previous year. There were 80,393 offences, compared with 62,518 in 2015-16 - the largest increase since the Home Office began recording figures in 2011-12. The biggest rises were in disability hate crimes (a 53 per cent rise) and transgender hate crimes (up 45 per cent). The Home Office said that these rises were due to better crime recording and more people coming forward.

In 2016-17, 62,685 (78 per cent) were race hate crimes; 9,157 (11 per cent) were sexual orientation hate crimes; 5,949 (7 per cent) were religious hate crimes; 5,558 (7 per cent) were disability hate crimes and 1,248 (2 per cent) were transgender hate crimes. The Crown Prosecution Service revealed on 16 October 2017 that the number of those accused of committing a hate crime who ended up in court had fallen by 1,000 in the last year, despite the 20 per cent rise in the number of reports.[157]

The EU has stoked up the ultra-right in Britain and across Europe. A tiny number of fascists here threatened our unity by committing hate crimes. Blaming Brexit for hate crimes was like blaming Islam for terrorism. Imputing guilt by association was always an undemocratic procedure.

Some seemed unable to tell the difference between opposing the neoliberal policy of uncontrolled immigration and hating immigrants, opposing a bad policy and having a bad ethic. Some accused millions of their fellow-citizens of racism and xenophobia, but in reality, even after the referendum that supposedly expressed and aggravated these vile traits, the World Values Survey found in 2018 that Britain was more racially tolerant than most European societies.[158] The European Commission ranked Britain third in Europe, narrowly behind Sweden and Denmark, 'in saying that they would be happy to have an immigrant as a neighbour, colleague, friend or family relation'.[159] The Commission's 2018

Eurobarometer survey found that Britons were generally more welcoming to immigrants than the average European.[160]

We opposed the policy of uncontrolled migration from the EU, yet some in the pro-EU camp confused this with the immoral targeting of immigrants. Opposing uncontrolled immigration was not the same as ending all immigration. (Just as controlling your food intake is not the same as ending your food intake.) Nor was it the same as being hostile to immigrants. The ultra-left falsely identified opposition to mass migration with xenophobia. The ultra-left also falsely identified opposition to EU membership with xenophobia. Ultra-lefts used smears of racism to cover their support for the employers', and EU, policy of the free movement of labour, which was the twin of the employers' policy of the free movement of capital. The slogan 'British Jobs for British Workers' could only be deemed racist on the assumption that only white workers were British.

An 'anti-racism' leaflet denounced an 'anti-foreign, anti-European mentality' identifying opposition to EU membership with xenophobia. Similarly, Elizabeth Fekete, Director of the Institute of Race Relations, referred to 'the anti-EU, anti-migrant cause'.[161] But calling for Britain to leave the EU was not racist or xenophobic. Barrister Afua Hirsch claimed that "The anti-human rights act sentiment that existed then, in the mid-2000s, is a direct antecedent of the anti-European sentiment that exists today."[162] No proof of this was apparently needed; it was stated as a self-evident, incontrovertible truth.

On 2 June 2016, Jeremy Corbyn defended those concerned about high levels of immigration: "I've already talked about how some industries are affected by the undercutting of wages and the action that can be taken to tackle that. But some communities can change dramatically and rapidly and that can be disconcerting for some people. That doesn't make them Little Englanders, xenophobes or racists. More people living in an area can put real pressure on local services like GPs surgeries, schools and housing. This isn't the fault of migrants. It's a failure of government."

Many of the Labour Party's new members clung to the unpopular view that there should be no borders and they insulted those who disagreed with them as old white racist bigots. A popular meme showed an EU supporter saying, "I just don't understand it. Throughout the entire campaign, I called at least 120,000 people racist, and yet we still lost."[163]

In a fine example of open prejudice, the UK's former Ambassador to the EU, and leading supporter of the EU, Lord Kerr of Kinlochard, who drafted the EU Constitution/Lisbon Treaty, said, "In my view, immigration is the thing that keeps this country running. We native Brits are so bloody stupid that we need an injection of intelligent people, young people from outside who come in and wake us up from time to time."

Professor Michael Cox, editor of Palgrave Macmillan's series 'Rethinking World Politics', wrote of the EU, "even to raise difficult questions either about its design, coherence or effectiveness almost seemed to cast those who did so into the camp of the no-nothings [sic!] and the troglodytes." [164] Professor Richard Dawkins wrote, "It is unfair to thrust on to unqualified simpletons the responsibility to take historic decisions of great complexity and sophistication." [165] The supposedly progressive thinker Slavoj Zizek said, "Direct democracy is the last Leftist myth." He said that referendums are impractical for resolving transnational challenges, and that he would prefer 'the appearance of a free decision, discretely guided' by a discerning elite.[166] This contempt for the masses, who are, please remember, other people, lost the pro-EU camp the support it took for granted.

Immigration

Transnational corporations used the free movement of labour enshrined in EU treaty since 1957 to exploit migrant workers and employees 'posted' from one country to another, where they were employed on worse terms and conditions than local workers. ECJ rulings derived from the EU Posted Workers Directive, the 2005 Services (Bolkestein) Directive and the Business Transfers Directive protected this widespread and systematic abuse of workers.

The EU dogma of free movement gave 450 million people the right to move to, live and work in Britain. As a member of the EU, we had no way to prevent migrants from the other EU member states from coming to live and work here as and when they wished. The euro stifled the job hopes of millions of Europeans, so many of them looked to us for a chance of work. There were six EU members where the average wage was less than a third of our minimum wage and another eight where it was less than a half. The accession countries had average wages lower than our minimum wage. So, many of their people were likely to want to come here. The reverse did not apply.

In 2011, the European Commission called for a 'Global Migration Approach', to encourage even more migration into EU countries 'to meet its projected labour needs via targeted immigration of third country nationals', when unemployment in the EU was 20 million.

Who wanted the free movement of labour? The employing class. Who supported it? President Juncker called for No Borders. By contrast, the Leave campaign was about controlling our borders, not closing them. In the Schengen countries, where the EU allowed no controls on immigration, the far right was on the rise. In Britain the far right had only derisory levels of support.

EU immigration policy was set by whichever member government opened the door widest – Spain in 2005, Germany in 2015, when Merkel decided to admit one million refugees to Germany and therefore to Europe, without consulting her EU partners. Any EU member state could make anyone in the world a citizen and then every other EU member state had to accept that person as a citizen. When we were in the EU, any

EU citizen could come here to settle, work, claim benefits and use the NHS. [167] We had no control over whether that individual's presence was economically beneficial, conducive to the public good or in our national interest. We were not allowed to screen new arrivals for qualifications, extremist links or past criminality. The USA fingerprinted all foreign arrivals, so that it could identify anyone trying to use a false ID. But in Britain we did not even fingerprint illegal immigrants trying to enter from France.

Even Cameron's Director of Communications Craig Oliver said, "When you sit down and explain to any reasonable person that in order to be part of this international organisation you have to accept immigration into your country that is unlimited no matter what the circumstances, most people would say, 'That is crazy.'"[168]

On 28 June 2016, Sadiq Khan said that it was important not to 'demonise' the 1.5 million Londoners who voted for Brexit. He said, "While I and millions of others disagreed with their decision, they took it for a variety of reasons and this shouldn't be used to accuse them of being xenophobic or racist. We must respect their decision and work together now to get the best deal for London." He showed exemplary generosity of spirit.

Professor Jonathan Hearn acknowledged that using nationalism "as a covering term for objectionable ethnic chauvinism will not do." He wrote that Brexit "mobilizes national identities not simply in terms of ethnicity and culture but also in terms of the adequacy of democratic government, of people's rule over themselves. ... to deny the democratic impulse behind this nationalism is an act of wilful misrecognition."[169]

An Ipsos-MORI poll of 11-14 June 2016 found that the public thought, by 55 per cent to 27 per cent, that immigration had had a bad effect on the NHS. Worcester and Mortimore commented, "It is particularly noteworthy that this powerful message was accepted by so many who do not seem to have been anti-immigration as such. The belief that the NHS had suffered cannot therefore be explained away as those who oppose immigration for other reasons rationalising their beliefs, or trying to find a respectable excuse for opinions they might otherwise be embarrassed to hold. It was a key claim of Leave supporters and in the circumstances must be judged to be more a driver of, than driven by, wider opposition to immigration. One consequence of this was that accusing all those voters with doubts about immigration of xenophobia or racism, as happened explicitly and implicitly during the campaign and afterwards, could only anger them and deepen still further their impression that Cameron and his team were playing dirty as well as being out of touch with real concerns of the public, which in the circumstances were both dangerously alienating impressions to give."[170]

In January 2017 Vince Cable made the case for immigration controls: "I have serious doubts that EU free movement is tenable or even desirable. British opposition to immigration is mainly colour-blind. But the benefits accrue mainly to migrants themselves (and business owners). It is also reasonable for Remainers to accept that there should be controls, as for non-EU migrants. That is also where public opinion is. Long-term social survey analysis suggests that the demand for effective immigration control coexists with greater tolerance of diversity. There is no great argument of liberal principle for free EU movement; the economics is debatable; and the politics is conclusively hostile."[171]

May said, "Free movement of labour cannot be allowed to continue." She said the Brexit vote sent a very clear message about the need to control immigration. Net migration needed to come down to sustainable levels. In July 2017 the Prime Minister said, "free movement will end in March 2019."

But Corbyn told the *Guardian*: "my view is that if we have a single market with free movement of capital, there has to be free movement of labour." Asked if there could be an upper limit for immigration, he said: "I don't think you can have one while you have the free movement of labour." He said, "More migration is good for us." He said that limiting migration would 'sow division' in the country. He said, "There is nothing wrong with people migrating to work across the Continent." A Corbyn spokesman said, "We are not concerned about numbers. It is not our objective to reduce the numbers, to reduce immigration." John McDonnell told the Labour Party conference on 27 September 2016, "We will seek to preserve access to the Single Market for goods and services. Today, access to the Single Market requires freedom of movement of labour." So, the 'internationalist left' allied with international capital in backing the EU's free movement of labour.

The European Court of Justice controlled our ability to require migrants to have proper identification issued by the government. An EU directive forbade systematic verification of whether EU citizens were lawfully resident in Britain: "verification shall not be carried out systematically."[172] The Court ruled in 1999, "EU citizenship is destined to be the fundamental status of nationals of the Member States." The Court did not see itself as bound to follow international law, not even the resolutions of the UN Security Council.

In English law, there was no right to asylum: we were not legally obliged to accept asylum seekers. We had the power and the right to refuse admission to nationals of other countries. Our courts have ruled that the unqualified right to exclude them was an essential attribute of national sovereignty. And this was in line with the practice of all other states. As Guy Goodwin-Gill and Jane McAdam wrote in the definitive book on the status of the refugee in international law, "State practice ... permits only one conclusion: the individual still has no right to be granted asylum. ... Freedom to grant or to refuse permanent asylum remains ..." [173] Professor of international law J. G. Starke wrote of "the untrammelled nature of the discretionary right of a State of proposed refuge to grant or withhold the grant of asylum, as the case may be, according to its own domestic laws, policies, and practices."[174]

The ECJ could control how member states applied the 1951 UN convention on asylum and refugees because the Charter incorporated it into EU law. So we had no control over how we implemented the Convention. The Charter contained a freestanding right to asylum, article 18(1).

The UK opted into the First Qualification Directive, 2004/83/EC. Chapter III of this Directive committed member states to apply the Geneva Convention as set forth in the Directive. The ECJ had the ultimate authority to interpret the Directive. The ECJ's rulings governed our Court of Appeal's judgements. In 2000 the UK Court of Appeal decided that France and Germany were not 'safe places' to send refugees, and that the then Home Secretary had acted unlawfully in ordering three asylum seekers to be returned to France and Germany. This prevented Britain deporting thousands of failed asylum seekers. Austria and Greece have since been added to the UK list of 'no return' countries.

Inside the EU, under EU rules, reducing EU immigration was illegal. So Cameron restricted non-EU immigration, which included almost all refugees. EU rules made us prioritise EU migrants over refugees. Outside the EU our options were open, we were free to decide our immigration policy, we could, if we wanted, stop prioritising EU migrants over refugees.

Syria is the biggest source of refugees – 3.88 million have fled the country. 2.59 million had fled Afghanistan, 1.1 million had fled Somalia, 2.6 million had fled Iraq, 309,000 had fled Libya. What did these countries have in common? NATO had attacked them all. NATO started the wars that caused mass migration. The EU supported these wars, so the EU was part of the problem. The root cause of the current mass migrations was NATO/EU military and economic aggression against those countries. International financial institutions' policies fuelled emigration.

Counter-revolutions have also caused mass migration. Ten million have fled Eastern Europe's new EU dependencies in the last 20 years. They voted for exit, but only with their feet.

A good policy was to conclude agreement with 'sending countries', as in 2008 when Italy concluded a 'Friendship Agreement' with Libya. The Libyan government agreed to step up border controls and to accept 'expelled foreigners' from Italy in exchange for $5 billion in infrastructure projects over 25 years. So, in May 2009 Italy began to intercept boat migrants on the high seas and return them to Libya and conducted joint Italian-Libyan naval patrols in Libyan territorial waters. This dramatically cut the number of boats attempting the journey from Libya. Irregular boat migrants to Sicily (including Lampedusa, the tiny Italian island just off the North African coast) and Sardinia fell by 55 per cent in the first half of 2009 compared to the same period in 2008. But the actions brought protests from human rights groups and the European Court of Human Rights declared the Agreement in breach of the European Convention on Human Rights, putting a stop to this policy.[175]

The UN should set up refugee camps in the countries next to those countries generating migrants and the UN should work to end the wars generating the migration. Instead of giving Turkey billions of euros, the UN should give this money directly to the United Nations High Commission for Refugees to provide education facilities and a humane existence to the people in the refugee camps.

Some pro-EU people said that if we voted to leave, the Calais camps would move to Kent. The 2003 Le Touquet agreement kept Britain's border controls in Calais in place. On 21 July 2016 May said: "We have discussed the Le Touquet agreement, and President Hollande and indeed interior minister Cazeneuve have both been very clear from their point of view that they wish the Le Touquet agreement to stay. I want the Le Touquet agreement to stay." The French president added that the agreement was useful to both countries: "We consider it as our duty ... to apply it and also to improve it."

The coalition government cut net non-EU immigration from 217,000 in December 2010 to 143,000 in December 2013 by clamping down on the abuse of student visas, raising the income threshold for people wanting to bring in spouses and effectively banning low-skilled immigration from outside the EU. Governments can control immigration. Would-be migrants from Commonwealth countries were hardest hit by the EU's free movement of labour rules, because non-EU immigration was the only kind that the government could control. The EU in fact discriminated against immigrants from Asia, Africa and Latin America, prioritising immigration from Eastern Europe. So, the EU discriminated in effect against non-whites. EU citizens, overwhelmingly white, enjoyed a constitutional right of free movement: non-EU citizens, largely non-white, did not.

Under EU law, we had to put to the back of the queue family members from Commonwealth countries, behind anyone who was granted citizenship by any other EU country. EU law gave all EU citizens the automatic right to enter the UK on producing a passport. But non-EU citizens were subject to immigration control and required leave to enter the UK.[176] We could not control immigration overall when there was free movement to Britain from EU member countries.

Terrorists and other criminals

The EU's border agency, Frontex, warned that terrorists were exploiting the EU's porous borders to enter Europe. It stated that EU member states reported a record 1.82 million illegal border crossings in 2015 – six times higher than the previous record set in 2014. Frontex admitted that the figure was an underestimate as so many migrants 'continued their journey without being detected', and that a 'staggering number' of EU citizens had travelled to Syria to fight for ISIS. "Between 3,000 and 5,000 Europeans, who gathered fighting experience in terror camps [in Syria], are back in Europe," the Director of Europol Rob Wainwright said. He said that the number of foreign fighters returning from Syria represented the biggest threat to Europe 'in more than 10 years'. 850 British citizens joined ISIS in Syria or Iraq. 130 have been killed. 400 have returned. More than 300 were still there.

Frontex concluded that the EU made us less safe. It said, "The Paris attacks in November 2015 clearly demonstrated that irregular migratory flows could be used by terrorists to enter the EU ... there is a risk that some persons representing a security threat to the EU may be taking advantage of this situation ... there is clearly a risk that persons representing a security threat may be entering the EU."[177]

The Cameron government backed Turkey's joining the EU and encouraged the rest of the EU to grant visa-free travel to Turks. This would put our national security at risk: Turkey supported thousands of ISIS terrorists in its territory. The former head of Interpol, Ronald Noble, said that the EU's internal borders policy was 'like hanging a sign welcoming terrorists to Europe'. He observed that dismantling Europe's borders created 'an international passport-free zone for terrorists to execute attacks on the Continent and make their escape'.

Inside the EU, EU laws constrained the grounds on which we could exclude or remove foreign criminals and those whose presence was not conducive to the public good. We could not strip British citizenship from criminals who acquired it fraudulently. The Charter of Fundamental Rights added more dangers. The Charter prevented us from removing foreign criminals and terrorist suspects if it would violate their 'private or family life'. We could not remove EU citizens because of their criminal convictions or on grounds of punishment, public revulsion or deterrence.[178] We could not even deport convicted murderers. For example, in 2007, Mr Justice Collins ruled that it was unlawful under EU law for us to remove convicted murderer Learco Chindamo.

The European Court of Justice controlled how our intelligence services combated terrorism. The Court overruled our laws on counter-terrorism. ZZ was an Algerian/French national who had lived here between 1990 and 2005. In 2005, the Home

Secretary, Charles Clarke, refused him readmission on return from a trip to Algeria and expelled him on the grounds of public security. The Special Immigration Appeals Commission explained, "We are confident that the Appellant was actively involved in the GIA [Algerian Armed Islamic Group], and was so involved well into 1996. He had broad contacts with GIA extremists in Europe. His accounts as to his trips to Europe are untrue. We conclude that his trips to the Continent were as a GIA activist."[179] But it then ruled that EU law stopped the government from excluding ZZ from Britain.

We were also constrained from removing terrorist sympathisers, as shown by the government's failure to deport Chaymae Smak. A Moroccan national, Smak was convicted of conveying a SIM card into prison for her father-in-law, convicted terrorist Abu Hamza al-Masri, and sentenced to a year in prison.[180] The Secretary of State decided to deport her. On 4 February 2016, Advocate General Professor Maciej Szpunar delivered an opinion stating that it was contrary to the EU Treaties to deport Smak because she had a child who was a British citizen.[181] Another example: we were required to readmit a Romanian rapist, Mircea Gheorghiu, whom the Home Secretary had expelled, and grant him permanent residence.[182]

On SkyNews, on 2 June 2016, Cameron claimed "of course it isn't freedom of movement if you are a criminal, it isn't freedom of movement if you are a terrorist." On ITV, he asserted "we can stop anyone at our border, EU nationals included, and if we think they are a risk to our country, we don't have to let them in." Not so; the Home Office had conceded that there was indeed 'free movement of criminals'.[183]

The European Court of Justice controlled our ability to deport violent criminals or terrorists. Leaving the EU let us exempt the intelligence agencies from EU law, immediately improving national security. Leaving let us deport EU citizens whose presence was not conducive to the public good, enabling us to remove convicted murderers, violent criminals, rapists and terrorist sympathisers, like Abu Hamza's daughter-in-law, regardless of what the European Court said. The EU's 2004 citizenship directive said that the free movement of people in the EU could be restricted on grounds of 'public policy, public security or public health'. But the directive also said, "previous criminal convictions shall not in themselves constitute grounds for taking such measures."

If we reverted to the European Convention on Extradition that applied to us before the EU established the European Arrest Warrant, we could better protect our people. The Convention's signatories include non-EU members Switzerland, Norway and Iceland, and non-European countries like Israel, South Africa and South Korea. Or we could adopt either the Australian or the US extradition agreements with the EU, which gave these countries more ability to protect their people and to deny spurious extradition claims. For example, Australia's Extradition Act of 1988 required an Australian judge to determine whether an extradition was valid using criteria that included prima facie evidence.

Immigration's effect on wages

The Migration Advisory Committee, the Economic Affairs Committee of the House of Lords, the Department of Communities and Local Government, the Bank of England and the Department of Economics at University College London (UCL) all found that immigration had a small but significant negative impact on the wages of the worst paid.[184] The Bank of England study concluded: 'the biggest effect is in the semi/unskilled services sector, where a 10 percentage point rise in the proportion of immigrants is associated with a 2 percent reduction in pay'.[185]

Len McCluskey of Unite wrote in the *Guardian*, "In the past 10 years there has been a gigantic experiment at the expense of ordinary workers. Countries with vast historical differences in wage rates and living standards have been brought together in a common labour market. The result has been sustained pressure on living standards and a systematic attempt to hold down wages and cut the costs of social provision for working people. That is why, for trade unions, control of the labour supply in an industry or across society has always been the core of our mission, to ensure that workers get a fair share of the wealth they create."[186]

Professor David Metcalf, chairman of the home secretary's migration advisory committee, said that low-skilled migration benefited employers and exerted a downward pressure on the pay of low-skilled workers. Sigmar Gabriel, Germany's Economics Minister, said, "the EU's policies are depressing the earnings of low paid workers and pensioners." Professor Robert Rowthorn wrote that "unskilled workers have suffered some reduction in their wages due to competition from immigrants." He also highlighted the pressure on public services.[187]

Lodewijk Asscher, leader of the Dutch Labour Party, warned, "Wage-lowering labour migration in Europe nowadays leads to unequal competition between workers." Janice Morphet, in her passionately pro-EU book, acknowledged that "in-migrants are being placed into the economy and mitigating rises in wage costs due to labour shortages."[188] She accepted that immigration had a dampening effect on wages.

As Professor Richard Layard, a key figure in creating the Labour party's jobs policy, wrote, "There is a huge amount of evidence that any increase in the number of unskilled workers lowers unskilled wages and increases the unskilled unemployment rate. If we are concerned about fairness, we ought not to ignore these facts. Employers gain from unskilled immigration. But the unskilled do not."[189]

Christian Dustmann, Uta Schönberg and Jan Stuhler concluded, "Whereas 69.7% of immigrant arrivals to the UK would be classified as high skilled based on their reported education, only 24.6% are effectively high skilled, suggesting that far from a supply shock for high skilled workers, immigrant arrivals to the UK were a supply shock in the market for low skilled workers."[190]

Robert Peston pointed out that "If you were a British bricklayer or electrician, it is simply implausible that there was no impact on your earning power when large numbers of Polish bricklayers and electricians initially turned up. The influx of all this migrant labour also made it much easier for companies to employ people on the shortest possible and least secure contracts – zero-hours contracts, agency contracts and so on – and this has been harmful to the welfare of the indigenous British workforce, too." He also observed that, "Immigration has shifted the balance of power between company and worker too far in the direction of the boss."[191]

Halligan and Lyons wrote, "EU membership gives firms access to unlimited flows of low-wage unskilled migrants – who are then subsidised by the state via tax credits – benefitting big businesses disproportionately." [192] Benjamin Martill and Uta Staiger noted "the downward pressure on wages in the UK resulting from high levels of immigration after the 2004 'big bang' accession ..."[193]

Joseph Stiglitz wrote, "And yet, while many might deny it, an increase in the supply of low-skill labour leads – so long as there are normal downward-sloping demand curves – to lower equilibrium wages. And when wages can't or won't be lowered, unemployment increases. This is of most concern in countries where economic mismanagement has already led to a high level of overall unemployment. Europe, especially the eurozone, has been badly mismanaged in recent decades, to the point that its average unemployment is in double digits. Of course, there was much talk about the net benefits of inward migration. For a country providing a low level of guaranteed benefits – social protection, education, health care, and so forth – to all citizens, that may be the case. But for countries that provide a decent social safety net, the opposite is true."[194]

Lord King, the former Bank of England Governor, said: "Because we've had very large immigration into the UK, employers in the UK have stopped investing in training unskilled people in Britain." He continued, "You can't blame employers for that because they have no incentive to do so – but it's not served the interests of unskilled, low-educated people in the UK." [195] Private sector employers had invested too little in the science, technology and IT skills of British people, which led to constant pleas for such jobs to be given priority in immigration. Public spending constraints often led to greater immigration, particularly of nurses, paramedics, care workers and science and maths teachers.

The Commission's online recruitment scheme advertised hundreds of thousands of jobs across the EU. In July 2014 Cameron promised to stop British jobs being advertised there. In October 2015, the site was still advertising 122,214 jobs in Britain.

Philip Whyman, Mark Baimbridge and Andrew Mullen observed, "a majority of the new jobs created in the United Kingdom over the past decade have gone to migrant workers, preventing further reductions in unemployment and depressing wages below the levels which would otherwise have resulted from tight labour markets. Indeed, the Bank of England has expressed its viewpoint that immigration has played a positive effect in restraining inflationary effects within the UK economy precisely because it has caused slower-than-anticipated wage growth." [196]

Our current growth relied not on increasing productivity but on adding numbers to the labour market. But this reliance on a free and flexible market in labour reduced employers' incentive to invest in training or in innovation. This low productivity in turn helped to keep wages down.

Jason Farrell and Paul Goldsmith summed up, "The argument goes like this: the availability of a large pool of immigrant labour tends to result in lower wages, fewer incentives for firms to train their workers, lower productivity, more housing shortages and increased inequality within a country. It also raises the benefits bill in the UK, because the lower wages are topped up with tax credits, also known as 'in-work benefits', which would be reduced if wages had to improve because that pool of available immigrant labour was reduced. ... The same issue could be said to apply to the NHS and state education, which would, apparently collapse without immigrant labour. This situation, though, might have been caused by a long-term government policy of employing cheap, willing immigrants rather than improving pay and conditions so that Britain can train and retain its own workers. This strategy furthermore deprives developing countries of workers with those skills, meaning there are some African countries who actually give Britain more aid, in terms of the involuntary donation of trained medical staff, than Britain gives them."[197]

As Martin Wolf pointed out in the *Financial Times* on 29 April 2016, "High net immigration imposes significant negative externalities: greater congestion, more stress on social services, higher land prices and a need for significant investment in infrastructure and housing." Of course, there were many reasons for the difficulty of getting housing in the UK, but uncontrolled immigration increased the demand for housing. The House of Commons Library admitted, "A fixed housing stock inevitably results in immigration placing upward pressure on rents and/or prices."[198]

The 2013 British Social Attitudes Survey found that 62 per cent of Londoners thought that immigration should be reduced, and so did 69 per cent of Scots. The Migration Observatory reported that 65 per cent of those aged 50 and above favoured reducing immigration 'a lot', but so did 51 per cent of respondents aged 16-29. An April 2016 YouGov poll for ITN found that 71 per cent thought that immigration was too high. Even 65 per cent of LibDem voters thought so. It found that majorities of 18- to 25-year-olds, of black and minority ethnic Britons, of Londoners, of Scots – all wanted to reduce immigration. About 80 per cent of the country agreed that immigration was out of control and that something like an Australian points system was a good idea. This was true across party lines. If the referendum had just been a decision on immigration, Leave would have won by a mile.

ICM research for British Future in September 2017 found that there was much common ground on which voters agreed. Half of those who voted Remain would like to reduce low-skilled immigration from the EU. Around two-thirds of voters would support a system that delivered the control over low-skilled EU migration demanded in the referendum through an annual quota. That included 71 per cent of Leave voters and 60 per cent who had voted Remain, as well as 75 per cent of Conservatives and 57 per cent of Labour voters. Just 14 per cent disagreed with this approach to immigration.

An Open Europe study of popular opinion on immigration, published in December 2017, concluded, "Our data shows no significant support for an immigration system that assessed entry on the basis of factors such as race, religion or country of origin – these were consistently rated the least important criteria to consider." [199] The authors explained, "The overwhelming hostility to continued large-scale immigration, especially from the EU, relates only weakly to hostility to immigrants. We encountered racism or nativism very rarely. A better way to understand it is that immigration for our groups was associated with a labour market and benefits system they see as dysfunctional, and because of stagnant wages has failed to improve living standards for many people over the last decade. Our attendees ... thought - and, importantly, expected - that turning off the immigration tap would make employers improve wages and conditions for British workers, rather than preferring to ship in what they saw as pliable immigrants willing to work for low pay and in inferior conditions." [200]

No control in the EU

The OECD said that the only way to meet Cameron's promise to cut migration to the tens of thousands was to Vote Leave: "tighter controls in the UK could lead to a reduction of net migration from EU and non-EU countries to below this level. ... After Brexit, immigration is likely to be restricted more significantly." The House of Commons Library agreed: "If the UK were to leave the Single Market, it would be free to impose its own controls on EU/EEA immigration; for instance, it could choose to apply the immigration controls that currently apply to non-EU/EEA nationals. This would restrict economic migration to predominantly high-skilled migrants (via a points-based system) and reduce the flow of migrant workers doing low-skilled jobs."[201]

During the referendum campaign, Cameron told us that a points system would 'trash the economy'. Yet in his 2005 general election manifesto he had promised, "We will introduce a points-based system similar to the one used in Australia. This will give priority to people with the skills Britain needs." Until 2016 he pledged to control immigration, but in 2016 he told us that controlling immigration would be disastrous.

Cameron won the 2010 general election on his pledge to cut immigration to 'tens of thousands' with 'no ifs no buts'. But he knew that inside the EU we could not control immigration: as he said, "When it comes to the free movement of people, we need powers to be returned to this country." The 2015 Conservative manifesto said: 'Our commitment to you: ... keep our ambition of delivering annual net migration in the tens of thousands ... Continuing this vital work will be our priority over the next five years." On 8 June 2016 George Osborne told Andrew Neil this was an ambition, not a commitment.

Immigration reached 330,000 in 2015 alone, which proved that we could not control immigration while we stayed in the EU. Yet in the referendum campaign Cameron claimed that "we can remain in the EU and control immigration." In the leaflet distributed to all UK households ahead of the June 2016 referendum, the Cameron government said "we control our own borders" in the EU. We did not. Being outside Schengen meant EU nationals must show a passport as they entered the UK. But they still had the right to live, work and claim benefits here. His Home Secretary disagreed with him: May said, "Free movement makes it harder to control immigration ..."

Cameron had told us in his 2014 Conservative conference speech that the free movement of people would be at the heart of his renegotiation strategy: "I will not take no for an answer and when it comes to free movement I will get what Britain needs." But when he went around Europe's capitals trying to get the deal he wanted to keep us in the EU, the EU's leaders refused even to discuss a limit on immigration. He got no for an answer and when it came to free movement he did not get what Britain needed. His friend Steve Hilton commented, "I think that the demands were relatively modest and even those modest demands were treated with total contempt."

The numbers

Before 1997, net immigration was rarely more than 50,000 a year. Nick Clegg on 9 March 2004 told us that immigration from Eastern Europe would not be an issue for the UK. Blair told the CBI in April 2004, "there are half a million vacancies in our job market and our strong and growing economy needs migration to fill these vacancies." So, in 2004 his government opened the gates to immigrants from the new EU member countries of Eastern Europe, leading to the biggest influx in British history.

The government even waived temporary restrictions on migration from the newer, poorer EU accession countries. The governor of the Bank of England deliberately promoted this to 'lower wage growth and control inflation'.[202]

On 19 May 2017 Blair told Andrew Marr "the majority of EU immigrants came post-2008." No, 15,000 came in 2003, 87,000 in 2004, 104,000 in 2006 and 127,000 in 2007. When asked if the government knew that the numbers would rise, he claimed, "No, we didn't know the numbers." Yet his government in 2004 forecast 5,000-13,000 migrants a year from the new EU members of Eastern Europe. Former Home Secretary Jack Straw admitted in 2013 that Labour had made a 'spectacular mistake' in lifting the controls in 2004. In 2016, the number of workers from the 2004 accession countries living in the UK passed one million.

220,000 EU nationals moved to the UK during the year to the end of September 2017 – about the size of Wolverhampton's population. If we added those issued with a national insurance number to work here the number rises to 497,000, the size of Liverpool's population. There were 3.6 million EU nationals living here in June 2016; in September 2017 there were 3.8 million.

The EU wanted to grow. There were five recognized candidates for membership: Turkey (applied in 1987), Macedonia (applied in 2004), Montenegro (applied in 2008), Albania (applied in 2009) and Serbia (applied in 2009). Cameron wanted Turkey to join the EU, with its population of 75,000,000, Macedonia with 2,000,000, Montenegro 600,000, Albania 2,800,000, and Serbia 7,000,000. The UK government was to pay these countries a total of £1.2 billion between 2014 and 2020 as part of the EU fund to help them join the EU. Turkey, Montenegro and Serbia have started accession negotiations. The EU also recognised Bosnia-Herzegovina and Kosovo as potential candidates. Bosnia-Herzegovina has formally submitted an application for membership, while Kosovo has a Stabilisation and Association Agreement with the EU, which generally preceded the lodging of membership application.

In June 2014 the EU signed an Association Agreement with Moldova, with visa-free travel. Two million Moldovans (almost half the population) work abroad. The EU proposed an Association Agreement with Ukraine which included 'a visa-free travel regime for the citizens of Ukraine'. Ukraine had 45 million people, with average monthly wages of $120 and monthly pensions of $40.

On 6 April 2016 the Dutch people voted against the proposed Agreement with Ukraine by 61 per cent to 38 per cent. Turnout was 32.2 per cent, above the 30 per cent threshold required for the referendum to be valid. Dutch Prime Minister Mark Rutte said that as a result the ratification of the Agreement 'can't simply go ahead'.

The 7 March 2016 EU/Turkey Agreement made clear that all EU member states needed to lift visa restrictions on Turkey by June. By the EU deal, Turkish citizens all got the right to enter the EU without restriction. Cameron said this did not apply to us. But the European Council of 17-18 March confirmed that: "Following the decisions of the Heads of State of government of 7 March" the European Council "calls for the full implementation of the EU-Turkey statement". The Council also stated, "the EU and Turkey reconfirmed their commitment to re-energise the accession process" for Turkey to become a full member. On 18 March, Cameron committed to 'accelerating' Turkey's accession. He could always have neutralised the issue by promising to veto Turkey's joining the EU.

Outside the EU, no outside body can draw up laws on our behalf. We will be able to elect those who draft the laws and make the decisions and if we oppose the laws and policies that they put forward, we can kick the rascals out. Outside the EU, we will be able to decide what immigration policy we want to adopt, and we will be able to change it when we decide that it does not suit our needs.

Chapter 6 - Foreign and defence policy

The EU and wars

The first step towards the EEC was the 1951 European Coal and Steel Community. The US government wanted this as part of its effort to rearm Germany against the Soviet Union.[203] So the EEC was not born as a peace project. Supporters of the EU often claim that it alone has saved us from wars between the nations of Europe, but this kind of war has almost vanished across the world.

The EEC was born in the middle of France's dirty colonial war against Algeria (1954-62). The EEC endorsed this war. Later, it triggered the wars which destroyed Yugoslavia. After the downfall of the Soviet Union, Yugoslavia, unlike the other Eastern European countries, refused to allow NATO forces to be based in the country and refused to apply to join the EEC. This defiance could not be permitted, so the EU and NATO aimed to break Yugoslavia apart. In October 1991, when Yugoslavia was still united, the EEC announced that all the Yugoslav republics 'are sovereign and independent with international identity'. The EEC declared that the borders between Yugoslavia's six republics were international borders and said that the majority people in each republic, not the Yugoslav people, had the right to self-determination. The EEC cancelled its 1980 trade agreement with Serbia and Montenegro, ending most of their foreign trade.

In December 1991, the EEC said it intended 'to recognise the independence of all the Yugoslav republics' and Germany recognised Croatia. The EEC together with Thatcher followed suit. A civil war broke out between those trying to keep the country united and those trying to break it up. When the Yugoslav government deployed its army to hold the country together, the EEC called this 'illegal'.

In January 1992, the Bosnian government held a referendum on secession, approved by the EEC. In April the

EEC recognised the Republic of Bosnia and Herzegovina, which sparked the next phase of the war.

Next on the NATO/EEC agenda was Iraq. The EEC and its leading members backed Bush and Blair's illegal attack on Iraq. The EEC resolution of February 2003 was an ultimatum demanding Iraq's 'unconditional cooperation', which opened the way to war. The EU posed as progressive but sided with reaction. For example, when Israel attacked Gaza in 2009, the EU lamented the casualties on 'both sides' and called on 'both parties' to end hostilities.

Next, the EU endorsed Cameron and Sarkozy's 2011 war against Libya. George W. Bush welcomed Libya's decision to end its unconventional weapons programme, declaring that "leaders who abandon the pursuit of chemical, biological and nuclear weapons, and the means to deliver them, will find an open path to better relations with the United States and other free nations." Better relations? The EU governments of Britain and France attacked the country, wrecked it, and gave it over to feuding Islamist extremists who murdered its leader. The next year the EU was awarded the Nobel Peace Prize! A North Korean official commented at the time that the "Libyan crisis is teaching the international community a grave lesson." Later the EU funded Islamist militias in Libya, militias which thrived on a new slave trade.

Herman van Rompuy, then president of the EU Council, told us, "Europe's greatest enemy today is fear. Fear leads to egoism, egoism leads to nationalism and nationalism leads to war."[204] Nationalism leads to war? So, nationalism caused the war on Libya, not the pro-EU governments of Britain and France? The EU was an agreement to export wars, to unite for wars against poor countries in Africa and the Middle East. NATO and the EU attacked these countries not because they were Muslim countries, not because NATO and the EU were motivated by fear of Islam or by racism against Arabs, but because these countries defended their national independence and sovereignty, their right to control their own resources.

The bigger and the more centralised the EU became, the more it threw its weight about. The EU not nationalism meant war. The EU not Brexit was the source of war.

The EU has been imposing sanctions on the DPRK since 2006, causing food shortages. On 22 December 2017 the UN Security Council unanimously voted for more sanctions. Its Resolution 2397 cut 90 per cent of the DPRK's oil supplies and demanded the expulsion of 150,000 North Koreans working in other countries.

President Trump threatened at the United Nations, of all places, "to totally destroy North Korea ...", so it was no wonder that the DPRK sought a nuclear deterrent. In December 2017 South Korean and US forces conducted a mock invasion of the DPRK, to 'remove weapons of mass destruction', under Lieutenant General Thomas Vandal.

When the cold war ended, Ukraine became independent. As part of the deal, Ukraine gave up its large nuclear arsenal and in return Russia, Britain and the USA guaranteed its integrity. US Secretary of State James Baker assured Gorbachev that, in return for the Soviet Union's agreement to the reunification of Germany: "NATO will not expand one inch east of Berlin." NATO assured Russia that it would not invite Ukraine to join the NATO. But in 2008 President Bush tried to fast-track both Ukraine and Georgia into NATO and the EU offered them security 'cooperation'. The EU agreement offered to Ukraine in 2013 excluded Russia as a mutual trading partner and included 'military and security' terms binding Ukraine to NATO. The EU's 2014 Association Agreement called for Ukraine's 'ever-deeper involvement in the European security area'.

In February 2014 the US government and the EU carried out what George Friedman, Head of Stratfor, 'the Private CIA,' called 'the most blatant Coup in History'. The current Ukrainian President, Petro Poroshenko, also admitted that it was a coup.

In 2015 Ukraine's government, the Russian government and the Donbass region all signed the Minsk peace agreement to re-integrate Donbass into Ukraine. But on 18 January 2018 Ukraine's parliament tore up the treaty by declaring its support for taking Donbass back by military force. Ukraine's government also committed itself to conquering the Crimea, whose people had voted by more than nine to one in March 2014 to rejoin Russia.

The EU's advance into what was always recognised to be a contested neighbourhood provoked the conflict in Ukraine. Russia had lost 700,000 square miles of territory since 1991. The EU had gained more than 400,000 of these square miles. The other 300,000 were largely in Ukraine. The EU, not Russia, was the expansionist power.

As part of the largest build-up of NATO troops in Eastern Europe since the Cold War, the Baltic States, Poland, Romania and Bulgaria hosted soldiers from across NATO's 29 member states. British, French and Dutch forces were in Estonia. German troops lead the NATO forces in Lithuania. British soldiers are also deployed in Poland as part of a US-led NATO mission, supported by the Romanian army. British Typhoon jets from RAF Conningsby are deployed in Romania to support NATO's Southern Air Policing mission.

In 2016, military spending in Western Europe rose by 2.6 per cent on the previous year. Spending in Central Europe rose by 2.4 percent. The Baltic States spent $900 million on the military in 2005. By 2019 they will be spending more than $2 billion. Poland is also expanding its arms spending. Sweden is increasing its military spending and reintroducing conscription.

Mrs May said on 25 January 2017 that "The days of Britain and America intervening in sovereign countries in an attempt to remake the world in our own image are over." She condemned torture and suggested that Britain could limit its intelligence sharing with the USA because of President Trump's support for waterboarding. She also said: "There is nothing inevitable about conflict between Russia and the West. And nothing unavoidable about retreating to the days of the Cold War."

In October 2015, the European Parliament endorsed a report calling for the abolition of the UK's seat on the UN Security Council. Brussels wanted the EU to become a permanent member of that body, with one permanent seat and one single vote.

The US government imposes sanctions against most of the world's countries, to prevent their development as rivals; especially it imposes permanent punitive sanctions against socialist countries. The EU is applying sanctions against 36 countries, including two of its own members, Poland and Hungary, and against Cuba, the DPRK, Venezuela, Belarus, Russia, and Eastern Ukraine. The EU and the USA often impose far more severe sanctions on top of any UN sanctions. On 17 February 2018 Prime Minister May promised to carry over all the EU sanctions.

The EU's European Endowment for Democracy, launched in December 2012, was modeled on the US government's National Endowment for Democracy. In 2015 the EU founded the East StratCom Task Force, a team of 450 journalists and academics based in more than 30 countries whose remit was to expose Russian 'fake news'. But East StratCom has often labelled any criticism of non-Western immigration to EU as pro-Kremlin disinformation, even when neither the media nor the content has any relation to Russia. Alberto Alemanno, a professor of EU law and regulation at the business school HEC Paris, who has launched a complaint over Brussels' fake news initiative to the EU's internal watchdog, said, "The approach taken by the EU on fake news is in breach of the freedom of expression and citizens' right to be informed. The European Ombudsman - an independent and impartial body - should open an investigation and hold the [European] Commission to account for withholding critical information from the broader public."

The Pentagon's Defense Intelligence Agency issued a report in June 2017, 'Russia: Military Power: Building a military to support great power aspirations'. It said, "Moscow seeks to promote a multi-polar world predicated on the principles of respect for state sovereignty and non-interference in other states' internal affairs, the primacy of the United Nations, and a careful balance of power preventing one state or group of states from dominating the international order. To support these great power ambitions ..."[205] Since when is promoting respect for sovereignty, for non-interference and for the United Nations proof of great power ambitions?

The EU army

In 2000, EU leaders from Britain, Germany, Italy and Poland called for a European army. But from the start, these plans were enveloped in a cloud of denial. Romano Prodi, a previous President of the European Commission, said, "When I was talking about the European army, I was not joking. If you don't want to call it a European army, don't call it a European army. You can call it 'Margaret', you can call it 'Mary Ann', you can call it any name." Before the referendum, the *Guardian* told us that 'Claims from the leave side about moves to unify Europe's armed forces are nothing more than fantasy.'[206] Lord Ashdown said the idea of an EU army was 'nonsense'. The author of a recent book on EU defence policy argued strenuously that the EU was not creating a European army and then wrote, "However, there can be no denying that what is being created is a European armed force, for use on behalf of the European Union and the international community."[207]

Chancellor Merkel said in 2010 about the post-2008 debt crisis: "we have a shared currency but no real economic or political union. This must change. If we were to achieve this, therein lies the opportunity of the crisis ... And beyond the economic, after the shared currency, we will perhaps dare to take further steps, for example for a European army."[208]

The 2009 Treaty of Lisbon, in its Protocol on Permanent Structured Cooperation, called on all EU members to 'contribute to the vitality of a renewed Atlantic alliance' as a rationale for embracing a 'more assertive Union role'. As Donald Tusk, the president of the EU Council, said "whoever attacks the European Union harms America."

Permanent Structured Cooperation - PESCO - was another step towards the EU taking control of military matters. In December 2017 President Juncker tweeted, "She is awake, the Sleeping Beauty of the Lisbon Treaty: Permanent Structured Cooperation is happening. I welcome the operational steps taken today by Member States to lay the foundations of a European Defence Union. Our security cannot be outsourced."

The May government said it would not join PESCO, but Sir Stuart Peach, the Chief of Defence Staff, wanted us to 'keep the door open' to full membership. The government wanted to participate in the EU defence programmes which were the foundations of PESCO even after we left the EU. It was willing to pay into the European Defence Fund and to participate fully in the European Defence Research Programme and the European Industrial Development Programme.

This would require us to make substantial payments to the EU, to adhere to single market rules in the sphere of defence, and to concede some military decision-making power to the EU. Major-General Julian Thompson warned that this "would bind the UK to collective decision making ... heavily controlled by the EU Commission." Government participation in these programmes and defence companies' participation in supply chains could tie us into EU defence schemes, undermining our national independence. The government wanted to continue and even enhance its co-operation with EU member countries on matters of defence and security.

Germany aimed to increase its military spending to more than €35 billion by 2019 and comprehensively modernise its army. By 2020, it aimed to spend 53 per cent more on military equipment than it did in 2016. It pledged to increase its armed forces to 200,000. An EU army, headed by Germany, would be a formidable force.

In 2017 Germany took matters into its own hands and integrated units from the armies of Romania, the Czech Republic and the Netherlands into its armed forces. Romania's 81st Mechanized Brigade joined the Bundeswehr's Rapid Response Forces Division, while the Czech 4th Rapid Deployment Brigade, the Czech Army's spearhead force, joined the Bundeswehr's 10th Armored Division. One Dutch brigade joined the Bundeswehr's Rapid Response Forces Division, and another joined its 1st Armored Division.

Germany had joint military units with six of its nine neighbouring countries, including a Franco-German brigade. Germany was the nucleus of the Eurocorps, set up in 1992. France, Belgium, Luxembourg, Spain and Poland were also permanent members. Germany was also in the German/Polish/Danish corps and a German/Dutch corps.

The EU has a European Defence Agency, an EU Common Security and Defence Policy, an EU Security and Defence Implementation Plan, an EU Defence Action Plan, an EU Defence Industrial Development Strategy, a European Defence Research Programme, a European Defence Technology Industrial Base and an EU Network of Defence-Related Regions. The EU pursued all this to expand 'EU sovereignty' across defence, in Juncker's words. All were part of the EU's military plan. All required obedience to EU authority.

The Commission's EU Defence Action Plan said, "A stronger European defence requires Member States' joint acquisition, development and retention of the full-spectrum of land, air, space and maritime capabilities."[209] Juncker said in March 2015, "You would not create a European army to use it immediately. But a common army among the Europeans would convey to Russia that we are serious about defending the values of the European Union."

Germany's Defence Minister declared in September 2016, "It's time to move forward to a European defence union, which is basically a 'Schengen of defence'." She said, "There will be a comprehensive air defence." Juncker in his State of the Union speech of 14 September 2016 called for a common military force 'in complement to Nato', a European army.

In Juncker's State of the Union speech of 13 September 2017 he said, "I want our Union to become a stronger global actor. I want Member States to look at which foreign policy decisions could be moved from unanimity to qualified majority voting. The Treaty already provides for this, if all Member States agree to do it. And I want us to dedicate further efforts to defence matters. A new European Defence Fund is in the offing. As is a Permanent Structured Cooperation in the area of defence. By 2025 we need a fully-fledged European Defence Union."

He said that the EU "should also move towards common military assets, in some cases owned by the EU." On 26 September 2017 President Macron supported Juncker, saying, "Europe must have a joint intervention force, a common defence budget and a joint doctrine for action." In March 2018 Guy Verhofstadt said, "Most importantly, we have to swiftly build a Defence Union, as a European pillar of NATO. For decades, we have relied on the US and failed to invest in modern defences and the integration of our capacities. Many European politicians refuse to make the case to the people for a European defence and security capacity ..."[210]

In May 2018 the Commission urged "a European defence research programme within the next multiannual financial framework post 2020. This programme ... may need an estimated annual budget of EUR 500 million ... This amount would place the EU among the top 4 of defence research & technology investors in Europe." The Commission wanted the EU to become a player in defence research on the scale of a nation state. The size of this proposed budget meant it would supplant the national defence spending of most member states. The Ministry of Defence started to push for us to join the EU's defence research project Preparatory Action on Defence Research, which required long-term UK adherence to EU rules.

Britain's defence research spending was about £1.8 billion per year. We were the leading defence research power in Europe with the highest level of defence research related exports. This status was due not to the European Defence Agency but to our long history of defence research, military spending and scientific excellence. The EDA had a budget of £27 million, to which we paid the second highest amount, paying more than a tenth of its budget. The EU's High Representative Federica Mogherini explained, "Improving CSDP responsiveness requires enhanced civil/military intelligence to support anticipation and situational awareness, through the Single Intelligence Analysis Capacity (SIAC) as the main European hub for strategic information, early warning and comprehensive analysis." Our intelligence services are to feed into this EU intelligence hub.

EU law has weakened the UK's surveillance regime. It has struck down key powers that MI5, SIS and GCHQ rely on to keep us safe. In July 2015, the Divisional Court in London annulled the Data Retention and Investigatory Powers Act 2014 as inconsistent with the EU's Charter of Fundamental Rights. In November 2015, the Court of Appeal referred the UK's surveillance regime to the European Court of Justice for a decision as to whether it will be allowed, stressing that the ECJ's decisions 'will remain central to the validity of all future legislation enacted by the Member States in this field', which showed the extent of EU powers over our intelligence services.

The EU's External Action Service produced the Security and Defence Implementation Plan (SDIP), and the EU Commission produced the European Defence Action Plan

(EDAP). The May government approved the two plans at EU Council meetings in November and December 2016. EU Council staff stated that the government approved as a full member, that there were no exemptions and that Britain had 'full rights and responsibilities' as a signatory.

The Foreign Office's statement in the government's *Strategic Defence and Security Review* of December cited the possibility of 'continued UK involvement in EU Common Security and Defence Policy (CSDP)'. At the EU Council's 15 December 2016 meeting, the Prime Minister endorsed the creation of a permanent operational planning and conduct capability at the strategic level. Sir Alan Duncan, Minister of State at the Foreign Office, told the MPs of the European Scrutiny Committee that there was 'support from other EU states for UK engagement in EU defence policy after Brexit' and he wanted to 'avoid hampering such future cooperation'.

The EU's first centralised defence budget, the EU Defence Fund, is to be supported by billions of euros from the European Investment Bank (EIB) whose rules the EU is rewriting to prioritise defence funding. Britain is the joint-largest shareholder in the EIB, so this means that the EU is reassigning our money. This Defence Fund will be able to offer free money to British firms to join EU-led procurement projects, giving these firms a financial incentive to demand involvement in the EU's 'defence single market'.

In the European Defence Technology Industrial Base, defence procurement will be coordinated by a European Defence Agency. Because it sees the close connection between defence supply and defence policy, the EU wanted a single military procurement policy. Compliance with EU defence directives is a condition of participating in the EU's defence industrial schemes. This was a threat to our highly developed military manufacturing and research complex, which is a very large element of our remaining industrial base.

At present, we were 'permitted' to choose our own domestic suppliers in shipbuilding and in aircraft and other manufacture, but the EU wanted to open all defence contracts to 'cheapest-wins' EU-wide competition. The ECJ has already reduced the scope of Article 346 and the EU Council can at any time amend the defence items that it covered. The EU was also tightening defence asset production rules to create an EU defence market in which member state governments would find it impossible to protect domestic defence jobs and industry, Scottish shipyards for example.

So British companies were tied into defence procurement deals which required adherence to EU defence policy. When we leave the EU, we regain defence autonomy, but the companies would still be hostages to EU policy and political pressure.

The government's National Shipbuilding Strategy of September 2017 fully adheres to the latest EU rules on cross-border defence tendering. About one third of naval ships (frigates, destroyers and aircraft carriers) are reserved as Britain-only build while all others (such as patrol, mine-countermeasure, hydrographic, amphibious vessels and Royal Fleet Auxiliary) will be open to international tender. The GMB union complained that the strategy 'does not go far enough' in allocating shipbuilding to our shipyards. This EU procurement policy squeeze also applies to building helicopters, armoured personnel carriers, artillery, aircraft or firearms, and to conducting research.

The EU Commission has told the government that because 'decisions over EU Defence Union were taken unanimously', Britain is expected to 'play its full role while it remains a member'. So, we appear to be fully involved in EU Defence Union plans via SDIP and EDAP until we leave in 2019, and the speed and nature of these plans make it much more difficult to get out of the EU defence union. Our only remaining veto in defence was in the final 'defence union', where responsibility and command over military forces is wholly and permanently switched to the EU Commission and EU Council.

The government is also participating in a trial of the EU's Coordinated Annual Review of Defence. This is a financial mechanism whereby the European Commission appraises our defence budget plans to integrate member nations' militaries. Ministers have now indicated that we might stay in this and in EU Battlegroups (which place UK forces under EU Council policy control) and even play a 'partial' or 'project' role in PESCO. May said on 17 February 2018 that we should be open to deploying our defence resources 'with and indeed through EU mechanisms'.

In sum, since November 2016, the government has signed us up to all parts of the EU's defence union except one, without any vote by MPs. These include finance, a command centre and a central budget. If we stay in them, or if any of them go into an exit treaty, as the government wants, we will not have left the EU. EU military integration, a single EU foreign and security policy, along with an EU treasury with a single budget and a single all-EU currency, all add up to a single EU state. It would no longer comprise individual member states. They would all be swallowed up into a United States of Europe. As former British Prime Minister Tony Blair said, "It is not about peace today, it's about power."[211] The key to peace in Europe is not to create an armed supranational federation, but to build a strong democratic pro-independence culture in every European country.

Now we have decided to leave the EU, we should stay outside its defence schemes and should certainly not go along with any of them as a sweetener in the negotiations. Britain's armed forces would be more effective, under more democratic control, and more able to retain their distinctive capabilities and ethos outside the EU's defence structures.

Europol

Europol is an EU agency created in 1994 which calls itself 'the European Union's law enforcement agency'. But Europol does not enforce the law in any conventional sense. It has no executive powers, makes no arrests, does not proactively collect intelligence and does not undertake counter-terrorism operational activity. It has no power to either instigate or engage in counter-terrorist operations. Europol's European Counter Terrorism Centre was set up on 25 January 2016 to 'provide operational support to member states'. But it had just 39 staff members.

Our membership of the EU and Europol is more beneficial to the EU than to us regarding security and counter-terrorism. Leaving both will have little, if any, impact on our national security or counter-terrorism capabilities. 14 non-EU states, including the USA, Canada and Norway, cooperated with Europol, without being members. So could we. Europol's Director Rob Wainwright said that a post-Brexit Britain could still cooperate with Europol from outside the EU. We can continue to work with Interpol, with the Organisation for Security and Co-operation in Europe, with the United Nations Office on Drugs and Crime and with the International Criminal Court. After we leave, we will continue to participate fully in global and European bodies that exist to exchange intelligence and share best practice on national security and counter-terrorism (for example, the 'Club of Berne' and the Police Working Group on Terrorism). Participation does not depend on being in the EU.

Mark Rowley, Britain's most senior national counter-terrorism police chief, when asked whether co-operation between Scotland Yard and anti-terrorism agencies in Europe had lessened since the Brexit vote, said 'on the contrary it had improved'. Andrew Parker, the head of MI5, dismissed claims that leaving the EU would affect cooperation with European intelligence services.

The Irish border

The long-established Anglo-Irish Common Travel Area, which goes back to 1923, is a matter exclusively for the British and Irish governments and is not an EU matter. Irish people will continue to move freely between the two islands and across the North-South border in Ireland as they have always done. The British government's negotiating directives said, "Existing bilateral agreements and arrangements between Ireland and the United Kingdom, such as the Common Travel Area, which are in conformity with EU law, should be recognised."

The governments of both the UK and the Republic of Ireland have committed to not erecting a hard border on the island of Ireland. Irish Taoiseach Enda Kenny said on 2 November 2015 of the UK-Irish border, "Neither I, nor the Prime Minister, desire to limit the freedom of people on both sides of the Irish Sea to trade, to live, to work, to travel freely across these islands. Therefore, we have agreed that the benefits of the Common Travel Area be preserved."

The head of Irish customs has said that it is 'practically 100% certain' there would be no customs facilities along the border. Jon Thompson, Permanent Secretary at Her Majesty's Revenue and Customs, agreed, "it is perfectly possible that absolutely nothing happens at the border." He told the Brexit Select Committee that a streamlined customs arrangement could 'cover the vast majority of the trade between Northern Ireland and Ireland' and that any checks could be 'intelligence-based' and 'well away from the legal border'. Even the European Commission confirmed in November 2017 that there was no need for physical border checks in Ireland.

Passenger information is already collected because the Republic is not part of the Schengen passport-free zone. So, border checks can be carried out electronically. All that is needed is proper information-sharing between British and Irish border forces. Such cooperation is already strong. A UK-Ireland Border Working Group should be established alongside existing high-level cooperation to plan, supervise and evaluate progress.

We already run one of the world's most efficient customs systems. In 2016, the World Bank ranked us fifth in the world on customs performance. The World Bank Logistics Performance Index for fifteen developed countries showed that in 2016 98 per cent of all goods were cleared with no border checks and the median clearance time of the other 2 per cent was one day – most within a few hours.

General transport costs have already fallen to very low levels due to containerisation and computerisation of customs procedures, and the 'virtual border' - mandatory under WTO rules - has nearly ended border costs. Further, services were more than 40 per cent of our exports and trade in services was not subject to border formalities and was weightless. Technology minimised friction at the present customs borders.

A customs border will be required but the border can be almost invisible. Measures can be adopted to reduce its visibility drawing on the experience of the customs union border between Sweden and Norway. Cross-border trade along Ireland's internal border comprises mostly goods related to the food and building industries which can be documented online and cleared via an automated e-border, so trucks can cross without needing to stop. Physical inspections of non-EU shipments were extremely rare. In practice, containers were opened only when intelligence indicated illegal activity. For instance, in the port of Bristol only two containers had been opened in 2015 and two in 2016. Inspections – when exceptionally required – should take place at dedicated zones away from the border, with UK checks recognised by Ireland and vice versa. Almost all customs declarations were received electronically and could be lodged before goods arrived. The same approach should be extended to shipments from the EU.

Most countries let traders submit their customs documentation electronically in advance of the goods arriving at the border. Nearly all the submissions of the EU's own Single Administrative Document (SAD) for declaring imports and exports were made online. This meant that most trade arriving from countries that were members of neither the single market nor the customs union had little or no delay at the border when entering the EU. There was no reason for this to change after we left the EU.

A report on the use of electronic customs clearing and border checks, commissioned by the Constitutional Affairs Committee (AFCO) of the European Parliament and undertaken by the EU Commission's Directorate General for Internal Policies, showed how electronic border arrangements could work.[212] The report's author is the EU's own customs expert, Lars Karlsson, the former Director of World Customs Organization, and Deputy Director General of Swedish Customs. This study identified international standards, best practices and technologies that could be used to avoid a 'hard' border as well as case studies that provided insights into creating a smooth border experience. Modern technology means that borders do not need physical customs posts, not even cameras. Karlsson envisaged the use of mobile phone and GPS technology to track HGVs, together with the computer-based customs clearing which is the norm across much of the world. Karlsson stated that this would be 'a border without any new infrastructure… what you would describe as a frictionless border'. This solution offered a template for future UK-EU border relationships.

The National Audit Office reported in June 2018, "HMRC expects it will take a further three months to scale up the operational CHIEF [Customs Handling of Import and Export Freight] system. If it successfully completes this work, HMRC should have the system capacity to handle customs declarations no matter what the outcome of negotiations between the UK and the EU. HMRC is confident that CHIEF will be able to handle the increased volume of declarations, and that it remains a reliable system that is suitable for a short term contingency arrangement."[213]

Annual EU-Switzerland trade was a hundred times greater than Northern Ireland-Republic of Ireland trade, yet the many Swiss border crossings to the EU were often completely unmanned, despite Switzerland being in neither the EU's single market nor its customs union. In 2012 the Swiss estimated that their total EU-Switzerland border costs were just 0.1 per cent of trade value. Border frictions were non-existent because their products met EU standards.

The US and Canada were not in a customs union, yet more goods crossed the US/Canadian border each year than did the EU's external border - with no delays. In the port of Felixstowe, there is not a customs officer in sight, yet it handles £80 billion of trade a year - £77 billion more than the Irish border - without a hitch. They use a tried-and-tested digital cargo-tracking system developed in Felixstowe, known as Destin8, which has worked so well for more than a decade that it processed most of the non-EU maritime trade coming into this country. So there would be no need for checkpoints or customs officials at the border.

A poll taken on 29-31 May 2018 found that, if people had to choose between leaving the customs union and avoiding a hard border between Northern Ireland and the Republic, 41 per cent in Great Britain said they would leave the customs union, 32 per cent said they would stay to avoid a hard border, and 27 per cent didn't know. [214] Three quarters of Conservatives and Leave voters in Great Britain agreed that the border issue was being "deliberately exaggerated by politicians and others to suit their own political agenda."[215] The EU was indeed trying to use nationalists in Scotland and Ireland to break Britain apart.

Taoiseach Leo Varadkar said on 18 July, "President Juncker and my EU colleagues have on many occasions said that they wouldn't require us to put in place a physical infrastructure and customs checks on the Border between Northern Ireland and Ireland."

If Northern Ireland alone were to remain in a customs union with the EU, this would prevent it from benefitting from future trading arrangements put in place by the rest of the UK after Brexit. Prioritising the 23 per cent of Northern Irish trade with the EU (including the Republic of Ireland) over the 77 per cent with Britain and the rest of the world would clearly be a mistake.

Our leaving the EU will not damage the 1998 Good Friday Agreement. The passing references to the EU in the Agreement's text allow of no such interpretation. The Agreement was a bilateral agreement between the British and Irish governments and a multilateral agreement by most of Northern Ireland's political parties. The EU was not a party to the Agreement. On 17 January 2017 the Supreme Court rejected the claim that Brexit undermined the Agreement on the grounds that the Agreement covered Northern Ireland's place in the UK but not its place in the EU. Former leader of the Ulster Unionist Party David Trimble has said that it "is not true that Brexit in any way threatens the peace process ... There is no reason it can't continue to be policed without hard barriers, even after Brexit."

More wars

Born in colonial wars, the EU was still enmeshed in colonial wars. Between 2003 and 2013 the EU launched 32 'crisis management' missions. Most managed to make the crises worse. Seven were in Former Yugoslavia, 16 in Africa, 2 in Palestine, and one each in Ukraine, Afghanistan, Iraq and Indonesia. The EU has six ongoing military operations – Bosnia Herzegovina since 2004, the Central African Republic, two in Mali and two in Somalia. In 2018 French troops were still fighting in Mali, Chad, Niger, Mauritania and Burkina

Faso. The EU is to spend £50 million backing a regional force which is supposed to replace the French force.

Foreign policy must be under democratic control. This would be far more peaceable than parliament was. An *Independent* poll of July 2009 found that 52 per cent of the public wanted the immediate withdrawal of troops from Afghanistan. Yet on 9 September 2010 in the first specific vote on the military campaign in Afghanistan, MPs voted by 310 to 14 to keep the troops there. So just 2 per cent of all MPs represented the views of the majority of the public.

On 22 March 2011 MPs voted by 557 to 13 for intervention in Libya. That same day a ComRes poll found that 53 per cent of the public opposed intervening in Libya and only a third backed military action. Again, just 2 per cent of MPs represented the views of the majority of the public.

In 2013 Cameron planned to invade Syria. But when MPs asked their constituents for feedback they were besieged by emails 'overwhelmingly opposed' to intervention. A 28 August *Daily Telegraph* poll found only 11 per cent backed joining the war in Syria. On 28 August YouGov found that the British public opposed military action in the form of missile strikes by two to one. A YouGov poll in *The Times* of 29 August suggested that only 22 per cent supported missile strikes. On 29 August MPs voted against Cameron's proposed military intervention in Syria, for once in line with public opinion.

Time and again, the British people have shown that increasingly they back peace, while our supposed representatives preferred to vote for war. But if we want peace, we must take control of our country's affairs. Without control, we cannot have peace. We should not delegate powers over the vital matters of war and peace to those who oppose our commitment to peace.

It was a basic principle of international law that countries must not interfere in each other's internal affairs; other countries must not threaten, never mind attack, the lives and liberties of any of our citizens or of those under our protection. So we should ensure that our country no longer interferes in other countries' internal affairs. We need to respect the sovereignty and territorial integrity of all other states and to promote peaceful relations with other countries. We need to promote the primacy of the United Nations, and to help to build a balance of power where no one state or group of states dominates the international order. We should never seek to advance our interests at the expense of others. While pursuing our own independent development, we need to respect the legitimate concerns of other countries, especially the interests of developing countries and of our neighbours.

Chapter 7 After the referendum

Taking control, taking responsibility

After the June 2016 referendum, some supporters of the EU called for a second referendum. Some also claimed that the referendum was no more than an opinion poll. But if the 2016 referendum was only a glorified opinion poll, how could a second referendum be any different? The EU does not like referendums, but if it is forced to allow one, and if the vote goes the wrong way, it is suddenly very keen on a second one. The EU bullied Denmark and Ireland into holding second referendums. Do they think that they can bully the British people into changing their minds? If we voted to return to the EU, we would never be allowed another vote, in case we were to change our minds to leave again.

Blair said in September 2017, "We have to respect the referendum result to change it." He told the BBC's John Humphrys in January 2018, "a fresh referendum … as opposed to 2016 – would be a choice between two alternatives." Did we have no choice in 2016? Blair wanted the second referendum to include the option of staying in the EU. If we had voted to Remain, would he be insisting on a second referendum and insisting that it must include the option of leaving? Cameron and Osborne repeatedly said that the British people should not expect another vote on the EU for at least a generation. At Leave campaign meetings nobody ever suggested calling for a hasty second referendum to ask the people again if we lost. Everyone was prepared to accept that if we lost this battle, we would prepare for the next, as we did after the 1975 referendum. If we had voted to stay in, we would have expected us to stay in, until we decided otherwise.

Nobody suggested that if we lost we should go to law to overturn the referendum decision. Nobody suggested that we should use Parliamentary procedure to slow down or halt the normal day to day business of the EU in the UK.

Our decision was a severe blow to the EU project of 'ever closer union'. To the EU, leave did not mean leave. They were doing all they could to stop us leaving. The EU wanted the Court and the Commission to keep control of the law, control of the money we sent the EU, and control of policies for any other contingencies – a very wide and open-ended set of demands. They wanted us to be subject to the EU even after an agreement was reached. The EU demand that its jurisdiction be maintained was a wrecking demand; it was at odds with their claim to want a clean break.

Our democratic majority decision to leave the EU cost it a tenth of its income. It will have a shortfall of up to £13.2 billion. We subsidised the EU, so its leaders were angry because their countries would have to pay more or get less, or both. If we were one of the biggest net recipients of EU funds, rather than one of the biggest net contributors, would the EU be insisting on paying its debts to us before anything else could be agreed? On 29 November 2016 Witold Waszczykowski, Poland's foreign minister, said that "Brexit may never happen and Britain should stay in the European Union for as long as possible. Poland's interest [is] that Britain remains a member of the EU and pays into the bloc's budget for as long as possible." He said that the EU27 all agreed on one thing: that Britain should pay as much as possible, for as long as possible.

On 8 February 2017, the House of Commons approved the European Union (Notification of Withdrawal) Bill by 494 to 122. A clear majority of MPs - 498 to 114 - voted to trigger Article 50.

This was a procedural bill to put into law changes that followed from our no longer being a part of the EU's legal order once we have left the EU. It did not repeal any EU legislation; it did not change any policies. As the *Financial Times* put it, "The bill is a largely technical measure ..."[216] The bill merely enabled the redrafting of laws. For instance, it would change references to EU regulatory bodies to which we would no longer be subject into references to the relevant British regulatory bodies. The bill explicitly precluded its temporary powers from being used in any way that would affect our Human Rights Act 1998. Claims that the government could use these powers to cut workers' rights or human rights were unfounded. The law affected by the Withdrawal Bill was itself overwhelmingly brought into force as secondary legislation. The Bill merely went some way to reversing this process.

When India achieved independence in 1947 it incorporated all British imperial statutes into law and then proceeded, at its leisure, to remove such measures it did not need or did not like. We will do likewise - incorporate all EU laws, directives and regulations into law and then remove those measures we do not need or do not like.

On 29 June 2017 MPs rejected, 322 to 101, Labour MP Chuka Umunna's amendment backing membership of the EU single market and customs union. On 11 September Parliament voted for the EU Withdrawal Bill by 326 votes to 290. This Bill ended the supremacy of EU law here by repealing the European Communities Act of 1972. Another important milestone was passed.

Jeremy Corbyn insisted that Labour MPs voted against the Bill. Seven of them bravely voted for it. Corbyn claimed that the Bill was a 'power grab' by the government because new laws could be created using statutory instruments and so would not be properly scrutinised. But using statutory instruments was a method all governments routinely used to enact the details of new law. In fact, the last Labour government doubled the number of statutory instruments to introduce new law. The Bill guaranteed our rights in law once we are outside the EU. If the Bill had not been passed, those rights would not have been carried into our law and on day one of independence - 29 March 2019 – those rights would have vanished. Labour, claiming to defend workers' rights, would have left us with no rights!

Voting against the Bill was voting against the democratic majority decision of the British people. If the Labour Party truly accepted the outcome of the referendum – as it stated in its election manifesto – then its MPs were obliged to back the Bill that implemented our decision.

The division was not between leavers and remainers but between the growing majority for independence and the dwindling minority for the EU. The YouGov poll of 17 November 2016 found that 59 per cent of people thought that Britain would leave the EU by 2020. 68 per cent thought that Britain should go ahead with Brexit, the same as in October. People who voted to Remain were evenly divided: half thought the government had a duty to carry out our decision and leave; half wanted the government to ignore or overturn our decision. When asked to rank Britain's aims in exit talks, most put first the need to respect the referendum decision. A quarter of Remain voters agreed. 59 per cent thought that calls for a second referendum were illegitimate.

The *Guardian* acknowledged in its editorial of 2 December 2016, "Remain is still losing rather than winning support. There is no appetite for a second referendum." After citing anti-Brexit headlines from the pro-EU *Financial Times*, *The Times* and the *Independent* that supposedly showed mass support for a second referendum, Worcester and Mortimore commented, "While pro-EU newspapers would rather lead on wishful thinking than news, it is perhaps unlikely that their readers will ever fully understand why they lost the referendum or what motivated and still motivates the Leave voters."[217]

An Opinium survey of January 2017 found that 52 per cent of voters believed that Britain 'made the right decision in deciding to leave the European Union' and 39 per cent did not. An ICM poll for *Change Britain*, reported on 17 February 2017, confirmed that 68 per cent of voters wanted the government to 'get on with implementing the result of the referendum', compared to just 15 per cent who disagreed.

More Remain voters (42 per cent) agreed with the statement than disagreed (33 per cent), up from December 2016, when 26 per cent of them agreed, against 40 per cent who disagreed.

The YouGov poll of 26-27 March 2017 found that 44 per cent of those polled agreed with the statement, "I support Britain leaving the EU, and the British government should ensure that Britain does leave the EU." 25 per cent agreed with the statement, "I did not support Britain leaving the EU, but now the British people have voted to leave, the government has a duty to carry out their wishes and leave." 21 per cent agreed with the statement, "I do not support Britain leaving the EU and the government should ignore the result of the referendum or seek to overturn it in a second referendum." Ten per cent said they did not know. So, in sum, 69 per cent thought that Brexit should go ahead.

A June 2017 YouGov poll suggested that 70 per cent of the public thought that Brexit needed to happen. Only a fifth of us thought we should stay in the EU on its current terms of membership, or with more powers handed over to the EU. Just 2 per cent thought that we should unite with the rest of the EU to form a single government.[218]

The 16 July 2017 survey of 1,000 people for the Tony Blair Institute for Global Change, by research firm Luntz Global Partners, found that given the choice of a 'hard Brexit', 'soft Brexit' or a second referendum, most people chose the first. More than 40 per cent favoured a clean break, fewer than 40 per cent wanted a 'middle way' and only a fifth wanted another vote. Asked whether 'Brexit must mean Brexit', with Britain leaving the EU even if no deal had been agreed with Brussels, 56 per cent agreed, with 25 per cent against and 19 per cent unsure. 75 per cent said they believed Britain's immigration policy was too open, compared with just 4 per cent who said it was too closed.

A project by the London School of Economics and Oxford University surveying 3,293 people (reported 11 August 2017) revealed that when the British public were asked in detail what they wanted from the negotiations, there was more support for harder Brexit options because Leavers and a significant number of Remainers backed them. There were relatively low levels of support for the policies that would amount to a 'soft' Brexit – single market membership, ongoing EU payments, free movement, and staying under the jurisdiction of the ECJ. 67 per cent of respondents preferred 'no deal' to soft Brexit, while 68 per cent opted for 'hard' over 'soft' Brexit.

Most Remain voters wanted a clean Brexit in which Britain took control of its borders, ended the jurisdiction of the ECJ and paid little or nothing to leave the EU. 51.3 per cent of Remain voters backed a Brexit deal which delivered full control over immigration and led to smaller numbers of EU immigrants. Among Remain voters, 54.7 per cent said that they did not think we should hand over any money to the EU. 52.2 per cent of Remain voters did not think Britain should be subject to the ECJ.

Neither Remain nor Leave voters wanted to pay a large 'divorce bill' to the EU when we left. Remain voters were even less willing to pay up than their Leave counterparts. Both groups strongly objected to a bill of £50 billion or £70 billion. Leave voters were just about happy with a bill of £20 billion or less, while Remainers would accept £10 billion. It was clear that most Remain voters accepted Brexit.

A Sky Data poll of 12 October 2017 asked people which came closer to their views on Brexit - No deal is better than a bad deal? 74 per cent agreed. Any deal is better than no deal? 26 per cent agreed.

A 2018 survey found that most Remain voters wanted national control over tax, immigration policy, agriculture and fisheries and environmental policy and opposed decisions on these matters being taken at the EU level.[219]

A 12 June 2018 poll from BMG for Change Britain found that an overwhelming majority of voters – and clear majorities of Remain and Labour voters – said that Britain must be completely free to strike its own trade deals after Brexit. 71 per cent of all voters agreed that we must be free to negotiate our own trade deals with other countries without any involvement of the EU, which meant not being part of any form of customs union. 64 per cent of Labour voters demanded the freedom to strike new trade deals. 60 per cent of Remain voters agreed. A majority of Remain voters also agreed that Brexit meant taking back control of trade policy, and 58 per cent of Remainers said that the referendum result must be respected.

But the May government was negotiating on its knees. The EU and its supporters here are pressing us to make a deal by a deadline, to have no option for walking away from a bad deal, to pay £40 billion up-front for the privilege of leaving, and to let their Court run the whole process. If you are selling your house, do you tell potential buyers that you must sell it by the end of the week? Do you tell them that you have no alternative? Do you offer to pay them a fee (any amount they decide) to buy it from you? Do you then offer to let their lawyer draw up the agreement?

The harder we fight to evict the EU, the more completely we defeat the pro-EU forces, the closer we get to independence. We need to ensure that we leave completely, cleanly and fully, on 29 March 2019. Our referendum decision on 23 June 2016 was our declaration of independence. We must gear the next phase of the struggle to the 29 March 2019 target date, our independence day, just as we focused on 23 June 2016. We must press the politicians into making leave happen, just as we pressed them into conceding a referendum. The next stage should be about what we do with our independence.

Cooperation not assimilation

Those who wanted us to stay in the EU often called those who wanted to leave 'isolationists' and claimed that we would never again cooperate with anybody over anything. On the contrary, outside the EU we are free to cooperate with other nations for agreed purposes. Outside the EU, we still cooperate with the nations of the world through the 90 or so international agreements to which we are party.

We were not isolationist. We were not turning our back on our nearest neighbours. We were not severing cultural ties with European civilisation. Leaving the EU was not about isolation but about independence. We were leaving an organisation that was not in our best interests, so that we can develop mutually beneficial relations with its member countries on a new and better basis of mutual respect. Independence did not preclude cooperation; in fact, genuine independence was a condition of genuine cooperation. Even Jacques Delors said, "If the British cannot support the trend to more integration in Europe, we can remain friends but on a different basis." We will still be able to work for peace and non-discrimination; we will still be able to oppose crime, people-trafficking, bank corruption and tax havens. Leaving one dysfunctional, self-aggrandising body was not leaving the world.

The EU was not about cooperation but about assimilation. We belonged to more than 90 international cooperative bodies. Only one of them wanted to absorb us into a single state. There is a difference between cooperating with other nations and being merged into a single European Union state. The EU is like the Borg in *Star Trek: The Next Generation* - an alien force which seeks to assimilate all other life forms, under cover of cooperating with them.

The European Commission said, "the main goal of the EU is the progressive integration of member states' economies and political systems." The Commission wants complete Economic Union, Monetary Union, Financial Union, Fiscal Union and Political Union by 2025 at the latest. This will 'be developed within the framework of the European Union', so it would have applied to us too.

Cameron told us that the EU was only a market, just as Heath had told us that the EEC was only a market. Cameron only ever talked about the EU as a market. He ducked every question about the EU as a political union. But what market needed its own flag, its own national anthem, its own passport, its own bank, its own currency, its own supreme court, its own parliament and its own army (a 'strategic necessity', said the European Commission)? The EU was not a market, it was a political union.

Jason Farrell and Paul Goldsmith pointed out, "Intergovernmentalism involves arrangements where nation states cooperate with each other on matters of common interest in situations and conditions they can control. States are free to cooperate or not and have the ability to set the level of cooperation. This is often operated through states having a veto, enabling them to block any proposal presented by other parties. So, for example, although the UK is part of NATO and the United Nations, it retains a veto over actions these organisations can take, and whether or not to approve these actions. Crucially, these circumstances involve no loss of sovereignty.

"Supranationalism, however, sees states delegating some responsibility for decision-making to a body or decision-making forum that stands above the nation state. States lose their right to veto and agree to be bound by the majority decisions of cooperating states and thus lose some control. This means that in some circumstances states may have to go along with a policy that contravenes their particular preferences. Essentially, supranationalism takes inter-state relations beyond cooperation towards integration. ... The European Union from the start was more supranational: a law-making body making laws directly applicable to Britain and whose laws are superior whether Westminster approves of them or not."[220]

As Anthony Coughlan explained, "Supranationalism - from Latin supra, 'above' - is where Nation states surrender their authority to a superior entity that rules them and has legal primacy over them ... Supranationalism is the opposite of internationalism, which is a benign and progressive concept. Internationalism – from Latin inter, 'between' – implies the pre-existence of sovereign Nation states. It refers to relations of co-operation between the states that constitute the international community, but with each controlling and deciding its own domestic and external affairs in accordance with the wishes of its people. Recognition of states based on the right to self-determination of nations and peoples is a basic principle of modern democracy and international law. Supranationalism, in contrast to internationalism, implies a hierarchy, with the supranational level on top. Internationalism implies legal and political equality between the parties. Properly understood, internationalism is opposed to all forms of chauvinism and xenophobia."[221]

Nationalism holds societies together against the divisive forces of ethnic or religious rivalry. Rejecting nationalism brings not internationalism but division. A fear of returning to the national scale of governance – and, ultimately, a fear of the domestic electorate – undergirded some opposition to Brexit. The EU gave governance to elites insulated – by design – from popular control, which locked in anti-democratic policies. Restoring popular control had to involve leaving the EU and revitalising national democracy.

Most European elites were quite happy with a mode of governance that maximised their autonomy from their own electorates while minimising their popular accountability. This typically included the British elite, which was why so few of them were pro-Brexit. As Cameron said in 2010, Britain was dominated by 'an elite who thinks it knows best', 'people have lost control' and 'the politicians have forgotten, the public are the master, we are the servant'. By our referendum vote, the British people asserted control and showed that they, not the elite, were the master.

Our leaving the democracy-denying, austerity-enforcing EU should encourage other countries to do so too. It also makes it harder for reactionary governments across the EU to impose the EU's austerity policies. The EU project will sunder, as across the continent people increasingly opposed it. People, inspired by Brexit, called for referendums, for democracy. 58 per cent of Italians wanted a referendum, 53 per cent of Dutch said they would vote leave.

The EU - a state, but not a democratic one

One of the euro's creators, Hans Tietmeyer, said in 1988, "Like a marriage made in heaven, EMU must last forever because there is no way out. Monetary union is therefore a monetary community of destiny."[222] John Major said in 1995, "The often unspoken fear of many people – we should address it honestly and clearly and examine it - is that Europe might develop into a super-state, an overarching Government with no national veto, no control over our own borders, prescriptive decisions, a single currency imposed and the nation state retreating to a wholly subordinate role. That fear exists out there... and we should recognise the fact that it exists ... I for one would find such a Europe wholly unacceptable for this country. I do not believe that it is remotely likely, but, if that were to be the future, it would not be a future that would be suitable for this country."[223]

Chancellor Merkel said in 2012, "Without doubt, we need more and not less Europe. That's why it is necessary to create a political union." She said, "The task of our generation is to complete economic and monetary union, and to build political union in Europe, step by step." She has said, "We need a political union, which means we must gradually cede powers to Europe and give Europe control."

European Commission chief Jose Manuel Barroso said on 10 July 2015, "We are a very special construction unique in the history of mankind ... Sometimes I like to compare the EU as a creation to the organisation of empire. We have the dimension of empire."

As French President François Hollande asked us in October 2015, "Do you really want to participate in a common state? That's the question." As he said, "The only road for those who are not convinced of Europe is to leave Europe.... It is the logical path."

The EU took advantage of our leaving by pressing on with its aims of developing a European Defence Force and of installing a Eurozone budget run by a Eurozone finance minister. They put forward a 'Roadmap Towards a Complete Economic and Monetary Union'. They intended to create a euro area system of Competitiveness Authorities, complete the Banking Union and create a European Fiscal Board. They wanted to launch the Capital Markets Union, designed to expand security trading, which would promote the interests of banks, fund managers and security traders at the expense of both savers and users of funds. By 2025 they intended to make the convergence process more binding, set up a macroeconomic stabilisation function for the euro area, integrate the European Stability Mechanism into the EU law framework and set up a euro area treasury accountable at the European level. They noted that "The process towards a deeper EU is nonetheless open to all EU members." They aimed to make EMU 'attractive for other EU Member States to join if they are ready to do so'.

In January 2014, Commission Vice-President Viviane Reding expressed the Commission's ambition: "we need to build a United States of Europe with the Commission as government." [224] Martin Schulz, President of the EU Parliament, wanted to move the EU swiftly to a 'one government' federal constitution. He wanted ever-closer European integration to turn the EU into a 'United States of Europe' by 2025. "I want there to be a constitutional treaty to create a federal Europe," he said on 7 December 2017. He wanted a single state, but not a democratic one: he said, "It is not the EU philosophy that the crowd can decide its fate."

Economist Otmar Issing decried the EU Five Presidents' Report's proposal of a 'fiscal entity', warning that this would create a rogue plenipotentiary with unbridled powers over all EU member nations, beyond democratic accountability. Such a system would end the budgetary sovereignty of the member states and would violate the principle of no taxation without representation, forgetting the lessons of the English Civil War and the American Revolution.

The EU imposed on member states the 'European Semester'. Each year, the Commission analysed EU member states' proposed budgetary, macroeconomic and structural reforms and gave them country-specific recommendations for the next 12-18 months. These were always neo-liberal policies, austerity policies, poverty policies. Every EU member was subject to the economic governance of the Six-Pack, the Two-Pack and the Fiscal Treaty.

Many said that they wanted a reformed EU. Some wanted 'progressive' forces to take power in the leading EU member-states then make the EU mend its ways. The contradiction was obvious. On the one hand, they did not believe that they could mobilise a few tens of millions of people in their own societies for these ends. Yet, they believed that they could mobilise hundreds of millions of people across the whole of Europe for the same ends. Incredibly, they further believed that they could achieve this simultaneously across a range of countries, so that the national positions of all the EU member-states would converge. In reality, it was easier to mobilise across one nation than across 27, and easier to act unilaterally not multilaterally.

Some of the left did not believe that most people supported better policies, or that they could persuade them to do so. They thought that the only way to ensure that 'left-wing' preferences could win was to rely on an undemocratic institution to 'lock them in'. Delors told the TUC that in this way the EC would be an alternative route to socialism. Bu the EU, far from locking in the road to socialism, locked in capitalism, treaty by treaty. Staying in the EU blocked any escape route from its treaty-bound pro-capitalist policies. The EU constitution, its treaties, could only be changed by the unanimous agreement of the member states, which made reform virtually impossible.

Some said, 'Another Europe is Possible'. Fair enough, but another EU was not possible. Many opposed the EU as it was but wanted to stay in it for 'what it could be', favouring a possible ideal over the actual reality. Some wanted us to stay in the EU but reduce its powers. But there was never an option of 'stay in and reduce the EU's powers'.

More realistically, Jan-Werner Müller wrote of "the illusion that European integration was once about realising social democratic ideals. The business of Europe has always been business ... It is clear that 'democratising Europe' is purely a cosmetic matter at this point. It also means that there won't any longer be even the tiniest illusion that the decisions Europeans take at the ballot box will have any influence on the political programme carried out by Brussels."[225] An EU of corporations is not a Europe of nations.

Philip Whyman, Mark Baimbridge and Andrew Mullen argued that the EU had four built-in blocks to progressive reforms. It did not have the budget or the economic tools to achieve a social Europe. None of its institutions backed such a policy. Capitalist forces in the member states thwarted any moves in this direction. And pro-capitalist forces in the EU's institutions, especially in the Commission and the European Central Bank, also opposed such moves. They concluded, "individual countries or groups of countries would find it nigh impossible to reform the European project from within because of this quadruple lock. Indeed, thwarting West European socialism in this manner was one of the main reasons why capitalist forces in Europe and the United States supported the European project during the Cold War Order and the New World Order and why they continue to do so. In short, any attempt to construct a Euro-Keynesian regime would have to overcome these four problems."[226]

As Christopher Bickerton pointed out, the EU's 'aim is to liberate national governments from the stranglehold of organized labour'.[227] He continued, "membership consolidates national governments in their relations with their own, increasingly discontented national populations. Across the Eurozone, the political consensus lies behind the need for monetary and fiscal austerity. Budget deficits and outstanding government debt need to be brought down to manageable proportions in order that economic growth returns to Europe. At the same time, budgetary reductions need to be accompanied by an acceleration of ongoing labour market and welfare state reforms if the reductions are to be sustainable: across the Eurozone, governments are looking to reduce state expenditures in the area of pensions and employment. The advantage of Eurozone membership is that it provides national governments with protection from domestic challenges to this consensus. Recalcitrant populations, unsure why they should pay for what are considered to be reckless spending actions of the financial sector, are in different ways challenging the actions of national governments. ... Pan-European policymaking has the advantage of limiting the scope for societal penetration of executive-level decision-making."[228]

Larry Elliott wrote, "Those who say a different Europe is needed are right in their analysis. The problem they have is in explaining how this different Europe comes about, particularly given that the direction of travel for decades has been entirely in the opposite direction, towards a destination where budgets have to balanced, where countries have to deflate their way back to growth, where the nation state must bend the knee to market forces and competition and where neoliberal ideas hold sway. A Corbyn-led government could make a success of reform and remain, but only if it could win the support of the European Commission, the European Central Bank and a Council of Ministers, none of which are exactly awash with kindred spirits. It would require treaty change to bring about a different Europe, which seems unlikely."[229]

When the *Wall Street Journal* in 2012 asked Mario Draghi, the President of the European Central Bank, "Do you think Europe will become less of the social model that has defined it?" Draghi confirmed, "There was no alternative to fiscal consolidation. The European social model has already gone."[230]

Whyman, Baimbridge and Mullen pointed out that "the retrenchment of Western Europe's welfare states and the failure to create a unified EU-level welfare state in their place has fatally undermined the ESM [European Social Model] concept and the dream, held by many social democratic and socialist political parties, trade unions and other progressive forces, of constructing a Social Europe."[231] They concluded, "there is no such thing as an ESM."[232]

Its Treaties, not its peoples, governed EU policies. There was no link between our votes and their power. Voters could not remove failed rulers or reform failed policies, so the EU was not reformable. Against the Treaties, we had zero influence: as President Juncker told us in 2015, "There can be no democratic choice against the European treaties." When we could not change the laws, we had no democracy. Merkel said, "The debt brakes will be binding and valid forever. Never will you be able to change them through a parliamentary majority."[233] As the EU Commissioner for Employment, Social Affairs and Inclusion said, "Eurozone membership and democracy are no longer compatible." The EU was by its very nature hostile to national democratic control of power.

Barroso said, "There is no sovereignty any more. Only the markets are sovereign."[234] There was indeed a clear conflict between the domination of markets and the demands of democracy, because markets were international and global, while democratic decision-making and the institutions of social protection were national and local.[235] As the former Governor of the Bank of England, Lord King, pointed out, "The crisis of European Monetary Union will drag on, and it cannot be resolved without confronting either the supranational ambitions of the European Union or the democratic nature of sovereign national governments. One or other will have to give way. Muddling through may continue for some while, but eventually the choice between a return to national monies and democratic control, or a clear and abrupt transfer of political sovereignty to a European government cannot be avoided."[236] He pointed out, "monetary union has created a conflict between a centralised elite on the one hand, and the forces of democracy at the national level on the other."[237]

Bob Crow, the late General Secretary of the Rail Maritime and Transport union, had warned that the euro would "mean more privatisation, the destruction of our social services and an end to democratic control over our own economy …"[238] Instead we needed to have "democratic control over capital flows, our borders and the future of our economy for the benefit of everyone … The only rational course is to leave the EU so elected governments regain the democratic power to decide matters on behalf of the people they serve."[239]

As Richard Tuck observed, "The only thing which will allow the Left to roll back the last forty years of market entrenchment is opening up a space in which democratic politics can determine the shape of the British economy, and British society in general, as it did from the coming of universal suffrage until 1 January 1973. If at some point the electorate votes for Conservative policies, so be it; the policies can at least be reversed through the simple means of a general election, rather than through what we are finding to be the agonising process of breaking away from a supranational entity."[240]

Unelected bodies should have less power. So, the European Commission should have less power - and our vote to leave achieved that. The European Parliament with its undemocratic trilogue procedure should have less power - and our vote achieved that too. So, the referendum was a democratic process leading to fewer powers for unelected bodies. Quite a good result then surely, for democrats.

The June 2017 election

Both Tories and Labour were clear in their 2017 election manifestos that we will leave the EU and the jurisdiction of the European Court of Justice, regain control of our borders and leave the EU's single market and customs union. Labour's manifesto said, "Labour accepts the referendum result." Corbyn said that he accepted our decision and accepted an end to free movement, which gave many leave voters the confidence to vote for his party. Labour endorsed leaving the EU more clearly than some people have claimed, since it promised that "Freedom of movement will end when we leave the European Union", which was incompatible with membership of the single market, and it promised to create new trade agreements with the rest of the world, which was incompatible with membership of the Customs Union.

The vote for the Conservatives went up by 5.5 per cent, to 13,667,213. This was 2.3 million more votes than in 2015. It won the biggest vote share, 42.4 per cent, and the most seats, 318, with a majority of 56 over Labour. So, there was still a majority for a clean break from the EU.

The vast majority of the MPs elected, 580 of the 650, stood on pro-independence platforms which said that they respected the vote to leave the EU. The total votes for pro-leave parties (Conservative, Labour, UKIP, and the Democratic Unionist Party) were 27,428,582. Total votes for pro-EU parties (the LibDems, the SNP, Plaid Cymru, Sinn

Fein, and the Greens) were 4,278,245. This was a pro-leave majority of 23,150,337.

All the pro-EU parties lost votes. The LibDems' vote share fell to 7.4 per cent, its worst-ever general election showing, after they campaigned 'fighting every step of the way' against 'an extreme and divisive Brexit' and called for a second EU referendum as their flagship policy. They gained four seats, three of which were in Scotland where the vote for them was a vote against separatism and nothing to do with the EU. They lost deposits in the 375 seats where they got less than 5 per cent of the vote.

The SNP did especially badly. In Scotland, unionist parties got 63 per cent of the votes. The separatists got only 37 per cent, down from 50 per cent in 2015, losing half a million votes and losing 21 seats.

The referendum vote appeared to have released a public pressure valve on immigration. The 2017 general election was the first since 2001 (that is, the first since EU enlargement) when immigration was not among voters' most important issues. In the 2010 and 2015 general elections respectively, 53 per cent and 52 per cent of voters had cited immigration as one of the top three issues facing the country. In June 2017, only 34 per cent did. UKIP had its worst election night since 2001.

Some people did treat the 2017 election as a Brexit election. Many people voted Conservative precisely to uphold our decision for independence because the Conservative party was the parliamentary party that seemed the most committed to carrying out our decision. They did not necessarily vote for austerity. Many people voted Labour to oppose austerity, to support our public services, and not necessarily against independence. These were all good reasons; we needed to bring them together, to unite against austerity and for independence. There could be no end to austerity within the EU, no independence within the EU.

In the election the Labour party focused on opposing austerity and cuts, not on Brexit. Their vote rose by 9.5 per cent, to 40 per cent, 12,874,985 votes, 792,228 fewer votes than the Conservatives (and 4,535,757 fewer than the votes to leave the EU). There was much wishful thinking among Labour supporters, fantasising that the Tory minority government would collapse and let Labour form a government. In 1974 Labour formed a minority government. Many forecast that it could not last. It lasted till 1979.

The May government had no incentive to commit suicide. On 28 June the House of Commons passed the government's policy programme for the next two years, by 323 votes to 309, in the government's first important test.

Nothing in the election changed the referendum result, or the previous votes in the Commons to leave the EU.[241] On 11 June Corbyn said that we could not stay inside the single market after we left the EU. Also on 11 June, John McDonnell, when asked if Labour would support continued membership of the single market, said, "I don't think it's feasible … I think people will interpret membership of the single market as not respecting that referendum." Shadow Foreign Secretary Emily Thornberry said on 15 June: "The Labour position is this. We leave the European Union, which means we need to leave the single market." Speaking on the BBC's Andrew Marr Show on 18 June 2017, Chancellor Philip Hammond said, "We're leaving the EU and because we're leaving the EU we will be leaving the single market." He added, "We will leave the customs union when we leave the EU. That's a statement of legal fact."

Those who called for another referendum wanted us to stay in the EU. So did those who called for the free movement of labour and for staying in the single market. Staying in the single market, the European Economic Area, the 'Norwegian model', would mean still giving the EU billions every year and accepting the EU's free movement of labour.

The European Court of Justice

The government's paper *Enforcement and dispute resolution* said, "However, one common feature of most international agreements, including all agreements between the EU and a third country, is that the courts of one party are not given direct jurisdiction over the other in order to resolve disputes between them. Such an arrangement would be incompatible with the principle of having a fair and neutral means of resolving disputes, as well as with the principle of mutual respect for the sovereignty and legal autonomy of the parties to the agreement. When entering into international agreements, no state has submitted to the direct jurisdiction of a court in which it does not have representation."[242]

It concluded, "The precedents examined in this paper demonstrate that there are a number of additional means by which the EU has entered into agreements which offer assurance of effective enforcement and dispute resolution and, where appropriate, avoidance of divergence, without necessitating the direct jurisdiction of the CJEU over a third party. Such an arrangement, whereby the highest court of one party would act as the means of enforcing or interpreting an agreement between the two parties, would be exceptional in international agreements."[243]

It was almost unprecedented for a state which was a party to an international treaty to accept the jurisdiction of a court of the opposing party in adjudicating treaty provisions. Apart from the EU treaties and the EEA agreement, one would have to go back to the treaties between various European powers and China in the 19th century, under which European citizens were subject to the jurisdiction of extra-territorial courts set up by their own countries instead of being subject to Chinese jurisdiction. China rightly condemned these arrangements as 'unequal treaties' imposed on them by gunboats. The former ECJ judge Professor Franklin Dehousse agreed that the EU's proposals to keep ECJ jurisdiction over Britain were like the colonial 'leonine treaties imposed by England on China in the nineteenth century'.[244] He said that this sort of treaty would turn Britain into 'some kind of new 1930s Shanghai, where the EU citizens will benefit from multiple privileges'. A state was only sovereign if it acted on the principle of one people, one law.

In the EU's external agreements there was no instance in which a non-member state accepted direct ECJ jurisdiction over itself or its relations with EU. Even the EU's agreements with the tiny statelets of Andorra and San Marino did not accept ECJ jurisdiction and instead contained balanced bilateral arbitration arrangements.

Courts in different countries may look at and learn from each other's decisions. But no court was bound to follow a decision of a foreign court if, having weighed it up, in the end it could not agree with it. The ability of our courts to disagree with, and depart from, the decisions of foreign courts was an essential part of our sovereignty.

The House of Lords European Union Committee reached two conclusions in its March 2017 report on Brexit and the EU budget: "Article 50 TEU [Treaty on European Union] allows the UK to leave the UK without being liable for outstanding financial obligations under the EU budget and related financial instruments, unless a withdrawal agreement is concluded which resolves the issue." (Paragraph 135.) And, "The jurisdiction of the CJEU [Court of Justice of the European Union] over the UK would also come to an end when the EU Treaties ceased to have effect. Outstanding payments could not, therefore, be enforced against the UK in the CJEU." (Paragraph 133.)

"... it would be unheard of for a non-member state to agree to binding adjudication by the ECJ in an international agreement with the EU. No counterparty to an EU trade treaty or other treaty would agree to such jurisdiction and plainly the UK should not do so. ... once the UK withdraws from the EU it is in principle no longer bound by the jurisdiction of the

Court or its judgments, because the provisions of the Treaties conferring jurisdiction on the ECJ will no longer bind the UK. There is no provision on the Treaties conferring jurisdiction on the ECJ to continue to rule after exit on matters arising before exit, unlike in some other treaties."

The committee concluded, "The hierarchy of norms within EU law gives priority to the total withdrawal from the treaties at the end of the 2-year period under Article 50(3) TEU over and above any financial obligations imposed on the UK through EU secondary legislation. Public international law also supports the argument that no such obligations as are apparently being asserted exist, and further it is clear that an effective withdrawal from the EU does not depend on the fulfilment of any outstanding financial obligations prior to withdrawal. In the event of a dispute between the UK and the EU, the jurisdiction of the ECJ will no longer apply once the UK has withdrawn from the Union."

More threats

We did not vote for a 'hard' Brexit or a 'soft' Brexit, or any shades of comfort in between. We voted to leave. Now all who had the interests of the people at heart must unite to ensure that decision is respected and implemented.

We needed to stop paying and stop obeying. There was no need to offer the EU any money over and above our legal obligations. But the European Commission wanted us to pay into the Common Agricultural Policy until 2020 and pay for EU administration costs for 2019 and 2020, foisting on us a bill for 100 billion euros. But, as the House of Lords pointed out, legally speaking all our financial commitments to the EU were linked to our membership. So, they ended when our membership ended. No law or treaty compelled us to make payments to the EU on leaving it. This was also the EU's own legal advice. EU treaties said nothing about a leaving payment, not even Article 50.

Aristotle asked whether a democracy should be obliged to pay the debts of the tyrant that the democracy has overthrown. He answered, no, because when the community changed from tyranny to democracy, it was no longer the same community. So, it was not responsible for the tyrant's debts, just as it was not answerable for the tyrant's crimes. So we were not obliged to pay any money to the EU when we left.

Some sought to delay our leaving beyond 2019 and wanted transition deals with the EU that would hold us in the EU straitjacket for years to come. The EU's draft negotiating principles included, "The EU is open to a transitional membership agreement, but this must be very clearly defined, time-limited and dependent on the UK maintaining EU membership obligations." We did not need to agree transitional arrangements that prolonged the EU's power over us. We should leave on 29 March 2019, when the notice we gave under Article 50 ran out. As the EU 'fact sheet' said, "once triggered, [Article 50] cannot be unilaterally reversed. Article 50 does not provide for the unilateral withdrawal of the negotiation." And if no agreement was reached, "the EU treaties simply cease to apply to the UK two years after notification".

President Hollande said in 2016 that Britain must pay a high price for Brexit to discourage others from following suit: 'There must be a threat, there must be a risk, there must be a price ..." The French economy minister, Emmanuel Macron, warned in April that Britain would be 'completely killed' in trade talks if it voted to leave. Juncker said Britain's post-Brexit economy cannot be allowed to grow faster than the Eurozone. President Tusk of the European Council said his demands were not aiming at a workable agreement, but were to frighten us into begging to come back in. Merkel told Germany's industrial chiefs that they would not be allowed to lobby for a sweetheart Brexit deal and warned them not to mind if trade with the UK was disrupted for the higher good of damaging Britain.

"I'm sure the deserters will not be welcomed with open arms," Juncker told *Le Monde* on 20 May 2016, "If the British should say No, which I hope they don't, then life in the EU will not go on as before. The United Kingdom will have to accept being regarded as a third country, which won't be handled with kid gloves. If the British leave Europe, people will have to face the consequences – we will have to, just as they will. It's not a threat, but our relations will no longer be what they are today." Britain would pay a 'huge price' for its decision to prioritise controlling immigration ahead of retaining membership of the single market, the Dutch Prime Minister Mark Rutte said. EU leaders like Guy Verhofstadt were still determined to stop us leaving. He threatened in June 2018 that the EU would not ratify Brexit until 2038.

Charlie Elphicke MP and Martin Howe concluded, "there is no credible legal argument either for a liability on the UK to contribute to the EU's pension fund deficit, or for any liability to contribute to the EU's ongoing programmes after Brexit day on 29 March 2019. ... the EU's 'Own Resources Decision' and its 'Multiannual Financial Framework' are legally subordinate to the EU treaties, have no binding force in law independently of the treaties, and therefore cease to impose any legal obligation on the UK on the date when the Treaties themselves cease to apply to the UK under Article 50 TEU. ... there is no general practice in international law of States making or receiving balancing payments representing the net assets or liabilities of an international organisation when they join or withdraw from the organisation." [245] Yet the EU's negotiator Michel Barnier stated that the UK's obligation to pay a multibillion pound bill on leaving the EU was 'incontestable'.

For a national democratic renewal

On 8 December 2016, the House of Commons agreed by 461 votes to 89, a majority of 372, "That this House recognises ... that it is Parliament's responsibility to properly scrutinise the Government while respecting the decision of the British people to leave the European Union; ... recognises that this House should respect the wishes of the United Kingdom as expressed in the referendum on 23 June; and further calls on the Government to invoke article 50 by 31 March 2017."

152 Labour MPs voted for, 56 abstained and 23 voted against. So Corbyn led the majority of Labour MPs to honour our decision to leave the EU by passing a law triggering Article 50 as soon as possible. All the SNP MPs, the Green MP Caroline Lucas and most LibAnti-Dem MPs voted against.

On 20 December 2017, MPs voted to reject New Clause 13 by 320 votes to 114, an amendment tabled by Labour's Chris Leslie which would have allowed the UK to stay in the EU's customs union. This was rejected after Corbyn whipped his MPs to abstain on this vote (Frank Field, Kate Hoey and Dennis Skinner defied the whip and voted with the government)

That same day, MPs backed by 319 votes to 294 Amendment 381 which fixed the UK's departure time and date into law as 11 pm on 29 March 2019, and they voted 319 to 23 to reject Lib Dem Amendment 120 proposing a referendum on the final Brexit agreement.

A poll of people planning to vote Labour – conducted by YouGov for the Best of Britain campaign group, reported in the *Guardian*, 27 December 2017 – found 24 per cent said they may change their minds before the next election, and two-thirds of those who voted remain would be disappointed or angry if Labour said it would proceed with Brexit. 63 per cent of self-identified Labour supporters said they would be 'delighted or pleased' if Labour said it would stop Brexit and stay in the EU. Another 21 per cent would oppose such a policy.

Andrew Rawnsley wrote in the *Observer* of 12 February 2018, "the Brexiters ... told us that the ultimate point of it all was to restore sovereignty to parliament." No, it was not about restoring the sovereignty of parliament. That was not the question on the ballot paper. It was about restoring the sovereignty of Britain, about gaining independence, so that we did indeed take control of our country, take that control away from the EU and vest it in the people.

The people were sovereign over Parliament. When Parliament failed to uphold the nation's sovereignty, it set itself against the people. On 13 December 2017 the House of Commons voted 309/305 to hobble the government's ability to negotiate the way in which we leave the EU.

A ComRes poll for the *Daily Mirror* of 12 January 2018 found that the majority opposed calling a second EU referendum: 51 per cent were opposed, 43 per cent were in favour. After the 2010 election, many regretted that by voting LibDem they had put Cameron into No. 10, but nobody called for a rerun then.

An ORB International poll reported on 11 March 2018 found that 67 per cent agreed that "the EU is trying to bully the UK." 53 per cent said that they would vote to leave the EU if a referendum was held tomorrow. An ITV Wales poll reported on 19 March 2018 found Welsh opposition to a second EU referendum increasing to 49 per cent, as against 39 per cent wanting one.

A BMG poll published on 23 March 2018 showed that 57 per cent agreed that "the government should get on with implementing the result of the referendum to take Britain out of the EU and in doing so take back control of our borders, laws, money and trade", with just 22 per cent disagreeing. Those who agreed with getting on with Brexit outweighed those who disagreed, across all ages, regions and political parties. 18-34-year-olds agreed by 40 per cent to 29 per cent.

A 4 April 2018 poll by ComRes found that 65 per cent of those surveyed felt that "the result of the 2016 Referendum should be respected and the country needs to move on." 68 per cent thought that those who voted against quitting the EU 'should respect the majority' for leave. Even 38 per cent who had voted Remain in the 2016 referendum agreed that the Leave vote should be respected. 65 per cent of voters in the survey did not want a second referendum. The poll found that people were overwhelmingly optimistic about the country's prospects after the country left the EU.

At the Scottish TUC in April 2018, a motion calling for the UK to remain in the single market was defeated. Also in April delegates at the Communications Workers Union national conference rejected an attempt to back continued freedom of movement of labour.

In a poll taken on 29-31 May 2018, 4 per cent of all respondents said that they had changed their mind and would now prefer to remain in the EU. However, 25 per cent of Remain voters said it was right for Brexit to go ahead given the result of the referendum. 62 per cent of British voters, including 69 per cent of Conservatives, 76 per cent of Leave voters and 55 per cent of Remain voters, said that the Brexit negotiations and decisions about the UK's future outside the EU were happening too slowly.[246]

A YouGov poll of 19-20 June 2018 found that a majority, 45 per cent to 37, believed that once the negotiations were complete and the terms of our withdrawal had been agreed there should not be a referendum to accept or reject them. A majority of 39 per cent to 36 believed that it would not be legitimate for MPs to vote to reject the deal. A majority of 50 per cent to 29 believed that it would not be legitimate for MPs to vote against Brexit going ahead.

Robert Peston acknowledged that "It was the official position of the British state to remain in the EU, and the people said no. That cannot be brushed aside as just one of those things. ... it is to patronise our countrymen in a disgusting way to say they did not know what they were voting for."[247] And, "The votes for Trump and Brexit were not the ignorant mistakes of the misguided. They were declarations by millions of families that they will no longer tolerate the countries they love being run against their values and economic interests by a self-renewing elite."[248] So, Peston concluded, "it makes sense for most of us to attempt to make Brexit a success, in good faith ..."[249]

Rafael Behr of the *Guardian* in March 2018 asked why we were leaving the EU and answered, "Pour away all the snake-oil claims of the leavers and only one durable answer is left: because that is what people voted for. It is a better argument than many remainers seem to think. The referendum was, without question, a massive democratic event. There is not much mileage for pro-Europeans in complaining about sneaky methods used to persuade voters, and no merit at all in constitutional pedantry around the designation of the poll as 'advisory'.

"Leave won and there isn't consistent or reliable evidence that the result would be different if the country were asked again. Some minds might have been changed by the conspicuous political shambles of the May administration, but the process of being asked for a second opinion could also trigger a collective, bloody-minded doubling down. Some would certainly rally around the proposition: "What part of 'leave' didn't you people understand the first time?"

"Even if Brexit could be thwarted at the ballot box before next March – in a plebiscite rematch or a general election where the winning party has unambiguously campaigned on a pro-EU platform – the clock would not be reset to 22 June 2016. Another referendum campaign would not bring a harmonious truce to culture wars stoked by the last one. Some former leave voters might not mourn Brexit's demise. But plenty would feel betrayed and enraged.

"I have yet to hear a compelling remain message for people who had never voted before 2016, but who turned out on that

June day because they felt that at long last they could push a button and everything would change. What is the pro-European offer to someone who voted leave precisely so that the kind of people who campaigned for remain would have to listen to them for a change? Try the argument out loud: we're sorry you were angry that remote Westminster politicians appeared to despise your opinions, now please bear with us while we reverse the totemic decision you felt we couldn't ignore. It doesn't sound great."[250]

On 20 April 2018, a *Guardian* article by David Shariatmadari headlined, "On Brexit, the views of the 48% must be respected too. That's democracy." We never saw a *Guardian* article headlined, "On Brexit, the views of the 52% must be respected too. That's democracy."

Jaffa asked, "if just government is based upon the consent of the governed, what right to govern inheres in those who claim political rights not on the basis of equality but on the basis of their superiority?"[251] He commented, "There is no surer sign that a man is a knave or a fool than his claim to rule other men because he is wiser than they."[252]

American billionaire George Soros, the founder of the Open Society Foundation (OSF), gave more than £400,000 to fund the Best for Britain campaign, which advocated remaining in the EU, since the June 2017 election. Best for Britain tried to delegitimise our referendum decision by falsely alleging that the leave campaigns overspent, that they only won by lying, and that foreign interference swung the vote.

In May 2018 the House of Lords passed a series of wrecking amendments to the EU Withdrawal Bill. This was in defiance of the vote of the British people in the referendum. The House of Lords put itself on collision course with the people and put its own future on the line. One amendment gave Parliament a new option over the final deal – to vote it down and keep Britain in the EU. Viscount Hailsham's amendment added an instruction that "Her Majesty's Government must follow any direction in relation to the negotiations", the first time that Parliament has ever tried to mandate any government over treaty negotiations.

Lord Kerr's amendment made our commitment to the EU's customs union a precondition for the repeal of the European Communities Act 1972. If the House of Commons agreed to Kerr's amendment, it would override the repeal of the 1972 Act. The Pannick/Goldsmith amendment demanded the re-introduction of the Charter of Fundamental Rights. Lord Patten's amendment would put an Irish veto on the border question. Lord Wellington's amendment sought to remove the reference to 29 March 2019 as the Exit Day from the Bill. MPs rejected these amendments.

Confidence in the House of Lords has plummeted as 76 per cent of voters feel peers are 'out of tune with the will of the British people'. Even more said the House of Lords is an 'outdated throwback'. A *Daily Mail* poll, carried out by ComRes in May 2018, revealed that 58 per cent of voters believed that peers would be wrong to try to thwart Brexit, with 24 per cent thinking they should do so.

An unelected revising chamber had no right to overturn a democratic decision made through a referendum. As historian Ian Millhiser wrote, "The premise of any democracy is that the people must be trusted to make decisions for themselves, even if a small group of men with lifetime tenure believe that those people will come to regret their decision."[253] Back in 1776 Tom Paine decried the 'remains of aristocratical tyranny in the persons of the peers'.

No deal better than a bad deal

There was no need for the government to have any trade deals in place before we left the EU on 29 March 2019. Halligan and Lyons wrote, "Unless the EU sees that we are prepared not to sign an FTA, we will only be offered a bad one. Signing a bad FTA because we are desperate to 'get a deal' would disadvantage UK exporters and consumers for a long time.

That was David Cameron's mistake ahead of the June 2016 referendum. In trying to renegotiate the UK's relationship with the EU, he asked for very little and got even less. That's because he vowed to support ongoing EU membership whatever the terms."[254] No deal was indeed better than a bad deal. Negotiating up against a hard deadline would make any long-term agreement far worse than one reached under less time pressure.

Our trade deficit with the EU meant that if we traded with the EU without a deal, we would benefit from billions of pounds of import tariffs. A study by Civitas concluded that if we left without a deal and traded instead under WTO rules, companies in the rest of the EU would pay £12.9 billion a year in tariffs to export their goods to us, while our companies exporting to the EU would pay £5.2 billion a year. EU exporters would pay the relatively low WTO tariffs, which we could use to compensate UK exporters.[255] Germany, Spain, Belgium, Luxembourg, the Netherlands, France, Poland, Italy, Sweden, Denmark, Portugal and Finland all want low- or even zero-tariff trade to continue after we left the EU, because they all sold far more to us than we sold to them. Costs to the EU would be much greater than our costs if full customs cooperation with us were not secured. If we traded with the EU under WTO rules, maintaining tariffs on imports would give us bargaining power to negotiate lower EU tariffs in the future. Some sectors, such as autos, were so strong that a zero-tariff strategy might be warranted from the outset, or soon after we left the EU.

The European Common External Tariff could be accepted in practice, at an average of 2-3 per cent. Tariffs at this low level made little difference, which was why British exports had for some years been growing faster to countries outside the EU than to countries in the EU. But the EU could not increase these tariffs just to hurt Britain. The WTO had two rules of equal treatment. The first was the Most Favoured Nation (MFN) principle, which compelled the EU to treat all

WTO members equally. When we leave the EU, we too will have this right to equal treatment: the EU could not legally discriminate against us. WTO and World Customs Union agreements which the EU has signed prevented the EU punishing us for leaving.[256]

In addition, under Articles 3, 8 and 50 of the Lisbon Treaty, the EU had to negotiate 'free and fair trade' with non-EU countries. On leaving the single market/customs union under WTO rules, we would at once adopt the MFN tariffs that would at first be the same as we operate now. The MFN rules did not dictate the level of our tariffs – only the maximum tariffs that we could levy. We could cut or even end tariffs (if we treated all countries the same) thereby allowing us to avoid raising tariffs against the EU.

We and the EU were already signed up to the WTO agreement on Rules of Origin which committed all its signatories 'to ensure that rules of origin themselves do not create unnecessary obstacles to trade'.

The WTO had tough rules on non-tariff barriers (NTBs), such as laws setting technical and regulatory standards, requiring them to be non-discriminatory. The WTO brought all regulations and other NTBs under its National Treatment Principle, its second rule of equal treatment. All such measures applied equally to imported products and domestic products. Naturally, European internal laws would apply to British exports to Europe, which must be treated just like European domestic products. Above all, the WTO rules came without strings. They left Britain free to develop trade relations worldwide.

As the then Brexit Secretary David Davis said in Vienna on 20 February 2018, "Standards for products and services that originated from our own national bodies are adopted the world over, in a wide range of sectors. Eight out of ten of the most used and implemented standards worldwide, ranging from product quality to environmental management, originated in the UK. ... These fears about a race to the bottom are based on nothing, not our history, not our intentions, nor our national interest.

"Frankly, the competitive challenge we in the UK and the European Union will face from the rest of the world — where 90 percent of growth in markets will come from — will not be met by a reduction in standards. We will never be cheaper than China, or have more resources than Brazil. This challenge can only be met by an increase in quality, an increase in service levels, an increase in intellectual content. ...

"On safety at work, our industrial workers are the safest in Europe. The fatality incidence rate, as it is delicately known, is the lowest in Europe, thanks, not to European legislation, but to British laws initially passed in the early and mid-70s. Britain was one of the first Member States to introduce the right to flexible working hours for parents and carers in 2003 ... We ... are one of only three European Union countries to operate a tax disclosure regime.

"The United Kingdom was the first country in the world to set legally binding targets to reduce our greenhouse gas emissions. That saw us reduce our emissions by 40% since 1990 — faster than any G7 country or European country. And after Brexit, plans are in the pipeline for a new, independent body that would continue to uphold environmental standards."

But the Prime Minister was undermining Mr Davis. Early in July 2018 Mrs May declared her hand. She wanted from the EU an agreement based on the kind of agreement the EU had with Morocco. Her letter to Tory MPs spelt it out: "We are proposing that the framework for our relationship with the European Union should be an Association Agreement."

This kind of agreement was exactly what the European Parliament's Brexit Co-ordinator, Guy Verhofstadt, has been pressing for all along. It was also identical to the 2000 EU-Morocco Agreement. Both have a Free Trade Area exclusively for goods (including agri-foods) between the two parties. And ever since Morocco committed to this, it has become more and more absorbed into the EU's single market with every EU law and every European Court ruling – without having any say in how it developed.

The government's acknowledgment that refusal to follow EU rules 'would have consequences' for trade likewise echoed the EU-Morocco Association Agreement. Any Moroccan efforts to deviate from any EU law are thwarted by threats of attacks on trade. Similarly, if Britain tried to deviate from EU rules, the EU would threaten to tear up the whole agreement in order to enforce our obedience. Under the agreement's 'Common Rulebook' Britain would have to obey EU rules, and the European Court of Justice would continue to be supreme, just as it has been over Morocco.

The EU rejected all real negotiation as 'cherry-picking' because it always treated its four freedoms as indivisible, so conceding on any one freedom inevitably meant conceding on all the others. A single claw ensnared, and the bird is caught.

May also refused to commit to taking back full control of our fishing grounds. Similarly, the 2006 EU-Morocco Fisheries Partnership Agreement allowed vessels from 11 EU member states to fish in Moroccan waters. So Britain would not assert control of its own coastal waters.

The model was the EU's Association Agreement with Moldova. Article 403(2) reads, "The ruling of the Court of Justice of the European Union shall be binding on the arbitration panel." This Agreement contains specific obligations to match EU directives and regulations covering all the areas subject to ECJ rulings.

The EU has used Association Agreements as the basis of the six Western Balkan countries' moves towards joining the EU. All these agreements entailed accepting EU rules, acknowledging the European Court of Justice's supremacy, and agreeing to coercive mechanisms designed to enforce regulatory uniformity. These deals geared third countries' entire legal systems, trading horizons, standards and norms to the EU's.

The EU may well accept the government's proposal – after all, it is the EU's idea. If so, the government will have trapped us into an agreement which does not deliver any of the prizes of Brexit, breaches all the government's supposed red lines, and trashes our decision to leave the EU.

The government's White Paper (some called it a white flag) said, "The UK would make an upfront choice to commit by treaty to ongoing harmonisation with the relevant EU rules."[257] The government said it would be allowed to 'share its views with the EU as those EU rules are developed'.[258] And if we disagreed on anything, the government accepted that the EU could demand 'financial compensation' from us (more money from us), and could 'impose non-compliance measures' on us and 'reductions in market access'.[259]

It went on, "The UK's proposal is to agree a new Facilitated Customs Agreement with the EU. As if in a combined customs territory with the EU, the UK would apply the EU's tariffs and trade policy for goods intended for the EU. The UK would also apply its own tariffs and trade policy for goods intended for consumption in the UK."[260] There was no 'as if' – we would be in a customs union with the EU.

The *Sunday Telegraph* editorial of 8 July said, "Millions of people have indeed been betrayed, let down by a political class that had promised to implement the referendum … Last Friday felt like a political coup by the establishment." It was a 21st century style coup - a parliamentary coup, carried out in the name of 'democracy', a 'soft coup', as outlined by American political scientist Gene Sharp. Some in Parliament and the media were clearly working to create what the CIA called a 'coup climate', a sense of political crisis and confrontation, by spreading propaganda, waging 'psychological warfare', and encouraging businesses to stop investing in Britain.

As David Davis wrote to the Prime Minister, "the general direction of policy will leave us in at best a weak negotiating position, and possibly an inescapable one. The Cabinet decision on Friday crystallised this problem. In my view the inevitable consequence of the proposed policies will be to make the supposed control by Parliament illusory rather than real. ... the 'common rule book' policy hands control of large swathes of our economy to the EU and is certainly not returning control of our laws in any real sense."

The *Evening Standard* opined on 9 July that David Davis was "right to say that the proposed new 'business-friendly customs model' is tantamount to membership of a customs union with the EU in goods. He is right that adopting the 'common rule-book' on industrial and agricultural products 'hands control of large swathes of our economy to the EU'. He is right that talk of a 'parliamentary lock' on those rules is 'illusory rather than real' when the consequence of voting against any one individual rule would be to bring down the entire deal – and so will never happen. ... Mr Davis's resignation means Mrs May can no longer pretend that any of this is consistent with taking back control of our laws, our borders and our money."

Even after the biggest popular mandate in our nation's history, some pro-EU people colluded with the EU against their own nation. Academic A. C. Grayling told the EU's Guy Verhofstadt, "What would help the Remain movement in the UK is if the EU is very, very tough and uncompromising on a deal." Nicola Sturgeon's Scottish National Party proposed an amendment to the trade bill, "For the purposes of this Act, 'United Kingdom' does not include Scotland."

Opinium has conducted 13 polls since December 2016 which asked respondents: "Should there be a second referendum on Britain's membership of the EU once we know the terms the government has negotiated?" Most respondents consistently rejected the idea of a second referendum on EU membership. On average, exactly half of voters thought there should not be a second referendum, 36 per cent of voters thought there should, and 13 per cent were undecided.

Corbyn said early in July 2018, "It's not our policy to have a second referendum. It's our policy to respect the result of the referendum." But the pro-EU group Labour for a People's Vote wanted "a public vote on the deal with an option to remain in the EU." That meant disrespecting the referendum result.

In July 2018 Justine Greening MP proposed a second referendum. This was a transparent attempt to split the leave vote. She proposed three options, two for leaving the EU and one for staying in the EU. So those who wanted to stay in the EU could unite around the third choice, while those who wanted to leave the EU would be divided, some backing one pro-leave option, some backing the other. This was a blatant attempt to rig a new vote to give the pro-EU camp a chance to overturn our 2016 decision. Both the BBC and ITV headlined Ms Greening's proposal. The government at once rejected the proposal, because it knew that it could not win a second referendum.

Rebuilding Britain

Inside the EU we were trapped into its treaty-driven austerity policies and its treaty-determined privatisation policies. Outside the EU, we can decide to implement better policies. And now we must make that happen.

Leaving the EU will be good for Britain. Outside the EU, our economy will be stronger, we can protect our industries, our NHS and jobs, we stay out of TTIP, we trade better, we control our borders, we can rebuild Britain. The only way to get a trade-only deal with the EU was to leave it. The only way to get out of the EU's political structures was to leave it. The only way not to be in a single state was to leave it.

In 2000 the National Institute for Economic and Social Research said, "In conjunction with the potential gain from withdrawing from the Common Agricultural Policy and no longer paying net fiscal contributions to the EU, there is a case that withdrawal from the EU might actually offer our nation net economic benefits." The Governor of the Bank of England Mark Carney said in 2015, "there are risks from remaining in the European Union and risks particularly related to the development of the euro area."[261] Graham Gudgin, Ken Coutts, Neil Gibson and Jordan Buchanan wrote, "Per capita GDP is predicted to be higher by 2030 as a result of Brexit, as lower GDP is shared among a smaller population. The important factors in reaching this assessment are the lower exchange rate, and the assumption that interest rates will be lower than would otherwise have been the case. Austerity in public spending will also be tempered as a result of Brexit."[262]

Stiglitz observed, "The reality is that UK is not likely to be much worse off – and potentially even better off – so long as the divorce is not too unpleasant, and so long as Europe doesn't violate its obligations under the WTO rules (including the critical 'most-favored-nation' provision, which requires that one treats every nation, outside a common market, no worse than any other, so that the UK could not be treated any worse than the US). ... We should note that the United States and Canada have both prospered – indeed, they have been doing far better than the eurozone – without free migration between them, without being a single market, and without full economic integration."[263]

Of the 40 or so economic studies reviewed in the recent book, *The economics of Brexit*, a third suggested that Brexit would either lead to a net gain to our economy or that the costs and benefits were finely balanced and depended upon the relationship agreed between Britain and the EU.[264]

The government's 2017 industrial strategy committed it to raising R&D investment to 2.4 per cent of GDP by 2027, including £12.5 billion more public R&D investment by 2021-22; to investing £400 million in maths, digital and technical education; to creating a National Retraining Scheme including £64 million investment for digital and construction retraining; to increasing the National Productivity Investment Fund to

£31 billion by 2022-23 to develop transport, housing and digital infrastructure; to increasing electric vehicle infrastructure investment by £100 million; and to investing more in rural broadband and data accessibility.

Halligan and Lyons wrote, "most people understand and would accept the good sense of borrowing to invest. If we are to avoid a slowdown now, while positioning the UK for the opportunities presented by Brexit, we should use fiscal policy more proactively. The fact that the UK ill-advisedly ran budget deficits in years of strong growth does not mean we should necessarily cut spending in a downturn."[265]

For the EU Britain was the problem, the EU the solution. For us, the EU was the problem, Britain the solution. The question was, what next for Britain? Now we have voted to take responsibility for our country's future, what do we need to do?

We need to build a new Britain, but how do we each contribute, together, to make it happen? The vote was historic, our declaration of independence, but the job is not done. National liberation struggles are protracted struggles, with many ups and downs. Capitalism does not want independent countries to exist at all; as the whole 20th-century proved, it attacks socialist countries and any countries trying to run their own affairs.

Free trade meant the unfettered movement of capital, freed from all political, national, social or environmental controls. It meant the complete undisguised ascendancy of the capitalist class, the open, official subjection of society and production to the laws of capitalism. Competition abroad was constantly increasing, so cheapness must also increase constantly. So, wages must keep constantly falling. And how do employers effect this fall? By adding to the supply of labour and by reducing workers' rights. We should not embrace the market, neither the EU's single European market, nor the WTO's world market.

Mrs May praised 'free markets, free trade and globalisation', but these are the problems not the solution. They brought us the crash of 2008, the £1.2 trillion gifts to bail out the failed bankers, endless austerity, wage cuts, public spending cuts, an El Dorado for tax dodgers, ever more pollution, inequality, unemployment, homelessness and debt.

The EU was no ally in the fight against deregulation, privatisation and liberalisation, it was no ally in the struggles for workers' rights or for the environment (witness its collusion in Volkswagen's criminal behaviour over emission tests). As Turkuler Isiksel wrote, "Rather than bolstering the capacity of Member States to protect their vulnerable domestic constituencies against the pressure of global economic interdependence, the EU has worked to exacerbate these pressures."[266]

The banks lent governments cash, in return for huge payments in the future, while letting the governments keep the loans off their balance sheets and hide their growing debts. This was just like Gordon Brown's Private Finance Initiatives that he used to keep his borrowing off the books, while landing taxpayers, hospitals and schools with ever greater debts for the future. And the free market will bring us another crash. As Lord King observed, "Without reform of the financial system ... another crisis is certain, and the failure to tackle the disequilibrium in the world economy makes it likely that it will come sooner rather than later."[267]

The division is between those who want our country to be independent and those who want us to be dependent. What do we mean by independence? Independence is the democratic right of self-determination. It is political, economic and intellectual independence, independence of mind, independence from the employing class, from Parliament, from the EU. It is active, participatory, egalitarian democracy.

National sovereignty is a precondition for popular sovereignty. Popular sovereignty is the only basis for democracy, for a national democratic renewal. Democratic involvement leads to progress – as after the world wars and the 2016 referendum. Non-involvement leads to reaction.

We needed economic sovereignty: the power to own and run our own enterprises better than ever before; no more uncontrolled movement of labour; send no more money to the EU; leave the single market and the customs union; uphold workers' rights; no deals like TTIP; control our land and waters; one law for all; no rules from the European Court of Justice; out of the EU's drive towards a European army and a single budget enforced by the Six-Pack, the Two-Pack and the Fiscal Treaty.

We have specific plans: build a new Britain, build industry, buy British steel. We want high wages, high investment and high productivity. Acquired rights in employment law, health and safety, environmental protections and consumer rights, all stay.

We must build on positives to build support for independence. We have made our decision, to leave the EU, a brave, revolutionary act, but not a revolution. We declared our independence. Now we must make a success of this independence.

Independence is a once-in-a-lifetime event. Within the EU there is no alternative to the austerity of capitalism in decline; outside the EU everything is possible. Now that Britain is about to leave the EU, the only thing that is stopping us is us.

Chapter 8 Plans for industry and services

Manufacturing

An economy could not succeed without the capacity to produce. Every country needed an industrial base to produce the goods that people need. Countries need to be independent so that they can make their own decisions about what goods they need to produce. As the Morrisons' advert said, "What we make makes us who we are." Independence is necessary for industrial development and in turn industrial development promotes independence. The material needs of independence force governments to make industry a priority.

Data published in September 2017 showed that Britain was the eighth largest industrial nation with an annual output worth $249 billion. Manufacturing accounted for a tenth of our GDP and nearly a half of all our exports. It employed 2.7 million people and drove 68 per cent of business R&D spending. Much of our manufacturing was high-tech and high value-added and much of it competed successfully in world markets. It was intensive in skilled labour.

We needed to focus on quality, on becoming a high-productivity, high-skilled, high-wage economy.[268] Relying on price competition would instead put downward pressure on working conditions and living standards and would always be vulnerable to much cheaper overseas labour.

We needed an industrial strategy, with a balanced, robust and cheap energy policy, to lessen our dependence on imported energy. We needed to ensure that firms, government departments and local authorities bought British. We needed to develop a knowledge and innovation strategy through more investment in research and development, especially in university research. We should make apprenticeship schemes compulsory for British firms, as Germany and the Nordic nations did for their firms. We needed to design an immigration policy that met our needs, and plan the public services we needed to house, school and provide healthcare for all those living and working here. We needed to design support for our farmers. We needed to rebuild our fishing industry through controlling our own waters and implementing a new sustainable fisheries policy. We needed to promote growth and full employment, which would help to reduce inequality. We needed to rebuild our trade unions, based on the workplace, on the unifying material foundations of better pay and conditions, not on divisive idealist moralising.

Unite the Union stated, "... a long-term strategy for manufacturing is needed in which the government deploys every tool at its disposal. This must include direct investments, such as strategic use of the £200 billion public sector procurement budget. Investment and incentives for the training of skilled apprenticeships would not only benefit existing manufacturers and the supply chain, it would remove a vital barrier to re-shoring. The UK government must also retain the right to directly intervene in the defence of strategic industries. ... The government must not only retain its sovereign right to directly support and defend industry and UK manufacturing; it must exert the political will to do so. This must not be bartered away in negotiations for access to the Single Market or in any Free Trade Deal. ... The government must abandon the failed politics of austerity with direct investment in UK industry and infrastructure. Such investment should replace any lost EU funding while stimulating demand for manufacturing." [269] Infrastructure bonds could move our very substantial pension and life industry savings away from low-yielding gilts towards more productive uses.

State aid, infant industry protection and public ownership were harder to carry out, or were even banned, inside the EU. (Germany escaped this ban, because before the Treaty of Rome was ever signed, the British and US governments set up a system of state aid in Germany which allowed German governments to invest billions in its industrial sector through the state-backed KFW banking system.) And Germany's *Länder*, its provincial banks, were allowed to pour money into local industry. This state aid, not Germany's fabled free-market reforms, enabled Germany's swift postwar growth as an industrial power.

EU competition policy only allowed state aid if it did not distort fair and effective competition between companies in EU countries or harm the economy. EU Treaty provisions meant that the European Commission must approve all state aids, including to the public sector, as being compatible with the single market. The EU system also allowed corporations to challenge grants of state aid on competition grounds. Reforming this state aid regime would require treaty amendment, needing the accord of all member states.

The single market allowed state aid to industry or to a region only if it was market-compatible. EU rules prevented member countries setting the direction of an industry, a sector or the whole economy. WTO rules on state aid were far less restrictive than the EU's rules were. EU rules also forced nationalised industries to behave just like private firms. They had to act like 'a market economy operator'. The Commission ruled, "it is not relevant whether the intervention constitutes a rational means for the public bodies to pursue public policy (for example employment) considerations... The decisive element is whether the public bodies acted as a market economy operator would have done in a similar situation."[270]

But the market was not a good judge of efficiency. Well-directed state intervention could achieve better outcomes than the market did. As Joseph Stiglitz and Bruce Greenwald noted, "because the industrial sector not only has a greater capacity for learning but also more learning spillovers, encouraging that sector through protection or industrial policies can lead to higher growth and societal welfare."[271] And, "... there is an *infant economy argument for protection*. Growth and standards of living can be raised by *defying* a country's seeming comparative advantage and imposing trade restrictions that encourage industrialization."[272]

Stiglitz and Greenwald went on to advocate controls on the movements of capital and of labour: "If there are powerful arguments for broad barriers to imported industrial goods, those apply equally to restrictions on capital exports overseas and the import of financial services. In short this theory provides a new rationale for why capital and financial market liberalization may lead to lower rates of growth. Similar arguments also apply, we show, to labor exports overseas."[273]

But May said on 2 March 2018, "As with any trade agreement, we must accept the need for binding commitments - for example, we may choose to commit some areas of our regulations like state aid and competition to remaining in step with the EU's." As Corbyn perceptively commented on 5 March, "The Prime Minister's only clear priority seems to be to tie the UK permanently to EU rules that have been used to enforce privatisation and block support for industry."

As Unite observed, "The EEA has blocked Norway from subsidising the ailing ship building industry and prompted the part privatisation of the country's state run oil company."[274] EU policies on state aid also restricted social housing. The good policies in Labour's manifesto, like ending austerity and nationalising rail, could not be achieved while we stayed in the EU single market. As Edward Heath wrote in 1980, "The opponents of EEC membership inside the Labour Party know how much more difficult it would be to foist their brand of left-wing socialism on the British people if we remain part of a community based on the principles of free enterprise and the mixed economy."[275] Conservative MP Kenneth Clarke put it more succinctly in 1983, "The great thing about Europe is that it makes most of Labour's policies illegal." An EU internal strategy paper leaked to the *Financial Times* in February 2018 showed that the EU intended to tie Britain down after we left it by banning or curbing future moves to carry out an industrial strategy, under threat of sanctions.

But the EU certainly helped British companies in one way – by helping them to move abroad. EU grants helped Ford Transit to move to Turkey in 2013, helped Peugeot to move production to Slovakia, helped Crown Closures, Bournemouth to move to Poland, helped Gillette to move to Eastern Europe, and helped Texas Instruments Greenock to move to Germany.

Countries should be able to decide the size of their public sectors. But EU directives, which accorded rights of market access to corporations, forbade nationalising sectors such as gas, electricity, telecommunications and postal services. EU laws and treaties bound us into privatisation. For example, EU directive 91/440 enforced the privatisation of our railways and EU directives 97/67/EG and 2002/39/EG enforced the privatisation of our postal services. New public enterprises had to compete with private firms in a capitalist market. Repealing these directives would require a proposal by the Commission – the very instigators of EU 'liberalisation'. Article 59 of the Treaty on the Functioning of the European Union allowed the EU to liberalise services and since the 1980s it has done so in energy, transport, postal services, telecommunications, education and health.

Any such Commission proposal would require unanimous approval by the EU Council and the consent of the European Parliament. EU treaties granted companies the right of freedom of establishment, the right to establish branches and subsidiaries in other member states. The European Court of Justice would almost certainly ban nationalisation of branches and subsidiaries of companies based in other member states as a curb on the freedom of establishment. The Treaties also gave corporations the right to sue governments whenever any public monopoly, such as the NHS, infringed EU competition rules. The free movement of services meant that foreign companies, over which we had even less control, bought up our public services.

The free movement of capital, through the abolition of exchange controls, was supposed to get capital invested more efficiently throughout the EU. Instead money poured into speculation, real estate and construction.

The EU prevented us addressing the problem of soaring house prices in London. European Court rulings stopped us imposing residence requirements on property ownership. So, while we were in the EU we could not stop offshore companies buying UK property forcing up house prices. Offshore companies owned 100,000 properties. EU accounting rules said that Housing Association debt must be included in public sector debt, leading the government to impose the Housing Association sell-offs.

Steel

Without a regular local supply of steel, the heart of manufacture, manufacturing industry would be impossible. Since we joined the EEC/EU we have seen continuous decline in the steel industry, by 2010 it had less than a quarter of the capacity it had when we joined the EEC in 1972.

EU competition policy did not let the government support steel. Simon Boyd, a director at Reidsteel, Britain's largest steel construction company, said, "While we remain in the EU, the UK government we elect can do little to tackle the dumping of cheap steel or unfair state aid rules." Steve Webb, the Europhile former LibDem minister, admitted: "The issue there is you're not allowed to subsidise your own industry where they're competing with other peoples, and the EU come down particularly hard on steel, because the EU takes the view that there's too much steel capacity."

We should use British steel for the rail links HS2 (London-Birmingham then on to Manchester and Leeds) and for HS3 (Liverpool-Manchester-Leeds-Hull).

The EU-inspired green energy laws which priced steel out of the market were passed by the Labour government and maintained by the Tory government. When we joined the EU, we produced 4 per cent of the world's aluminium. Today it has practically all gone, thanks to plant closures brought on by the EU's dear power policies. Other EU member countries were not so foolish as to cripple their own industries.

Vehicle production

We were the HQ for seven main car manufacturers, eight luxury car manufacturers, seven Formula One teams, six design studios, 13 R&D centres and more than 100 specialist brands. We produced 1.8 million vehicles a year.

Before the referendum Nissan had threatened to leave Britain if we voted to leave the EU. Previously, it had threatened to leave Britain if we did not join the euro. But it did not leave. After the referendum, Nissan confirmed that it would build both the new Qashqai and the X-Trail SUV at its plant in Sunderland. This plant produced more than half a million cars a year – more than Italy's entire production in 2012. Nissan employed nearly 7,000 people in Sunderland, with a further 20,000 in the supply chain.

And in September 2017 Nissan said that it wanted to boost that production by 20 per cent, according to the authoritative Japan-based *Nikkei Asian Review*. It also said that it wanted to double the proportion of parts for its plant sourced in Britain from 40 per cent to around 80 per cent and that it would encourage parts manufacturers to site their own plants in nearby industrial parks. The *Guardian*, the *Independent* and the BBC's online news all failed to report this. The *Daily Mirror* made an uninformative reference in an article headlined 'Theresa May's futile Japan jaunt', saying that Nissan had reaffirmed its commitment to Britain and would use more British firms in its supply chain, but gave no details.

Jaguar Land Rover invested £12 billion in facilities and R&D between 2012 and 2017. It became our biggest car maker in 2015 and produced 544,401 vehicles in 2016, helping the industry to a 17-year production high. The greatest part of production was sold overseas, making it one of our largest goods exporters. Its chief executive pledged that JLR's design and technical development would continue to be based here. JLR planned to hire an extra 5,000 engineers and technical staff in 2018 for its factories in Castle Bromwich, Halewood and Solihull, increasing its workforce here by almost 15 per cent to 42,000.

German engineering giant Siemens also promised more investment in Brexit Britain. Siemens employed 14,000 people in Britain in high-skilled jobs including MRI scanners, transport signals, wind power, turbo machinery and health care diagnostics. CEO Joe Kaeser said: "We're here for the long-term and we don't let ourselves get jerked up and down. We're staying because the UK is a good place to do business. … We never said the UK is in bad shape if it leaves the EU." Siemens aimed to open a £27 million 3D-printing factory in Worcester, creating 50 skilled jobs. It said that the manufacturing facility would make metal parts for customers such as Rolls-Royce and British Aerospace as well as for its own factories and would aim to recruit engineers from the nearby universities of Birmingham and Warwick.

Today we are seeing the renaissance of the West Midlands, with more jobs being created than in any other region, a trade surplus with China, and businesses like HSBC UK choosing to relocate to the region. However, air pollution in the region causes 1,600 premature deaths every year and some roads have higher pollution levels than the insides of bus depots. Birmingham City Council has proposed a Clean Air Zone for the city. Some people have proposed an urban National Park around the Tame Valley in Birmingham and an urban green space like the New York Highline.

The region's manufacturers are already addressing the air quality problem. The latest diesel engine technology is the cleanest yet and is constantly improving. NOx and particulate emissions from JLR diesels are comparable to petrol, with 20 per cent lower CO_2 emissions.

Electric vehicles are the future, and the region's automotive companies have made plans. Geely has invested £300 million in building the new electric London taxi and electric vans in Coventry, GKN is investing tens of millions in developing eAxle systems, and JLR is spending hundreds of millions more on its Solihull plant to prepare it for the electric vehicle revolution. The government has supported these developments, funding the new Faraday Battery Institution at Warwick University to research electric battery storage technology.

The Local Industrial Strategy in the West Midlands is designed to grow this sector, where the region already has a world-class competitive advantage. New clean vehicles and components will be exported around the world, supporting thousands of jobs and keeping British engineering at the forefront of automotive manufacturing. We need a thought-through plan which gives our manufacturers the time to develop these new technologies and bring them into production.

Transport

Planning was indispensable for an integrated transport policy. Birmingham, for example, still needs an extensive well-integrated public transport network. Progress is happening – the building of HS2 and of new rail stations, improvements in the region's train services, the creation of new rapid bus routes with newer cleaner buses, and the extension of the Metro system across the region, creating a 'Crossrail for the West Midlands'. These infrastructure projects are on a scale which has not been seen in the region since the nineteenth century.

We needed to get more freight on the railways and get lorries off the roads. The great British train robbery of privatisation transferred billions of pounds to private rail operators and shareholders. Fares were the highest in the world.

Europe's sane, cheap travel was under threat from the EU's privatisation of European rail. The EU's Fourth Railway Package required market access to all passenger rail across the continent by 2019. It aimed to open the whole EU railway system to competition. Under EU rules, public rail companies must, like other public companies, operate under the same market rules as their private competitors. The EU was taking the worst model in the EU, the British, and imposing it on the best. As Mick Cash, the Rail Maritime and Transport union's General Secretary, said, "It would be ludicrous for a union like ours to support staying in a bosses' club that seeks to ban the public ownership of our railways, and attacks the shipping and offshore sectors."

We needed to expand airport capacity in London, Birmingham and new airports outside the south-east. International agreements allowed countries to be part of the Single Sky Agreement without being a member of the EU. Existing protocols for aircraft landing rights extended to many non-EU countries and were nothing to do with the EU. Freedoms of the air were not guaranteed by the EU but by a multilateral international treaty, the International Air Services Transit Agreement, signed from 1944 onwards by 133 countries. Norwegian and Swiss airlines, for example, had full access to the rest of Europe's aviation market - a status we could easily adopt. Yet in July 2017 the BBC's *Newsnight* seriously asked, 'Will Britain's planes fly after Brexit?'

Britain's space sector has been growing much faster than the overall British economy in recent years. In 2014/15 it was worth £13.7 billion and employed more than 35,000 people. More than three-quarters of Britain's space spending went to the 22-nation European Space Agency, which was not an EU body. Its Director-General Johann-Dietrich Woerner said that Brexit should have little or no impact on its programmes.

Energy

British enterprises will need to be more productive when we leave the EU and lower energy costs will be crucial. Key to achieving this will be secure and stable electricity supplies. A dash to become more reliant on imports was not the answer. Democratic national planning was indispensable for a rational energy policy. Professional bodies and trade unions needed to press for energy security, energy independence.

Aileen McHarg, Professor of Public Law at the University of Strathclyde, observed that Brexit "could also relate to the structure of the energy industries, for example, allowing more direct governmental involvement in energy decision-making, a stronger emphasis on energy planning rather than market-driven investment, a reintegration of energy networks with producers and suppliers, or restrictions on foreign ownership."[276]

EU Directives have forced us to close a third of our electricity generation capacity (coal and oil plants) in the years 2010-16. The Large Combustion Plants Directives of 1998 and 2001 were mainly responsible for closing many coal-fired electricity plants. The European Court forced us to quadruple the tax on installing energy-saving materials, such as solar panels and wind turbines.

We wasted hundreds of millions of pounds subsidising power stations to burn American wood pellets that did more harm to the environment by producing more greenhouse gases than the much cheaper coal they replaced. Britain was by far the biggest importer of wood pellets for heat and power in the EU, shipping in 7.5 million tonnes in 2016, mostly from the USA and Canada.

Britain's rising electricity imports were, in the short term, an easy way out for failed energy policies stretching back over a generation. Back in 2012, the Coalition government estimated that Britain would need 26GW of additional gas generation capacity by 2030 to plug any potential gap left by cloudy, windless days and to replace the output from closing coal, oil-fired and nuclear plants. On current trends, however, the UK was on track to build just 12GW of gas plants by 2030.

EU regulations have turned our productive, relatively cheap electricity industry, into a dearer one. EU energy policy forced us into more import dependence through interconnectors to the continent where before we were self-sufficient. Britain's interconnector imports from Europe increased by 52 per cent in the three years to 2016 and they will surge as new interconnectors are planned. In 2012, imports were expected to account for just 6 terawatt hours (TWh) of supply per year by 2030. But the 2016 forecast was that our electricity imports would rise from 21TWh to 77TWh in 2025, about a fifth of supply.

In the EU we could not stop the EU overcharging us for energy, because we had no sovereignty, no power to decide our own policies. Our energy costs were far higher than in other EU countries and higher than in our competitors. EU energy policy cost us £12 billion a year. A medium-sized business in Britain paid twice as much for its energy as a US one did. EU energy policy added £59 to household bills and £130,000 to medium-sized businesses' bills.

We needed our own nuclear industry. As energy expert Daniel Yergin wrote, "In a carbon-conscious world, nuclear power's great advantages are not only the traditional ones of fuel diversification and self-sufficiency. It is also the only large-scale, well-established, broadly deployable source of electric generation currently available that is carbon free."[277]

Privatisation fragmented nuclear R&D so there were few national bodies around which the supply companies could invest confidently for the long-term. Despite being the first country safely to develop a nuclear power plant, we did not have any domestic reactor design vendor. Foreign companies owned most nuclear power stations in Britain.

Cutting pollution

Diesel cars were far more polluting than petrol-driven ones, yet for 20 years the EU and successive British governments gave us incentives to buy them, because they emitted less carbon dioxide. As a result, diesel cars grew from just 7.4 per cent of Britain's car fleet in 2004 to a third – and half of new registrations. Three quarters of the ten million diesel cars sold worldwide each year were bought in Europe.

For years Volkswagen systematically and massively violated the legal limits on nitrogen dioxide by using default devices – algorithms that gamed the testing system. So, 600,000 American vehicles and 11 million European vehicles emitted nine times the allowable amount of the deadly gas. Volkswagen claimed that there were 'no fatalities involved', but the excess pollution emitted by their cars surely killed people. Nitrogen dioxide was estimated to kill some 23,500 people in Britain alone every year.

In October 2015 the EU voted against new tests that would have stopped car firms doctoring their emission results. The European Commission refused to act.[278] It then agreed with Volkswagen that it could exceed legal limits by 110 per cent until 2020. After that, the Commission will let Volkswagen exceed the legal limit by 50 per cent, indefinitely. In February 2016, the Cameron government backed these new EU rules.

Daniel Calleja, at the time director-general at the European Commission's internal market and industry department, wrote on 16 June 2015, "For the particular aspect of NOx emissions of diesel vehicles the European emission legislation therefore must be considered as an almost complete failure until now." This scandal showed how little the EU really protected our environment, consumer rights and public health. So did its public statement that its green targets were not binding. This helped to explain why air quality in Europe has not improved over the past fifteen years.[279]

Jeremy Corbyn claimed that the EU protected our environment and protected consumers. But the EU failed to protect us from the effects of Volkswagen's criminal behaviour. Harvard Professor John Gillingham summed up, "The motor industry is joined at the hip with its purported regulator, the EU. Caught red-handed by US authorities for engaging in activities detrimental to the health and welfare of the European public – the spewing of noxious fumes from more than 11 million automobiles over a period of many years – the Commission (amidst professions of concern and with deeply furrowed brows) punted and did its best to evade responsibility. Unlike the US Environmental Protection Agency, it did next to nothing to curtail the foul and illegal practice making exhaust pollution hazardous – let alone punish the malefactors. Nor, to its shame, did the self-anointed conscience of eco-Europe, the so-called European Parliament based in Strasbourg; it also caved in before the vehicle manufacturers."[280]

Some claimed that the EU had many years ago cleared up London's pea-soupers. We passed the Clean Air Act in 1956, which did the job years before we joined the EEC. Professor McHarg pointed out, "The majority of relevant EU environmental measures are already implemented in domestic laws and will therefore be unaffected by Brexit."[281]

When we leave the EU, we can continue to cooperate on environmental matters via the UN Environment Programme, the Kyoto Protocol and the UN Framework Convention on Climate Change. We will still be bound to the obligations of the 2015 UN Paris Agreement to 'strengthen the global response to the threat of climate change'. This is a treaty, a legally-binding framework for an internationally coordinated effort to tackle climate change.

The NHS

The Blair government invited US corporations in to run parts of our NHS. It introduced the disastrous Private Finance Initiative. It let the EU push the notorious Bolkestein Directive which sought 'liberalisation and deregulation of all service activity in Europe'.

The European Central Bank said in 2003, "A comprehensive institutional framework has been set up at the European level to coordinate and monitor ageing-related policies. ... This framework should be implemented in full to support governments in adopting appropriate policies at the national level."[282] It told us what health policies to implement: "Reforms should place both public pension systems and health and longterm care arrangements on a sustainable financial footing by limiting the public sector's exposure, enhancing private funding and setting incentives for efficient service provision."

It demanded the 'promotion of long-term contracts between providers of health services and the cost-covering institutions'. It said, "market forces can help to move towards efficient solutions." It demanded that public health systems 'focus on providing core services'. It called for governments to distinguish between 'essential, privately non-insurable and non-affordable services' and those where 'private financing might be more efficient'. This would limit free health care to accident and emergency care. It urged, "Greater private involvement in healthcare financing can be achieved, in particular, through patient co-payments, as already implemented in a number of countries." It told us to 'raise contribution rates, streamline services and secure private financing and funding'.

In 2005, the European Court of Justice ruled that health care provision was subject to EU market rules, and therefore to competition, regardless of national policy. This opened our NHS up to the privateers.

Europe's commissioner for health, Vytenis Andriukaitis, wanted a bigger role for the EU in health policy. He told a conference in Riga in June 2015: "I believe it will be nice to discuss the possibility to change the European Union treaties in the future." Andriukaitis added: "I think it will be very timely to raise questions" with the European Parliament and the EU Council. "Believe me, I can't imagine a more economically effective possibility than to manage health issues at EU level."

On the contrary, we needed to manage our NHS at national level and to stop the fragmentation and privatisation of health care. We needed proper planning of our NHS, especially of its staffing.

The NHS Sustainability Committee carried out a 9-month investigation into the future of the NHS between July 2016 and April 2017. It heard testimony from dozens of NHS witnesses, and received thousands of pages of written evidence. Their report came to the conclusion that "workforce strategy has been poor with too much reliance on overseas recruitment. … the Government should go to greater lengths to secure a reliable supply of well-trained professionals and other health and social care workers from within this country."

It quoted Ian Cumming, the Chief Executive of Health Education England, on the morality of relying on other countries – many poorer than ours – for healthcare workers: "We believe that, as the fifth-largest economy in the world, we have a moral duty to produce the healthcare workforce that we require for our National Health Service, and we should not be reliant on recruiting from other countries."

In December 2014 it was reported that 97,910 doctors registered with the General Medical Council (GMC) had received their primary medical qualification outside UK organisations – 37 per cent of the total. 29,010 had qualified in European countries. Ten per cent of nurses and midwives were educated abroad.

For example, the NHS employed 211 Malawian staff, 20 of whom were doctors. Yet Malawi, with a population of 17.2 million, had only 618 doctors. The number of doctors in Romanian hospitals fell from 21,400 in 2011 to 14,400 in 2013. The General Medical Council found that 2,140 doctors who qualified in Romania held positions in the UK. Romania spent £2.9 billion educating doctors, but other, richer countries got the benefit. The EU's attacks on Greece's health care system made 7,500 Greek doctors emigrate, many to EU member countries. Stiglitz observed, "Thus Germany and other European countries get improved health services, while the Greeks suffer from poorer access to doctors – after having invested millions of euros in their education."[283]

The NHS spent £2.5 billion a year on locum doctors and agency nurses. This spending exhausted financial resources that could have been better used educating and employing full-time staff. Instead, Osborne's tuition fees caused a drop in student nurses of a fifth. By 2018 we were still educating fewer doctors per head than Ireland or the Netherlands.

Since 2000, we have increased the number of nursing graduates by 50 per cent. We have doubled the number of places in medical schools since the late 1990s. But still, hundreds of eligible British students were turned down at over-subscribed UK medical schools. By reversing the public spending cuts in medical education, we could educate enough doctors and nurses to meet our needs, so we would not need to take from poorer countries their expensively-educated health care workers.

Addressing the BMA's staff, associate specialist, and specialty doctors' conference in 2016, the chair of the GMC Terence Stephenson said he was concerned that we chose "to remain so dependent on doctors from overseas... Not just from former Commonwealth countries but also from the European Union...I think we should become self-sufficient."

The interim chief executive of the International Council of Nurses, Professor Thomas Kearns, agreed that developed countries should not rely on overseas staff. He urged western nations not to 'destroy' the health systems of developing countries by draining them of nurses to address their own staffing problems. He said: "Nurses have always travelled to seek experience in other countries. However, there does need to be an ethical approach when countries plan their workforce. It makes very little sense to destroy or damage the health service in one jurisdiction, just to support our own." He also pointed out that health care organisations had spent too much time looking at recruitment in isolation, when effective workforce planning needed a focus on retention of staff too. It is not ethical for countries to try to grab the brains of the world.

Kearns noted the World Health Organization's estimate of a 12.9 million global shortage of healthcare workers by 2035 and said that every country had a responsibility to train and retain its own workforce. His message was also a timely reminder to Britain's health care unions to fight for pay and conditions – which were the key to retaining NHS staff.

In June 2018 the government announced an extra £384 million a week for the NHS in real terms over the next five years. The figure topped the £350 million a week that Vote Leave suggested we stop sending each week to Brussels and spend instead on our priorities. The money will largely come from the money that we will no longer be paying to the EU. It is a bigger increase than Labour promised at the 2017 election.

Research and higher education

One important gain from leaving the EU was escaping the EU's inhibiting approach to scientific experiment, which cramped our ability to be innovative and to benefit from the coming fourth industrial revolution. The House of Commons Science and Technology Committee found that, "At least part of the decline in UK trial activity is the result of the Clinical Trials Directive (CTD), which, since its adoption in 2001, has imposed a significant burden on anyone wanting to conduct a clinical trial within the European Union. Both Cancer Research UK and the Association of Medical Research Charities told us that it was 'widely' acknowledged that the CTD had 'contributed to the general trend of decreasing numbers of clinical trials in Europe' while failing to deliver significant benefits to patients."[284]

The EU did not allow genetically modified (GM) foods. President Juncker sacked the European Commission's chief scientific adviser for disputing the case against genetically modified organisms (GMOs). But almost all animal feed was GM because there was not enough non-GM feed in the world, and we cheerfully consumed these animals, with no ill effects.

Some raised concerns about chlorinated chicken. Chlorinating chicken helped to stop life-threatening human illness from salmonella and campylobacter. Every day we all consumed chlorine in our tea and coffee, from our tap-water, again chlorinated for safety. All our bagged salads were washed in chlorinated water and so were many of our vegetables, again with no ill effects.

Professor Gillingham commented, "Apart from the fact that they are chemically identical to the natural product, cheaper to raise, environmentally friendly, and medically harmless, public fears, easily fanned, of ingesting an unfamiliar product resulted in a ban. The GMO ban retarded the development of the European biotech industry generally, which, after promising beginnings, soon fell hopelessly behind its US counterpart."[285]

EU-backed information and communication technology projects all failed. IT companies like Nixdorf, ICL, Bull and Olivetti have all gone, despite support from the EU. Gillingham pointed out that the development of fifth generation (5G) telecoms technology and the arrival of the 'internet of things' promised vast productivity gains. But the EU stood in the way of the companies driving this change. Gillingham called the EU's stance 'guerrilla warfare', which was 'futile as well as self-defeating. It can only accelerate the rate of European decline.'[286]

The physicist Andre Geim, who won the Nobel prize for his work on graphene, said of the EU's science funding system, "I can offer no nice words for the EU framework programmes which ... can be praised only by Europhobes for discrediting the whole idea of an effectively working Europe."[287] Unite the Union urged, "Scientific research with direct application to manufacturing, such as graphene, must be supported through investment and must be at the heart of a new integrated, long-term industrial strategy."[288]

Many in research claimed that we got more research funds from the European Commission than other members did. But between 2000 and 2014 Belgium and Spain received the most funds per researcher. We came eighth. EU funds to British researchers those years averaged just 5.44 per cent of all our R&D spending.

Some claimed that leaving the EU would end all cooperation with Europe's educational institutions. This was not so. Erasmus, for example, involved 927 institutions in 37 countries, not just the EU's 27 members. In May 2018 the EU confirmed that the Erasmus+ programme would be opened to every country in the world. Non-EU Norway, Canada and Israel participated in Horizon 2020, the EU's main research programme, and it operated in more than 100 other states. The May government committed to underwrite any funding from Horizon 2020 for contracts awarded before Brexit to enable cross-border collaborations to continue unimpeded.

In June 2018 the EU agreed that we could participate in Horizon Europe, the EU's next R&D programme, which will run from 2021 to 2028. This will spend nearly 100 billion euros. Robert Lechler, president of the Academy of Medical Sciences, said, "I am delighted to see proposals to increase the budget for the programme and that the draft terms will enable third countries to fully participate in the programme." But there was a catch (there's always a catch). In research and development (as in so many other things) the EU wanted to have its cake and eat it. With researchers in the EU desperate to retain funding that will enable them to work with British researchers, the European Commission is saying it wants Britain to be part of Horizon Europe. But unfortunately and unsurprisingly, it is more than vague about how that would happen.

On 7 June the EU Commission put out a document on third-country access to Horizon Europe that appeared to open the door to Britain. EU Research Commissioner Carlos Moedas said the legal text behind the programme had been written "in a way so that we can include UK in the future as a third country. The doors are open for discussion. We didn't want to be that specific." Earlier in the week Budget Commissioner Günther Oettinger had been similarly encouraging – at first. Asked at a conference in Brussels about British participation in Horizon Europe he said, "We should be pragmatic and flexible to come to a solution on research."

So far, so good. But then he added, "...the UK should accept some of our fundamental rules and values." That's Brussels-speak for the free movement of labour. Pushed to be more specific, Oettinger made it clear that he was talking about Britain accepting free movement full stop – not exemptions for researchers. The proposals – still only proposals as they have to be accepted by EU member states – include a provision that would prevent third countries such as Britain taking out more money than they put in. And that would hardly make it worthwhile for Britain.

If the British government made the funds available directly, that would be easier to administer, and more importantly this would ensure the money is used to fund research that Britain wants. Under the existing seven-year programme, Horizon 2020, British scientists have been receiving about twice as much in grant funds as Britain puts in. That is because British science is so good, and because all Horizon 2020 funding is determined by the excellence of the proposal.

That has brought a flood of money into British universities, but the funding has not been cost-free to the British taxpayer, as every pound received by researchers reduced the British rebate from the EU by 66 pence. Instead of going begging to Brussels, the government should turn the tables and say to Brussels, "If you want to benefit from working with British research, what are you prepared to pay for it?"

The Times' Higher Education World University Rankings published in September 2017 put Oxford and Cambridge first and second. It found that seven of the top eleven universities in Europe were in the UK, with two more in non-EU Switzerland and only two, Germany's LMU Munich and Sweden's Karolinska Institute, in EU member countries. Britain accounted for 15.9 per cent of the world's most highly cited articles, despite having only 0.9 per cent of world population and 4.1 per cent of researchers. So, students and staff from EU member countries will still want to study and work in our universities.

The Department of Business, Innovation and Skills (BIS) invested £5.8 billion in UK science and research in the financial year 2015/16. By contrast, the European Research Council (ERC), the organisation that funded projects carried out through EU science networks, had a budget for 2016 of just £1.3 billion to fund all the 28 EU countries and the 13 non-EU countries that participated in its programmes.

In 2017 the government pledged £23 billion over the next five years to a new National Productivity Investment Fund, £2.3 billion for a Housing Infrastructure Fund, and £1.4 billion for affordable housing. The £23 billion will be spent on areas such as hi-tech research, funded by extra borrowing. A Treasury spokesman, lifting a phrase more commonly used by Labour, said this was 'borrowing to invest'. In the year after the referendum, investment in the tech sector was more than double that of our nearest rival Germany, at £2.4 billion.[289]

In its November 2016 submission to the House of Commons education select committee, Universities UK said,

"Universities UK (UUK) believes that, with the right support and investment from government - both now and in the future - universities can thrive outside the European Union. UUK welcomes the statements made thus far by Government on research, structural funding and EU students starting in 2016/17 and 2017/18."

It continued, "Our universities are a British success story, world-renowned, internationally competitive and a major economic asset, generating annual output of £73 billion for the British economy. Universities can play a central role in driving inclusive economic growth locally, regionally and nationally; improving productivity as part of a new industrial strategy; and strengthening our international trade and diplomatic relationships across Europe and the wider world. ...

"This paper includes a number of high impact policies and initiatives that Government could deliver to ensure that universities are best placed to maximise the UK's economic success and global influence outside of the EU in five areas:

☐ Encouraging students from around the world to choose to study in the UK

☐ Enhancing international research collaboration

☐ Making the UK an attractive destination for talented university staff

☐ Increasing public investment in research and innovation

☐ Supporting UK students and staff to access vital global opportunities."

Countries with systems of managed immigration, like Canada and Australia, were just as active as we were in scientific collaboration, recruiting a higher percentage of overseas researchers than we did within the EU. But it should be noted that the increased supply of lecturers from overseas was one of the factors that explained the lack of any pay increase for lecturers since 2004.

In 2018 University and College Union members across Britain acted in defence of their pensions, forcing Universities UK to agree that the pension scheme should continue with a future guaranteed pension promise. But this left open the question of whether the value of the current pension guarantee would continue to accrue for future pensionable service or be diluted. UUK proposed an 'independent pension panel' to review how the scheme's pension fund deficit had been arrived at. That deficit had fluctuated over time from £12 billion to £6.1 billion.

In 2000 the EU had introduced a market-related pension valuation method that had to be used in all occupational pensions. This method was rigged to show a deficit so huge that people gave up on a meaningful pension guarantee. The employers' attacks on pensions were coordinated through the EU's European Insurance and Occupational Pensions Authority. The EU should take its hands off the universities pension scheme. The pension panel needed to adopt a new method of valuing salary-linked pension guarantees, independent of the EU model.

The countryside and the Common Agricultural Policy (CAP)

The House of Commons Library concluded that the EU's CAP 'artificially inflates food prices'. Prices to EU consumers were on average 6 per cent higher than world prices. In some important products, the figure was far higher (e.g. beef and veal prices were 31 per cent higher).[290] The OECD estimated that EU agricultural tariffs cost EU consumers 10.7 billion euros in 2011.

The EU paid landowners and farmers £2.9 billion a year. 60 per cent of the money that came into the UK from the CAP went to the richest estates and farmers. Radomir Tylecote and William Cash concluded that the CAP "creates huge fraud and dumping that cannot be compensated by aid, and like the Common Fisheries Policy it creates poverty, hunger and immigration into Europe by people trying to escape its effects. The only people who benefit are the big farmers who have been turned into benefit-businesses."[291]

Outside the EU, we could support farmers in both the short term (as they adjusted to new competition) and in the long term (as we protected our environment), thereby doing better than under the CAP. The 1947 Agricultural Act had guaranteed prices for key agricultural products, which protected farmers and their workers from the ups and downs of the market. We should grow more of our own food and reduce our food import bills.

In 1995, the Royal Society for the Protection of Birds called the CAP 'the engine of destruction in the countryside'.[292] By contrast, the EU's respected Birds and Habitats Directives were largely based on our long-established laws on protected areas.

On animal welfare, we had stricter requirements than EU member states. The EU protocol on animals being sentient beings allowed bullfighting, veal farming, foie gras 'production', live exports for slaughter and cruel fur product imports. In 1992 the Conservative government sought to restrict the trade in live exports and refused licences to export sheep to Spain. The ECJ overturned this decision saying that it was contrary to EU rules on free movement of goods. Spain allowed calves to be reared in barren conditions without bedding. This was illegal in the UK where we applied tougher rules than the EU minimum. When we leave the EU, we will be able to end EU laws that allow the transfer of whale products through our ports and EU laws that allow the export of live animals across the Channel for slaughter.

The CAP is not only bad for Britain's farmers. It is also bad for the world's poorest countries.[293] The CAP, by dumping heavily-subsidised food onto Africa's desperately poor countries has destroyed Africa's ability to feed itself. The EU's Economic Partnership Agreements (EPAs) exposed African, Caribbean and Pacific countries to overwhelming competition from the world's most powerful companies. The Kenyan Institute of Economic Affairs noted the damaging effect of trade liberalisation on the East African Community member countries Kenya, Burundi, Rwanda, Tanzania, Uganda and South Sudan, especially on their manufacturing industries.

The EU imposed the world's biggest trade tariffs, of up to 183 per cent, on African farmers. These tariffs made food from Africa more expensive, so we could not buy food as cheaply as we could if we were outside the EU. The EU forced Europe's farmers to dump their excess farm produce on African markets. African countries' access to EU markets was conditional on no government support for local firms, opening public services to privatisation, free movement of capital and opening their resources to outside investors. For example, in 2014 the whole of Africa made nearly $2.4 billion from coffee exports, almost all raw beans. Yet Germany made $3.8 billion from coffee, without growing a single bean. Germany's coffee producers needed cheap, raw beans to make money, so there was no import tariff on these. But Germany imposed import tariffs on processed coffee because Germany made its money in the processing, branding, packaging and marketing.

Giles Merritt wrote, "Europe's farm support measures have, like those of the US, long had the effect of dumping subsidized EU food exports on African markets at artificially low prices with which Africa's smallholders could not compete. Of late, though, Europe has in the eyes of Africans, compounded this effect with new trade policies. The deadlock over the Doha Development Rounds – the World Trade Organization's unsuccessful multilateral trade liberalization negotiations – has produced a flurry of bilateral or regional deals that are imposing new burdens on African farmers.

"The EU, as the world's largest and most powerful trading bloc, has been in the forefront; it has negotiated what it calls Economic Partnership Agreements (EPA) to replace the non-reciprocal deals under which some categories of African commodities had preferential access to EU markets. Africans are instead being asked to end tariffs on at least eighty percent of their imports from the EU, but without compensating concessions from Europe."[294]

As Stiglitz pointed out, the EU, just like the USA 'reneged on their promise to reform trade rules to help the less developed countries grow ...'[295] So, "European and U.S. agricultural policies – maintaining massive subsidies in spite of all the free-market rhetoric – were depressing global agricultural prices, and from this the poorest people in the poorest countries, the farmers in sub-Saharan Africa, suffered enormously."[296]This resulted in "impoverishing millions in Sub-Saharan Africa and India."[297]

African trade unionists opposed the European Commission's attempts to impose a free trade deal on Africa. ITUC–Africa general secretary Kwasi Adu-Amankwah said that the proposed EPAs would allow European big business to continue to exploit the continent. He said that the colonial economic structure set up to export raw materials and import manufactures still existed and he called on Africa to reject 'the latest scramble' by European powers. As he noted, "Structural Adjustment foisted on Africa with the active involvement of the European Union has killed off the little industrial capabilities countries mastered immediately after independence."

He warned that the terms of the agreements would only make it harder for Africa to achieve the UN's 2030 Sustainable Development Goals. He pointed out, "As the tariffs came down on African raw materials, they went up for manufactures. It is highly disingenuous to conceive of a free trade between the poorest continent on earth and the world's most powerful trading bloc as the solution."

Some claimed that the EU was internationalist. But as far back as 1970, Action for World Development (founded by Oxfam and Christian Aid) published *The White Tribes of Europe* which concluded that "the present policies of the EEC are largely indifferent to the problems of world poverty and world development." In 1975 Labour MP Barbara Castle opposed Common Market membership because the EEC operated at the expense of the global poor. She lamented, "the largest and poorest countries ... are left out of this circle of privilege because their membership will not suit the trading interests of the European bloc ... This isn't the language of internationalism ... It is euro-jingoism."

The badly mis-named Department for International Development (DfID) promoted little real development away from over-reliance on primary agriculture and mineral extraction towards manufacturing and services. All developed countries reduced their poverty by raising incomes with higher-wage jobs in manufacturing and services. But by promoting premature trade liberalisation, deregulation and privatisation, and by joining the IMF, the World Bank and the WTO in outlawing key industrial policies, DfID's so-called 'aid' has held back developing countries from building their own manufacturing sectors. If DfID wanted to help to develop countries, it would be helping those like Tanzania and Nigeria, which, despite their faults, were trying to implement ambitious new industrialisation strategies. Both countries have rejected signing on to the EU's EPAs because the EPAs' rules block them from industrialising.

Former Labour minister Chris Mullin has said the EU's "aid programme is a disaster area. Most of it goes either to the undeserving or the not very deserving and takes forever to get there." Former international development secretary Clare Short argued that the European Commission ran 'the worst development agency in the world' and branded its operations 'an outrage and a disgrace'.

The EU's farm protection subsidies have penalised Africa's farmers, causing poverty and despair. EU trawlers hoovered up Africa's fish. The result of all these EU policies? Poverty, famine, disease, war, and mass migration. Outside the EU, we can remove barriers to farm and industrial exports from Africa and reach better trade agreements with Africa's countries.

The sea and fishing

Charles Clover, author of the excellent book on over-fishing 'The end of the line', wrote, "if there were a prize for the most disgraceful country or group of countries on Earth for pillaging the sea, the European Union would be the most favoured recipient."[298]

In 1995, 9,200 British fishing vessels landed 912,000 tons of fish; by 2016 just 4,607 vessels landed 683,000 tons, with a value of £920 million. Our imports reached 680,800 tonnes of fish and 92,500 tonnes of fish products, total value £2.784 billion, of which just under a third came from our EU neighbours. About 55 per cent of the total EU catch came from British waters, so we were buying back our own fish from our competitors.

The annual British fish catch was about 12 per cent of the total EU catch. When we reserve our waters for British fishermen, as was perfectly legal under the UN Law of the Sea, they would be able to land nearly £4.5 billion worth of fish.

The government has pledged to withdraw from the London Fisheries Convention. This will restore the entire Exclusive Economic Zone to which we were entitled under UN law. This will be welcomed by fishermen around the country, who have always overwhelmingly opposed the EU's Common Fisheries Policy.

By contrast, the SNP's wish for a separate Scotland to rejoin the EU would keep the fishing industry inside the CFP. Karmenu Vella, the European Commissioner for fisheries, confirmed that a new EU member state could not opt out of the CFP.

The Common Fisheries Policy's quota system for fishermen required that any catch made above the quotas assigned per species had to be discarded (usually dead) into the sea. This was a disaster. It is now enforcing a discard ban to which all our fishermen would be subject if we accept the EU's transition period. Suppose a fisherman has quotas for haddock, cod, hake and herring. As soon as he has caught his quota for *any one of these four*, he must return to port. So he is not allowed to catch his other quotas and will therefore make a huge loss on his trip. This is ruinous for the fisherman's business. Few of our fishermen could survive even a year of this policy, let alone the whole two-year transition period. The government has stated that this will bankrupt 60 per cent of the UK fishing fleet. So why is the government accepting the EU's transition period?

Fishing for Leave has produced a plan for fishing post-Brexit. [299] Vessels would be given a set number of non-transferable days at sea measured in hours per year. This provides forward planning and business stability by allowing fishermen to produce an annual business plan and would negate any 'race to fish'.

This days-at-sea system will produce a huge improvement in fisheries management. This will improve sustainability by working with the ecology of the UK's demersal mixed fisheries rather than trying to impose a rigid, ill-fitting system upon them. It encourages the adoption of a Conservation Credit system which would award extra time for species avoidance and selectivity measures. It will eliminate discards by removing the cause of discards. No fisherman wants to discard marketable fish - a time limit encourages retention of all catch. It will also improve safety. Vessels will be able to fish at the best times. The necessity to discard increased time at sea, crew fatigue and weather conditions worked.

It allows the UK a clean break from an EU quota system and relative stability shares with no recourse under international treaty law or human rights for the EU to claim current share outs. All future entitlements to the nation's fishing resources would remain with the nation. This avoids repetition of the quota trade. Fishing entitlements being only granted to active fishing vessel eliminates 'slipper skipper' quota traders and returns all fish entitlements to actual fishermen in the catching sector. Ending quota purchase/rent will release capital for investment.

The government's 2018 White Paper said, "Any decisions about giving access to UK waters for vessels from the EU, or any other coastal states will be a matter for negotiation." What was there to negotiate? If we are sovereign over our waters, we decide.

Britain leads in designating and managing Marine Protected Areas, with 23 per cent of UK waters protected, more than twice the UN's global target.

The government has announced its ambitions to double the fleet flying the Red Ensign flag, double the number of people taking maritime apprenticeships, and launch a new era of British ship building as part of a National Ship Building Strategy.

Planning for freedom

Nautilus International, the trade union representing maritime professionals, saw our vote to leave the EU as a unique opportunity to set ambitious goals for the future of the country's maritime industries.

Nautilus put forward ten aims:

1. Secure 100% financial support for the cost of training UK-resident seafarers to avoid a serious skills shortage within the next decade. The government support for the training of UK seafarers must be dramatically increased if the nation is to avoid a serious maritime skills shortage within the next decade. The real-terms value of the Support for Maritime Training scheme (SMarT) means that it now covers only around 36% of the costs of training, making the UK the second most expensive country in which to train officers. ... The average age of a UK seafarer is 58. Nearly 50% are over 50 and due to retire in the next 15 years. ...

Without a strong UK shipping industry and a healthy number of seafarers, the nation becomes dangerously dependent on the fleets of other nations for the supply of 90% of everything, including food, oil and gas for heating, and building materials. Those countries would then have the power to hold us to ransom by controlling the volume and price of goods entering or leaving UK ports through the manipulation of shipping rates or ocean carrier services, a hostile strategy known as 'sea strangulation'.

2. Review shipowner tax relief schemes (Tonnage Tax) so the UK remains attractive to owners whilst promoting the training and employment of UK-resident seafarers. ... more work has to be done, not only to incentivise companies to train more cadets but also to get them to commit to giving newly-qualified officers their first job, ensuring the government sees a return on its investment. ...

3. Maximise the employment of British seafarers in the UK, especially in: coastal shipping, passenger and freight ferry services, offshore windfarms, offshore oil and gas exploration and decommissioning ... The government must ensure these opportunities are used for the employment of British seafarers and not sold off to the lowest bidder. Local job content must be prioritised both ashore and afloat. ...

4. Develop a national maritime strategy with support from trade unions, government and industry. ... there are good examples to follow: the Netherlands, Singapore and Denmark all have national tripartite maritime cluster organisations working together to formulate national maritime strategies.

In the Netherlands the maritime cluster includes sea ports, maritime services, shipbuilding and repair, maritime supply industry, watersports, fisheries, dredging, offshore, royal navy, shipping and inland navigation. ... As a result of Maritime by Holland, the Dutch government provides tonnage tax incentives, social security and income tax rebates, and 100% support for the training of Dutch seafarers. In return, Dutch shipowners provide every cadet with a training place onboard and job when they qualify. ...

5. Encourage investment in UK maritime education and training so it retains its world-leading status. ... British maritime education and training is currently among the best in the world, but unless substantial investment in new technology is made, this position is under threat.

... In other countries, maritime cadets can be given hours of hands-on experience on state-of-the-art maritime simulators before they step onboard. They have access to engine room simulators, full mission bridge simulators, Electronic Chart Display and Information System (ECDIS) navigation, and liquid cargo handling simulators - all as part of their continual development. ... Research into the usability of different ECDIS systems is being carried out at the ECDIS Ltd training centre, in cooperation with Bournemouth University.

6. End support for the Red Ensign Group of registers and encourage British shipowners to return to the UK Ship Register. The Red Ensign Group (REG) is a group of ship registers that adopt the Red Ensign or a defaced version. Category one registers — unlimited tonnage and type — include the UK, Isle of Man, Bermuda, British Virgin Islands, Cayman Islands and Gibraltar. ...

Bermuda, Cayman Islands and Gibraltar registers are classified as Flags of Convenience (FOCs) by the International Transport Workers' Federation and many of them have been listed on the OECD list of offshore tax havens. The existence of the REG means the UK register faces significant unfair competition from flags which it actively supports. This undermines the UK Ship Register (UKSR) and does not encourage the owners of British ships to register in the UK. ...

Rather than being encouraged to use the UKSR, British ship owners can instead choose to benefit — via the REG — from all the quality and access to services provided by the UK register, including naval and consular protection, whilst paying lower fees, incurring little or no tax and avoiding UK laws. It also means the UK is actively involved in supporting the FOC and offshore tax haven system which undermines the desire for a global level playing field. ...

7. Improve the system for issuing foreign seafarers with Certificates of Equivalent Competency to deliver more opportunities for British seafarers on UK ships. ... the drive for more home grown jobs must include a preference for more domiciled seafarers on UK-registered ships. Leaving the EU should not be an excuse for British shipping companies to start looking outside of the EU for replacements for their current UK/EU/EEA workforce. This would have the effect of driving down wages and undermining the job security of the current workforce. ...

8. Apply the National Minimum Wage (and the National Living Wage) and the Equality Act to all vessels engaged in UK waters. Seafarers are presently the only group of UK workers who are excluded from the full protection of the National Minimum Wage (NMW) and equal pay legislation.

... Shipping companies have increasingly recruited foreign crews to profit from sub-national minimum wage pay rates and this must end. The government must act swiftly to address this imbalance and ensure all employee protection legislation applies onboard all vessels engaged wholly or mainly in UK waters.

Regulatory action must be taken to stop unscrupulous ship owners exploiting foreign seafarers and discriminating against UK seafarers ... Action must be taken to prevent social dumping of low-paid European and non-EU seafarers in British waters, as this undermines the employment and training of British seafarers. ...

9. Promote the employment of UK-resident seafarers on routes between UK ports (cabotage) including the North Sea offshore sector. ... After leaving the EU, the UK will not be bound by EU policy and should therefore develop an equivalent of the US Jones Act in UK waters. The Jones Act requires that goods and passengers transported by water between US ports be done on US-made ships, which are

owned by US shipping companies, and crewed by US seafarers. ...

10. Ensure all existing health, safety, environmental and employment legislation is maintained following the UK's withdrawal from the EU. ... UK shipping needs an industrial strategy which delivers better jobs, better pay and a plan for building the future. ..."

It concluded, "Now is the time to deliver on promises made during the referendum debate and deliver Jobs, Skills and a decent Future for UK maritime professionals."

This Charter for Jobs is a model for other trade unions, for professional associations, local government bodies and companies, all of which should be drawing up their own plans for their areas of work.

[1] Cited p. 315, James T. Kloppenberg, Toward democracy: the struggle for self-rule in European and American thought, OUP USA, 2016.

[2] See Jonathan Israel, The expanding blaze: how the American revolution ignited the world 1775-1848, Princeton UP, 2017.

[3] Cited p. xviii, Sean Wilentz, The rise of American democracy: Jefferson to Lincoln, W. W. Norton & Company, 2005.

[4] Cited p. 71, Sean Wilentz, The rise of American democracy: Jefferson to Lincoln, W. W. Norton & Company, 2005.

[5] Cited p. 95, Sean Wilentz, The rise of American democracy: Jefferson to Lincoln, W. W. Norton & Company, 2005.

[6] Cited p. 336, Harry Jaffa, Crisis of the house divided: an interpretation of the issues in the Lincoln-Douglas debates, Doubleday, 1959.

[7] Harry Jaffa, Crisis of the house divided: an interpretation of the issues in the Lincoln-Douglas debates, Doubleday, 1959, p. 307.

[8] Cited p. 209, Eric Foner, The fiery trial: Abraham Lincoln and American slavery, W. W. Norton 2011.

[9] See Jesse Norman, Edmund Burke: philosopher, politician, prophet, William Collins, 2013, p. 174.

[10] Cited pp. 130-1, Britain before the Reform Act: politics and society 1815-1832, Eric J. Evans, 2nd ed, Pearson, 2008.

[11] Cited p. 87, Britain before the Reform Act: politics and society 1815-1832, Eric J. Evans, 2nd ed, Pearson, 2008.

[12] Cited p. 126, Britain before the Reform Act: politics and society 1815-1832, Eric J. Evans, 2nd ed, Pearson, 2008.

[13] Sebastian Handley, Why Britain should be independent, accessed 12 December 2017.

[14] Lawyers for Britain, 'The referendum result is binding. Invoking Article 50: the Law, the Constitution and Politics'.

[15] See A. V. Dicey, Introduction to the study of the law of the constitution, 8th revised edition, Liberty Fund Inc., 1982.

[16] *Daily Telegraph*, 27 June 2016.

[17] R. G. Collingwood, Essays in political philosophy, ed D. Boucher, Clarendon Press, 1989, p. 106.

[18] Richard Tuck, Brexit: a prize in reach for the Left, 17 July 2017.

[19] Cited p. 255, Tim Shipman, Fall-out: a year of political mayhem, William Collins, 2017.

[20] Lord Attlee, Speech in the House of Lords on the British application to join the Common Market, 8 November 1962.

[21] Lord Attlee, Speech in the House of Lords on the British application to join the Common Market, 2 August 1962.

[22] Economic and Monetary Union, Foreign Office, 9 November 1970, FCO 30/789.

23 HM Government, *The United Kingdom and the European Communities,* (White Paper, Command 4715), 1971.

24 *Stoke on Trent v. B & Q* [1990] 3 CMLR 31 at 34.

25 Cited p. 430, Anthony Seldon and Peter Snowdon, Cameron at 10: the verdict, William Collins, 2016.

26 Giles Merritt, Slippery slope: Europe's troubled future, Oxford University Press, 2016, pp. 14 and 15.

27 Giles Merritt, Slippery slope: Europe's troubled future, Oxford University Press, 2016, p. 145.

28 Giles Merritt, Slippery slope: Europe's troubled future, Oxford University Press, 2016, p. 148.

29 Cited p. 135, Tom Gallagher, Europe's path to crisis: disintegration via monetary union, Manchester University Press, 2013.

30 Giles Merritt, Slippery slope: Europe's troubled future, Oxford University Press, 2016, p. 159.

31 Chris Bickerton, The European Union: a citizen's guide, Pelican, 2016, pp. 37-8 and 41.

32 Chris Bickerton, The European Union: a citizen's guide, Pelican, 2016, p. 40.

33 See Jason Farrell and Paul Goldsmith, How to lose a referendum – the definitive story of why Britain voted for Brexit, Biteback, 2017, pp. 128-9.

34 Cited p. 279, Larry Elliott and Dan Atkinson, Europe isn't working, Yale University Press, 2016.

35 30 June 1988, cited p. 110, Radomir Tylecote and William Cash, From Brussels with love, Duckworth New Academia, 2016.

36 Cited p. 246, Michael Hudson, Killing the host: how financial parasites and debt bondage destroy the global economy, CounterPunch Books, 2015.

37 Steps towards a deeper economic integration: the Internal Market in the 21st century, 2007, pp. 32, 30 and 48.

38 Steps towards a deeper economic integration: the Internal Market in the 21st century, 2007, pp. 51-2.

39 See Robert Peston, WTF, Hodder & Stoughton, 2017, p. 41.

40 Cited p. 274, Gavin Hewitt, Lost continent: the BBC's Europe editor on Europe's darkest hour since World War Two, Hodder & Stoughton, 2013.

41 TUC, Putting Brexit to the test, November 2017, p. 7.

42 Mervyn King, The end of alchemy: money, banking and the future of the global economy, Little, Brown, 2016, p. 248.

43 See Philip B. Whyman, Mark Baimbridge and Andrew Mullen, The political economy of the European social model, Routledge, 2012, p. 321.

[44] See Larry Elliott and Dan Atkinson, Europe isn't working, Yale University Press, 2016, p. 254.

[45] State of the Union Address, 25 January 2011.

[46] John Maynard Keynes, The means to prosperity, Macmillan, 1933, p. 14.

[47] Joseph Stiglitz, The euro: and its threat to the future of Europe, Allen Lane, 2016, pp. 183, 185 and 186.

[48] Joseph E. Stiglitz, The price of inequality, Allen Lane, 2012, p. 230.

[49] See The budget of the European Union: a guide,

http://www.ifs.org.uk/uploads/publications/bns/BN181.pdf
Based on HM Treasury (2015), 'European Union Finances 2015',
https://www.gov.uk/government/uploads/system/uploads/attachment_data/file/483344/EU_finances_2015_final_web_09122015.pdf

[50] House of Commons Library Briefing Paper Number 06455, 22 September 2016, EU budget and the UK's contribution.

[51] See https://fullfact.org/europe/our-eu-membership-fee-55-million

[52] OBR, March 2016; ONS, 5 November 2015.

[53] HMRC, 16 July 2015; ONS, 5 November 2015.

[54] Test Claimants in the Franked Investment Income Group Litigation v Commissioners of Inland Revenue, Case C-362/12; Commission v United Kingdom, Case C-640/13.

[55] Cited p. 54, Paul Krugman, End this depression now! W. W. Norton & Company, 2012.

[56] Simon Lee, Boom and bust: the politics and legacy of Gordon Brown, Oneworld, 2009, pp. 245-6.

[57] Joseph Stiglitz, The euro: and its threat to the future of Europe, Allen Lane, 2016, p. 316.

[58] Robert Peston, WTF, Hodder & Stoughton, 2017, p. 84.

[59] *Financial Times*, 25 May 2016.

[60] 26 October 2016, cited p. 19, Robert Oulds, What it will look like: how leaving the EU and the single market can be made to work for Britain, The Bruges Group, 2017.

[61] *The Times*, 10 November 2014.

[62] Philip Whyman and Alina I. Petrescu, The economics of Brexit: a cost-benefit analysis of the UK's relationship with the EU, Palgrave Macmillan, 2017, p. 43.

[63] BBC, The Andrew Marr Show, 6 January 2013.

[64] HM Treasury analysis: The immediate economic impact of leaving the EU, Cm. 9292, 23 May 2016, p. 4.

[65] David Cameron and George Osborne, Brexit would put our economy in serious danger, *Daily Telegraph*, 22 May 2016.

[66] Cited p. 382, Jason Farrell and Paul Goldsmith, How to lose a referendum – the definitive story of why Britain voted for Brexit, Biteback, 2017.

[67] See Liam Halligan and Gerard Lyons, Clean Brexit: why leaving the European Union still makes sense – building a post-Brexit economy for all, Biteback, 2017, p. 19.

[68] House of Commons Library, 18 September 2013.

[69] Kamala Dawar and Sübidey Togan, Bringing EU-Turkey trade and investment relations up to date? Directorate-General For External Policies Policy Department Workshop, May 2016, p. 27.

[70] See Michael Burrage, It's quite OK to walk away: a review of the UK's Brexit options with the help of seven international databases, Civitas, April 2017, pp. x-xi.

[71] Gerry Hassan and Russell Gunson, editors, Scotland, the UK and Brexit: a guide to the future, Luath Press, 2017, p. 176.

[72] See Michael Burrage, It's quite OK to walk away: a review of the UK's Brexit options with the help of seven international databases, Civitas, April 2017, p. xiii.

[73] Cited pp. 108-9, Liam Halligan and Gerard Lyons, Clean Brexit: why leaving the European Union still makes sense – building a post-Brexit economy for all, Biteback, 2017.

[74] Courtney Goldsmith, London won't lose its status as leading finance and legal centre after Brexit, professionals say, *City A.M.*, 21 December 2016; Simeon Djankov, Why London won't lose its crown as Europe's financial capital, *CAPX*, 1 September 2016; http://capx.co/why-london-wont-lose-its-crown-as-europes-financial-capital/; Simon English, Bankers heading off to Frankfurt? It's just a fantasy, *Evening Standard*, 11 October 2016; Joshua Chaffin, London's allure for European expats survives Brexit vote, *Financial Times*, 30 November 2016, and Bernard Goyder, The big casualties of Brexit: Economic doomsayers, *Financial News*, 24 August 2016.

[75] Michael Burrage, It's quite OK to walk away: a review of the UK's Brexit options with the help of seven international databases, Civitas, April 2017, p. xiv.

[76] Mervyn King, The end of alchemy: money, banking and the future of the global economy, Little, Brown, 2016, p. 230.

[77] Joseph Stiglitz, The euro: and its threat to the future of Europe, Allen Lane, 2016, p. 183.

[78] Anagnostakis v Commission Case T450/ 12, para [48].

[79] Cited p. 286, Gavin Hewitt, Lost continent: the BBC's Europe editor on Europe's darkest hour since World War Two, Hodder & Stoughton, 2013.

[80] Mervyn King, The end of alchemy: money, banking and the future of the global economy, Little, Brown, 2016, pp. 340-5.

[81] Joseph Stiglitz, The euro: and its threat to the future of Europe, Allen Lane, 2016, p. 285.

[82] See Liam Halligan and Gerard Lyons, Clean Brexit: why leaving the European Union still makes sense - building a post-Brexit economy for all, Biteback, 2017, pp. 142 and 275.

[83] See Kenneth Armstrong, Brexit time: leaving the EU, Cambridge University Press, 2017, p. 92.

[84] Joseph Stiglitz, The euro: and its threat to the future of Europe, Allen Lane, 2016, pp. 227-8.

[85] Joseph Stiglitz, The euro: and its threat to the future of Europe, Allen Lane, 2016, p. 411.

[86] John Locke, Second treatise on civil government, 1690, Chapter 8, Section 95.

[87] Cited p. 385, Sean Wilentz, The rise of American democracy: Jefferson to Lincoln, W. W. Norton & Company, 2005.

[88] Cited p. 383, Sean Wilentz, The rise of American democracy: Jefferson to Lincoln, W. W. Norton & Company, 2005.

[89] Eric Foner, The fiery trial: Abraham Lincoln and American slavery, W. W. Norton, 2011, p. 159.

[90] See Henry Jaffa, A new birth of freedom: Abraham Lincoln and the coming of the civil war, Rowman & Littlefield, 2000, p. 2.

[91] Fishing For Leave, The Brexit Textbook on Fisheries, February 2017, Section 1, p. 31.

[92] http://www.theguardian.com/politics/2013/aug/24/nicol a-sturgeon-scotland-better-off

[93] https://www.youtube.com/watch?v=AWfomb99QKw

[94] http://scotspolitics.com/interviews/nicola-sturgeon

[95] Scottish government, 'Scotland in the European Union', www.gov.scot/Resource/0043/00439166.pdf (November 2013).

[96] Kenneth Armstrong, Brexit time: leaving the EU, Cambridge University Press, 2017, p. 166.

[97] European Parliament Research Service, Article 50 TEU: withdrawal of a member state from the EU, Briefing, February 2016, p. 6.

[98] *Observer*, 6 November 2016.

[99] Tom Devine, The case for Scottish independence weakened by Brexit, *The Scotsman*, 22 August 2016.

[100] *Sunday Times*, 4 September 2016.

[101] *Mr. Burke's Speeches at His Arrival at Bristol and at The Conclusion of the Poll*, London: J. Dodsley, 2nd edition, 1775.

[102] Lord Ashcroft, Brexit, the border and the Union, Lord Ashcroft Polls, June 2018, pp. 29 and 28.

[103] See Michael Burrage, It's quite OK to walk away: a review of the UK's Brexit options with the help of seven international databases, Civitas, April 2017, p. 139.

[104] Cited p. 139, Gerry Hassan and Russell Gunson, editors, Scotland, the UK and Brexit: a guide to the future, Luath Press, 2017.

[105] Gerry Hassan and Russell Gunson, editors, Scotland, the UK and Brexit: a guide to the future, Luath Press, 2017, p. 103.

[106] See Robert Tombs, Brexit, Euroscepticism and the future of the United Kingdom, *New Statesman*, 24 July 2016.

[107] Cited pp. 262-3, Anthony Seldon and Peter Snowdon, Cameron at 10: the verdict, William Collins, 2016.

[108] See Robert Tombs, Brexit, Euroscepticism and the future of the United Kingdom, *New Statesman*, 24 July 2016.

[109] Cited p. 146, Tim Shipman, All out war: the full story of how Brexit sank Britain's political class, Collins, 2016.

[110] Harold D. Clarke, Matthew Goodwin and Paul Whiteley, Brexit: why Britain voted to leave the European Union, Cambridge University Press, 2017, p. 101.

[111] Equipping the Government for Brexit, Second Report of Session 2016-17, House of Commons Foreign Affairs Committee.

[112] Ed Rooksby, There is no left exit, *Jacobin*, 22 June 2016.

[113] Paul Mason, The leftwing case for Brexit (one day), *Guardian*, 16 May 2016.

[114] *Süddeutsche Zeitung*, 1 June 2016.

[115] See Kenneth Newton, May the weak force be with you: The power of the mass media in modern politics *European Journal of Political Research*, 2006, 45, 2, pp. 209-234.

[116] Psalm 146:3.

[117] Kenneth Newton, May the weak force be with you: the power of the mass media in modern politics, *European Journal of Political Research*, 2006, Vol. 45, No. 2, pp. 209-34.

[118] *Guardian*, 14 March 2017.

[119] *Washington Post*, 23 June 2018.

[120] See Martin Moore and Gordon Ramsay, UK media coverage of the 2016 EU referendum campaign, King's College London 2016, Figure 11, p. 119.

[121] Robert Worcester, Roger Mortimore, Paul Baines and Mark Gill, Explaining Cameron's catastrophe, IndieBooks, 2017, p. 13.

[122] David Goodhart, The road to somewhere: the populist revolt and the future of politics, Hurst & Company, 2017, pp. 19-20.

[123] Richard Tuck, Brexit: a prize in reach for the left, 17 July 2017.

[124] Federica Liberini, Andrew J. Oswald, Eugenio Proto and Michela Redoano, Was Brexit Caused by the Unhappy and the Old? September 2017, p. 14.

[125] Harold D. Clarke, Matthew Goodwin and Paul Whiteley, Brexit: why Britain voted to leave the European Union, Cambridge University Press, 2017, p. 173.

[126] *Shindler* and *Maclennan* [2016] EWHC [High Court of England and Wales] 957. See Kenneth Armstrong, Brexit time: leaving the EU, Cambridge University Press, 2017, p. 54.

[127] Kenneth Armstrong, Brexit time: leaving the EU, Cambridge University Press, 2017, p. 54.

[128] Robert Worcester, Roger Mortimore, Paul Baines and Mark Gill, Explaining Cameron's catastrophe, IndieBooks, 2017, p. 119.

[129] See Geoffrey Evans and Anand Menon, Brexit and British politics, Polity Press, 2017, p. 85.

[130] *Financial Times*, 18 July 2016.

[131] Michael Mosbacher and Oliver Wiseman, Brexit revolt: how the UK voted to leave the EU, New Culture Forum, 2016, p. 48.

[132] British Social Attitudes 34 - The vote to leave the EU, NatCen Social Research, 2017, pp. 16-7.

[133] In Gerry Hassan and Russell Gunson, editors, Scotland, the UK and Brexit: a guide to the future, Luath Press, 2017, p. 129.

[134] Cited p. 87, Robert Oulds, Everything you wanted to know about the EU, but were afraid to ask, Bretwalda Books, 2013.

[135] Anthony Coughlan, Tackling the EU empire: basic critical facts on the EU/eurozone, Better Off Out, 2016, p. 39.

[136] Hansard, 25 June 2007, col. 37.

[137] See Radomir Tylecote and William Cash, From Brussels with love, Duckworth New Academia, 2016, p. 140.

[138] *Daily Telegraph*, 14 October 2000.

[139] BBC News, 18 June 2007.

[140] See R (NS) v Secretary of State for the Home Department, Case C-411/10, para [120].

[141] (R (NS (Afghanistan)) v Secretary of State for the Home Department, Joined cases C-411/10 and C-493/10, para [120].

[142] Rugby Football Union v Consolidated Information Services Ltd [2012] UKSC 55, para [28].

[143] Cited p. 87, Gregor Gall, Bob Crow – socialist, leader, fighter: a political biography, Manchester University Press, 2017.

[144] See Johanna Kantola, Gender and the European Union, Palgrave Macmillan, 2010, p. 110.

[145] Liam Halligan and Gerard Lyons, Clean Brexit: why leaving the European Union still makes sense – building a post-Brexit economy for all, Biteback, 2017, p. 173.

[146] Gerry Hassan and Russell Gunson, editors, Scotland, the UK and Brexit: a guide to the future, Luath Press, 2017, pp. 112-3.

[147] Johanna Kantola, Gender and the European Union, Palgrave Macmillan, 2010, p. 7.

[148] Cited p. 132, Johanna Kantola, Gender and the European Union, Palgrave Macmillan, 2010.

[149] Johanna Kantola, Gender and the European Union, Palgrave Macmillan, 2010, p. 174.

[150] Johanna Kantola, Gender and the European Union, Palgrave Macmillan, 2010, p. 153.

[151] Johanna Kantola, Gender and the European Union, Palgrave Macmillan, 2010, p. 167.

[152] Johanna Kantola, Gender and the European Union, Palgrave Macmillan, 2010, p. 123.

[153] April 2016, pp. 2-3.

[154] Liam Halligan and Gerard Lyons, Clean Brexit: why leaving the European Union still makes sense – building a post-Brexit economy for all, Biteback, 2017, p. 173.

[155] *Daily Telegraph*, 16 May 2016.

[156] *Evening Standard*, 24 February 2016.

157 See Daniel Devine, The UK Referendum on Membership of the European Union as a Trigger Event for Hate Crimes. 5 February 2018. Available at SSRN: https://ssrn.com/abstract=3118190 or http://dx.doi.org/10.2139/ssrn.3118190

158 A fascinating map of the world's most and least racially tolerant countries, *Washington Post*, 15 May 2013.

159 Europeans remain welcoming to immigrants, *Economist*, 19 April 2018. See also Robert Ford, There's a remarkable change in the air – our hostility to migrants is on the retreat, *Guardian*, 19 May 2018.

160 Integration of immigrants in the European Union, Special Eurobarometer 469, 2018, pp. T2, T19.

161 Elizabeth Fekete, Europe's fault lines: racism and the rise of the right, Verso, 2018, p. 119.

162 In Goodbye Europe, Weidenfeld &Nicolson, 2017, p. 163.

163 Cited p. 158, Robert Worcester, Roger Mortimore, Paul Baines and Mark Gill, Explaining Cameron's catastrophe, IndieBooks, 2017.

164 Introduction, Nathaniel Copsey, Rethinking the European Union, Palgrave Macmillan, 2015, p. ix.

165 'David Cameron's Reckless Folly', *Prospect Magazine*, 6 July 2016.

166 Slavoj Zizek interviewed by Benjamin Ramm, *Open Democracy*, 1 July 2016.

[167] TFEU, article 20(2) (a).

[168] Cited p. 426, Jason Farrell and Paul Goldsmith, How to lose a referendum – the definitive story of why Britain voted for Brexit, Biteback, 2017.

[169] In William Outhwaite, editor, Brexit: sociological responses, Anthem Press, 2017, pp. 20 and 22.

[170] Robert Worcester, Roger Mortimore, Paul Baines and Mark Gill, Explaining Cameron's catastrophe, IndieBooks, 2017, pp. 128-9.

[171] Why it's time to end EU free movement, *New Statesman*, 4 January 2017.

[172] EU Directive 2004/38/EC, article 14 (2).

[173] Guy S. Goodwin-Gill and Jane McAdam, The refugee in international law, Oxford University Press, 3rd ed, 2007, pp. 414 and 416.

[174] J. G. Starke, Introduction to international law, 10th edition, Butterworth, 1989, p. 360.

[175] See Richard North, Flexcit: the market solution to leaving the EU, The Leave Alliance, 2016, p. 161.

[176] Immigration Act 1971, s. 3.

[177] Frontex, 5 April 2016.

[178] Directive 2004/38/EC.

[179] ZZ (France) v Secretary of State for the Home Department [2015] UKSIAC SC_63_2007.

[180] *Guardian*, 6 February 2016.

[181] Secretary of State for the Home Department v CS, Case C-304/14.

[182] Gheorghiu v Secretary of State for the Home Department [2016] UKUT 24.

[183] Home Office, 8 November 2014.

[184] See 'Limits on Migration: Limits on Tier 1 and Tier 2 for 2011/12 and supporting policies', Migration Advisory Committee, November 2010, Para. 7.88; 'The Economic Impact of Immigration', Vol. 1 Report, House of Lords Select Committee on Economic Affairs, 1st Report of Session 2007–08 (HL Paper 82-1) para 78; 'International Migration and Rural Communities', Department for Communities and Local Government, March 2011, 3.2.1; Stephen Nickell and Jumana Saleheen, 'The impact of immigration on occupational wages: evidence from Britain', Staff Working Paper No. 574, The Bank of England, December 2015; 'The Effect of Immigration along the Distribution of Wages', Centre for Research and Analysis of Migration, Department of Economics, University College London, Discussion Paper No 03/08.

[185] Stephen Nickell and Jumana Saleheen, The impact of immigration on occupational wages: evidence from Britain, Staff Working Paper No. 574, The Bank of England, December 2015.

[186] Len McCluskey, A Brexit won't stop cheap labour coming to Britain, *Guardian*, 20 June 2016.

[187] Robert Rowthorn, The costs and benefits of large-scale immigration, Civitas, December 2015.

[188] Janice Morphet, Beyond Brexit: how to assess the UK's future, by Policy Press, 2017, p. 87.

[189] Cited p. 47, Steve Moxon, The great immigration scandal, Imprint Academic, 2004.

[190] Christian Dustmann, Uta Schönberg and Jan Stuhler, The Impact of Immigration: Why Do Studies Reach Such Different Results? P. 47, *Journal of Economic Perspectives*, 2016, Vol. 30, No. 4, pp. 31-56.

[191] Robert Peston, WTF, Hodder & Stoughton, 2017, pp. 117-8.

[192] Liam Halligan and Gerard Lyons, Clean Brexit: why leaving the European Union still makes sense – building a post-Brexit economy for all, Biteback, 2017, p. 142.

[193] In the editors' introduction. Benjamin Martill and Uta Staiger, editors, Brexit and beyond: rethinking the futures of Europe, UCL Press, 2018, p. 12.

[194] Joseph Stiglitz, *Guardian* website, 7 July 2016.

[195] Radio 4's *Today*, 5 August 2017.

[196] Philip B. Whyman, Mark Baimbridge and Andrew Mullen, The political economy of the European social model, Routledge, 2012, p. 265.

[197] Jason Farrell and Paul Goldsmith, How to lose a referendum – the definitive story of why Britain voted for Brexit, Biteback, 2017, pp. 179-80.

[198] House of Commons Library, The economic impact of EU membership on the UK, 2013, p. 18.

[199] Henry Newman, Stephen Booth and Aarti Shankar, Beyond the Westminster bubble: what people really think about immigration, Open Europe, December 2017, p. 43.

[200] Ibid, p. 67.

[201] House of Commons Library, The economic impact of EU membership on the UK, 2013, pp. 18-9.

[202] Former Bank governor 'encouraged Eastern European immigration', *Guardian*, 24 November 2017.

[203] See Anthony Coughlan, Tackling the EU empire: basic critical facts on the EU/eurozone, Better Off Out, 2016, p. 5.

[204] https://www.consilium.europa.eu/media/27256/117692.pdf.

[205] Russia: military power: building a military to support great power aspirations, Defense Intelligence Agency, pp. 14-15.

[206] Jennifer Rankin, *Guardian*, 27 May 2016.

[207] Jolyon Howorth, Security and defence policy in the European Union, Palgrave Macmillan, 2014, p. 18.

[208] Charlemagne-prize speech, May 2010, cited p. 69, Anthony Coughlan, Tackling the EU empire: basic critical facts on the EU/eurozone, Better Off Out, 2016.

[209] Commission's EU Defence Action Plan, COM 2016 (950), p. 2.

[210] Europe needs a collective defence strategy to counter Russia, *Guardian*, 22 March 2018.

[211] In an interview with the *Irish Times*, 1 May 2017.

[212] Smart Border 2.0 – Avoiding a hard border on the island of Ireland for Customs control and the free movement of persons. Policy Department for Citizens' Rights and Constitutional Affairs, Directorate General for Internal Policies, PR 596.828 - November 2017.

[213] The Customs Declaration Service: a progress update, HC 1124 Session 2017–2019, 28 June 2018

[214] Lord Ashcroft, Brexit, the border and the Union, Lord Ashcroft Polls, June 2018, p. 6.

[215] Lord Ashcroft, Brexit, the border and the Union, Lord Ashcroft Polls, June 2018, p. 6.

[216] *Financial Times*, 14 July 2017.

[217] Robert Worcester, Roger Mortimore, Paul Baines and Mark Gill, Explaining Cameron's catastrophe, IndieBooks, 2017, p. 134.

[218] British Social Attitudes survey by NatCen, 28 June 2017, cited p. 356, Liam Halligan and Gerard Lyons, Clean Brexit: why leaving the European Union still makes sense – building a post-Brexit economy for all, Biteback, 2017.

[219] Noah Carl and Anthony Heath Should policies be decided at the European, national or sub-national level? Pp. 35-7 in Brexit and public opinion, ed Anand Menon, The UK in a changing Europe 2018

[220] Jason Farrell and Paul Goldsmith, How to lose a referendum – the definitive story of why Britain voted for Brexit, Biteback, 2017, pp. 16-17 and 20.

[221] Anthony Coughlan, Tackling the EU empire: basic critical facts on the EU/eurozone, Better Off Out, 2016, p. 6.

[222] Cited p. 199, Tom Gallagher, Europe's path to crisis: disintegration via monetary union, Manchester University Press, 2013.

[223] Hansard, Official Report, 1 March 1995; Vol. 255, c. 1062.

[224] Cited p. 69, Anthony Coughlan, Tackling the EU empire: basic critical facts on the EU/eurozone, Better Off Out, 2016.

[225] Jan-Werner Müller, Europe's sullen child, *London Review of Books*, 2 June 2016, pp. 3-6.

[226] Philip B. Whyman, Mark Baimbridge and Andrew Mullen, The political economy of the European social model, Routledge, 2012, pp. 172-3.

[227] Christopher J. Bickerton, European integration: from nation-states to member states, Oxford University Press, 2012, p. 108.

[228] Christopher J. Bickerton, European integration: from nation-states to member states, Oxford University Press, 2012, pp. 148-9.

[229] *Guardian*, 25 June 2017.

[230] See http://blogs.wsj.com/eurocrisis/2012/02/23/qa-ecb-president-mario-draghi/The Euro Crisis, Q&A

[231] Philip B. Whyman, Mark Baimbridge and Andrew Mullen, The political economy of the European social model, Routledge, 2012, p. 17.

[232] Philip B. Whyman, Mark Baimbridge and Andrew Mullen, The political economy of the European social model, Routledge, 2012, p. 221.

[233] Cited p. 5, James Heartfield, The European Union and the end of politics, Zero Books, 2013.

[234] Cited p. 13, Gavin Hewitt, Lost continent: the BBC's Europe editor on Europe's darkest hour since World War Two, Hodder & Stoughton, 2013.

[235] See Kenneth Armstrong, Brexit time: leaving the EU, Cambridge University Press, 2017, p. 279.

[236] Mervyn King, The end of alchemy: money, banking and the future of the global economy, Little, Brown, 2016, p. 237.

237 Mervyn King, The end of alchemy: money, banking and the future of the global economy, Little, Brown, 2016, pp. 343-4.

238 Cited p. 87, Gregor Gall, Bob Crow – socialist, leader, fighter: a political biography, Manchester University Press, 2017.

239 Cited p. 87, Gregor Gall, Bob Crow – socialist, leader, fighter: a political biography, Manchester University Press, 2017.

240 Richard Tuck, The current shambles, Briefings for Brexit, 7 August 2018.

241 See Liam Halligan and Gerard Lyons, Clean Brexit: why leaving the European Union still makes sense – building a post-Brexit economy for all, Biteback, 2017, p. 271.

242 Enforcement and dispute resolution: a future partnership paper, HMG, 2017, p.6.

243 Enforcement and dispute resolution: a future partnership paper, HMG, 2017, p.12.

244 Cited p. 116, Liam Halligan and Gerard Lyons, Clean Brexit: why leaving the European Union still makes sense – building a post-Brexit economy for all, Biteback, 2017.

245 Charlie Elphicke MP and Martin Howe, The withdrawal of the UK from the European Union, the Conservative European Research Group and Lawyers for Britain, September 2017.

246 Lord Ashcroft, Brexit, the border and the Union, Lord Ashcroft Polls, June 2018, p. 5.

[247] Robert Peston, WTF, Hodder & Stoughton, 2017, p. 9.

[248] Robert Peston, WTF, Hodder & Stoughton, 2017, p. 25.

[249] Robert Peston, WTF, Hodder & Stoughton, 2017, p. 10.

[250] Rafael Behr, Stopping Brexit is the right thing to do. But that doesn't mean it won't hurt, *Guardian*, 19 March 2018.

[251] Harry Jaffa, Crisis of the house divided: an interpretation of the issues in the Lincoln-Douglas debates, Doubleday, 1959, p. 338.

[252] Harry Jaffa, Crisis of the house divided: an interpretation of the issues in the Lincoln-Douglas debates, Doubleday, 1959, p. 337.

[253] Ian Millhiser, Injustices: the Supreme Court's history of comforting the comfortable and afflicting the afflicted, Nation Books, 2015, p. 265.

[254] Liam Halligan and Gerard Lyons, Clean Brexit: why leaving the European Union still makes sense - building a post-Brexit economy for all, Biteback, 2017, p. 131.

[255] See Liam Halligan and Gerard Lyons, Clean Brexit: why leaving the European Union still makes sense - building a post-Brexit economy for all, Biteback, 2017, p. 4.

[256] See House of Commons Library Briefing Paper 7694, 21 March 2017.

[257] The future relationship between the United Kingdom and the European Union Cm 9593, July 2018, p. 8.

[258] Ibid, p. 89, §22.

[259] Ibid, p. 90, §30, p. 90, §31, and p. 94, §40.

[260] Ibid, p. 16, §14.

[261] Evidence to Treasury Select Committee, 8 March 2015, Q993.

[262] Graham Gudgin, Ken Coutts, Neil Gibson and Jordan Buchanan, Defying gravity: a critique of estimates of the economic impact of Brexit, Policy Exchange, 2017, p. 9.

[263] Joseph Stiglitz, The euro: and its threat to the future of Europe, Allen Lane, 2016. pp. 347-8.

[264] Philip B. Whyman and Alina I. Petrescu, The economics of Brexit: A cost-benefit analysis of the UK's economics relationship with the EU, Palgrave, 2017, pp. 35-40.

[265] Liam Halligan and Gerard Lyons, Clean Brexit: why leaving the European Union still makes sense – building a post-Brexit economy for all, Biteback, 2017, p. 189.

[266] In Benjamin Martill and Uta Staiger, editors, Brexit and beyond: rethinking the futures of Europe, UCL Press, 2018, p. 243.

[267] Mervyn King, The end of alchemy: money, banking and the future of the global economy, Little, Brown, 2016, pp. 334-5.

[268] See Liam Halligan and Gerard Lyons, Clean Brexit: why leaving the European Union still makes sense – building a post-Brexit economy for all, Biteback, 2017, pp. 173-4.

[269] Unite the Union, Brexit on our terms: Unite strategy to defend manufacturing: jobs, investment and employment rights, October 2016, pp. 24-5.

[270] EU Commission, Commission Notice on the notion of State aid as referred to in Article 107(1) of the Treaty on the Functioning of the European Union, Notice 2016/C 262/01, p.18.

[271] Joseph Stiglitz and Bruce Greenwald, Creating a learning society: a new approach to growth, development, and social progress, reader's edition, Columbia UP, 2015, p. 7.

[272] Joseph Stiglitz and Bruce Greenwald, Creating a learning society: a new approach to growth, development, and social progress, reader's edition, Columbia UP, 2015, p. 24.

[273] Joseph Stiglitz and Bruce Greenwald, Creating a learning society: a new approach to growth, development, and social progress, reader's edition, Columbia UP, 2015, p. 8.

[274] Unite the Union, Brexit on our terms: Unite strategy to defend manufacturing: jobs, investment and employment rights, October 2016, p. 17.

[275] The Times, 9 October 1980.

[276] Gerry Hassan and Russell Gunson, editors, Scotland, the UK and Brexit: a guide to the future, Luath Press, 2017, p. 118.

[277] Daniel Yergin, The quest: energy, security, and the remaking of the modern world, Allen Lane, 2011, p. 403.

[278] John Gillingham, The EU: an obituary, Verso, 2016, p. 177-9.

[279] John Gillingham, The EU: an obituary, Verso, 2016, pp. 179-80.

[280] John Gillingham, The EU: an obituary, Verso, 2016, p. 247.

[281] Gerry Hassan and Russell Gunson, editors, Scotland, the UK and Brexit: a guide to the future, Luath Press, 2017, p. 120.

[282] The European Central Bank's Monthly Bulletin for April 2003, 'The need for comprehensive reforms to cope with population ageing'. See www.ecb.int/pub/pdf/mb200304en.pdf, pages 39-51.

[283] Joseph Stiglitz, The euro: and its threat to the future of Europe, Allen Lane, 2016, pp. 342-3.

[284] The House of Commons Science and Technology Committee, Third Report, 9 September 2013.

[285] John Gillingham, The EU: an obituary, Verso, 2016, p. 195.

[286] John Gillingham, The EU: an obituary, London, 2016, pp. 247-8.

[287] Times Education Supplement, 16 July 2015.

[288] Unite the Union, Brexit on our terms: Unite strategy to defend manufacturing: jobs, investment and employment rights, October 2016, p. 13.

[289] City A.M., 5 July 2017.

[290] OECD.stat Agricultural Support Estimates, Consumer nominal protection coefficient, 2015 figure.

[291] Radomir Tylecote and William Cash, From Brussels with love, Duckworth New Academia, 2016, p. 87.

[292] Cited p. 85, Radomir Tylecote and William Cash, From Brussels with love, Duckworth New Academia, 2016.

[293] See Liam Halligan and Gerard Lyons, Clean Brexit: why leaving the European Union still makes sense – building a post-Brexit economy for all, Biteback, 2017, pp. 224-5.

[294] Giles Merritt, Slippery slope: Europe's troubled future, Oxford University Press, 2016, pp. 97-8.

[295] Joseph Stiglitz, Globalization and its discontents revisited: anti-globalization in the era of Trump, Norton, 2018, p. xxxii.

[296] Joseph Stiglitz, Globalization and its discontents revisited: anti-globalization in the era of Trump, Norton, 2018, p. 341.

[297] Joseph Stiglitz, Globalization and its discontents revisited: anti-globalization in the era of Trump, Norton, 2018, p. xlii.

[298] Cited p. 79, Radomir Tylecote and William Cash, From Brussels with love, Duckworth New Academia, 2016.

[299] See Fishing For Leave, The Brexit Textbook on Fisheries, Section 2, pp. 61-2.

Bibliography

Alam, M. Shahid, Poverty from the wealth of nations: integration and polarization in the global economy since 1760, Macmillan, 2000

Bickerton, Chris and Tuck, Richard, A Brexit proposal, 2017 *https://thecurrentmoment.files.wordpress.com/2017/.../brexit-proposal-20-nov-final1....*

Bickerton, Christopher J., Brexit and the British growth model: towards a new social settlement, Policy Exchange, July 2018

Bickerton, Christopher J., European integration: from nation-states to member states, Oxford University Press, 2012

Bickerton, Chris, The European Union: a citizen's guide, Pelican, 2016

Brown, Tom, Tragedy and challenge: an inside view of UK engineering's decline and the challenge of the Brexit economy, Matador, 2017

Chang, Ha-Joon, 23 things they don't tell you about capitalism, Allen Lane, 2010

Chang, Ha-Joon, Bad Samaritans: the guilty secrets of rich nations and the threat to global prosperity, Random House Business, 2008

Chernow, Ron, Alexander Hamilton, Head of Zeus, 2016

Clarke, Harold D., Goodwin, Matthew and Whiteley, Paul, Brexit: why Britain voted to leave the European Union, Cambridge University Press, 2017

Davis, Mary, The chimera of workers' rights in the EU, https://www.thefullbrexit.com/analysis

Elliott, Larry and Atkinson, Dan, Europe didn't work: why we left and how to get the best from Brexit, Yale University Press, 2017

Farrell, Jason and Goldsmith, Paul, How to lose a referendum – the definitive story of why Britain voted for Brexit, Biteback, 2017

Foner, Eric, The fiery trial: Abraham Lincoln and American slavery, W. W. Norton, 2011

Furedi, Frank, Populism and the European culture wars: the conflict of values between Hungary and the EU, Routledge, 2017

Halligan, Liam, and Lyons, Gerard, Clean Brexit: why leaving the European Union still makes sense – building a post-Brexit economy for all, Biteback, 2018

Handley, Sebastian, Brexit: how the nobodies beat the somebodies, i2i Publishing, 2017

Hendy, John, The terrible tale of the EU and trade union rights, Trade Unionists Against the EU, 2016

Hewson, Victoria and Morgan, Austen, A hard question? Managing the Irish border through Brexit, *Irish Journal of International Law*, 2017, 20, 1, pages 38-52.

Institute for Public Policy Research, Time for change: a new vision for the British economy: the interim report of the Institute for Public Policy Research Commission on Economic Justice, September 2017

Jaffa, Henry, Crisis of the house divided: an interpretation of the issues in the Lincoln-Douglas debates, Doubleday, 1959

Jameson, Robert, Beyond Brexit: a positive vision for a successful post-Brexit economy, CreateSpace, 2017

Lapavitsas, Costas, The left case against the EU, Polity, forthcoming 2018

MacLeod, Christine, Heroes of invention: technology, liberalism and British identity, 1750-1914, Cambridge University Press, 2007

Martill, Benjamin, and Staiger, Uta, eds, Brexit and beyond: rethinking the futures of Europe, UCL Press, 2018

Mokyr, Joel, The gifts of Athena: historical origins of the knowledge economy, Princeton UP, 2002

Podmore, Will, British foreign policy since 1870, Xlibris, 2008

Podmore, Will, Reg Birch: engineer, trade unionist, communist, Bellman Books, 2004

Podmore, Will, The war against the working class, Xlibris, 2015

Podmore, Will and Nicholls, Doug, The EU: bad for Britain – a trade union view, Bread Books, 2005

Rakove, Jack, Revolutionaries: inventing an American nation, William Heinemann, 2010

Shipman, Tim, All out war: the full story of how Brexit sank Britain's political class, William Collins, 2016

Shipman, Tim, Fall-out: a year of political mayhem, William Collins, 2017

Stiglitz, Joseph, The euro: and its threat to the future of Europe, Allen Lane, 2016

Stiglitz, Joseph, Freefall: free markets and the sinking of the global economy, Allen Lane, 2010

Stiglitz, Joseph, Globalisation and its discontents revisited: anti-globalization in the era of Trump, Norton, 2018

Stiglitz, Joseph, The price of inequality, Allen Lane, 2012

Stiglitz, Joseph, The roaring nineties: seeds of destruction, Allen Lane, 2003

Stiglitz, Joseph, et al, The Stiglitz report: reforming the international monetary and financial systems in the wake of the global crisis, The New Press, 2012

Stiglitz, Joseph, and Greenwald, Bruce, Creating a learning society: a new approach to growth, development, and social progress, reader's edition, Columbia UP, 2015

Tuck, Richard, Brexit: a prize in reach for the left, 2017 *https://policyexchange.org.uk/pxevents/brexit-a-prize-in-reach-for-the-left/*

Tuck, Richard, Letters to the left on Brexit, 2016-18, available in Archive, www.thefullbrexit.com

Whyman, Philip B., and Petrescu, Alina I., The economics of Brexit: a cost-benefit analysis of the UK's relationship with the EU, Palgrave Macmillan, 2017

Whyman, Philip B., Baimbridge, Mark, and Mullen, Andrew, The political economy of the European social model, Routledge, 2012

Williams, Raymond, The long revolution, Chatto & Windus, 1961

www.thefullbrexit.com
www.briefingsforbrexit

Index